THE
100-YARD
WAR

THE 100-YARD WAR

INSIDE THE 100-YEAR-OLD MICHIGAN–OHIO STATE FOOTBALL RIVALRY

GREG EMMANUEL

John Wiley & Sons, Inc.

Copyright © 2004 by Greg Emmanuel. All rights reserved

Published by John Wiley & Sons, Inc., Hoboken, New Jersey
Published simultaneously in Canada

Design and production by Navta Associates, Inc.

Illustration credits: pages 132 (top), 133 (both), 134 (both), 136 (both), and 137 (top) courtesy of The Ohio State University Photo Archives; pages 132 (bottom), and 135 (both) courtesy of the Athletic Department Collection, Bentley Historical Library/University of Michigan; page 137 (bottom) photo by Brockway Sports; page 138 (top) courtesy of Molly Stevens; page 138 (bottom) courtesy of *The Michigan Daily*; pages 139 (top left) and 140 (top) photos by Jon Neff, courtesy of the *Michiganensian*; pages 139 (top right, bottom) and 140 (bottom) photos by Lauren Proux, courtesy of the *Michiganensian*.

For general information about our other products and services, please contact our Customer Care Department within the United States at (800) 762-2974, outside the United States at (317) 572-3993 or fax (317) 572-4002.

Wiley also publishes its books in a variety of electronic formats. Some content that appears in print may not be available in electronic books. For more information about Wiley products, visit our web site at www.wiley.com.

Library of Congress Cataloging-in-Publication Data:
Emmanuel, Greg.
   The hundred-yard war : inside the 100-year-old Michigan-Ohio state football rivalry / Greg Emmanuel.
     p. cm.
   Includes index.
   ISBN 0-471-67552-0 (cloth)
   1. University of Michigan—Football—History. 2. Ohio State University—Football—History. 3. Michigan Wolverines (Football team)—History. 4. Ohio State Buckeyes (Football team)—History. I. Title.
   GV958.U5284E45 2004
   796.332'63'0977157—dc22   2004005653

Printed in the United States of America

10 9 8 7 6 5 4 3

CONTENTS

1   Hate: The Early Years   *1*

2   Born and Bred   *25*

3   Cold War   *47*

4   Two Men and a Rivalry   *71*

5   Boys to Men   *109*

6   Broken Hearts and Ballooning Wallets   *141*

7   Go Bucks! Go Blue!   *163*

8   Countdown   *187*

9   One Hundred   *209*

10   Post-Game   *235*

Appendix   *253*

Notes   *261*

Acknowledgments   *273*

Index   *275*

Photographs follow page 131

HATE: THE
EARLY YEARS

It wouldn't be Ann Arbor if it weren't so freaking cold.

The calendar says November 21, 2003. Thanksgiving hasn't even arrived, but the late-night wind is making a February-like assault on any flesh that's foolishly been left exposed. It's a good night to be indoors, which works out well because that's where all the action is, anyway.

About halfway down a quiet street called Maynard, a bit off the beaten path and just behind the main drag, the tranquil mood changes as you approach a red brick building. It houses a bar called Scorekeepers. Even standing outside, you can hear a dull din, a hint of what's behind the wooden door.

Inside, Scorekeepers is a familiar-looking bar, with neon beer signs, watery drafts, and big TVs. In other words—if the name didn't already give it away—it's a sports bar. Just past the bouncer checking IDs up front is a large room that looks like a cross between a German beer garden and a ski lodge, with, of course, all the sports bar trappings. To the right is a bunch of small tables, and a long wooden bar abuts the wall on the left. In the back, a set of stairs leads to a second floor that has another bar and a pool table.

But you'd be hard-pressed to make it that far. The place is packed and it's damn loud, thanks to the *Slippery When Wet*–era Bon Jovi that's being played at arena-level volume and all the sports fans trying to talk over the music. This is really nothing unusual. After all, it's Friday night, and this bar is usually crowded and noisy on Friday nights.

Yet tonight Scorekeepers feels different. It *feels* significant. For proof, you need look no farther than the man standing about 10 feet from the door. You can't miss him: beneath a warm, beer-fueled flush, his taut neck muscles bulge grotesquely, almost threatening to rupture. On any other night, this might indicate that something is terribly wrong. Tonight, given the circumstances, it's perfectly normal. This is what a person looks like when he is yelling, very loudly.

His rage is directed at another man standing directly in front of him. You can't miss this guy either. His lips are tightly pursed together, as if he's trying to inflate a balloon or worse, prevent his own head from exploding. The men stand just inches apart, the gap between them bridged by flying spittle and incoherent obscenities.

They look remarkably similar, though, almost as if they could be best friends or even brothers. Both are white, in their early twenties, with short-cropped, light-colored hair and muscular, athletic builds. Both are wearing blue jeans—and sweatshirts.

And in the sweatshirts lies all the difference either man—or anyone in this bar, town, and state—needs.

The "neck" is wearing a blue sweatshirt with yellow letters, and Mr. Lips is wearing a red sweatshirt with gray letters.

Although they'd never met before this evening, their sweatshirts alone were enough to drive a permanent wedge between them. They knew when they first laid eyes on each other that they hated what the other man stood for—or, more precisely, who he rooted for.

One man is a fan of the University of Michigan Wolverines. And the other loves the Ohio State University Buckeyes.

In a little over 12 hours, these two football teams will run onto a field and, for all intents and purposes, settle the argument going on between these two fans, the gist of which is: whose team is better?

Tomorrow's contest is a regular season college football game, but the stakes are enormously high. A conference championship, a possible invitation to the national championship game and—most importantly—bragging rights are all on the line. That's why both of these men are so worked up. That's what makes one grown man get in another man's face. And that's ultimately what makes those neck muscles strain and twitch and those lips press together so severely.

But that's not even the half of it.

Arguments about sports occur every second of every day. Guys in bars yell at each other all the time. Opposing fans tell each other how much they "suck" and how their own team will kick the other team's ass. This is why sports bars exist in the first place—to be a venue for such behavior. And if you think about it, that's pretty much the driving force behind all spectator sports.

But there is another reason why tomorrow is not just any other game. There's history here. Lots and lots of history.

When the rivalry between the Buckeyes and the Wolverines began, the game of basketball was only six years old. The first World Series wouldn't be played until six years later. Any whisper of the NHL was still 20 years away, and the mighty NFL wouldn't come on the scene for another 24 seasons. In other words, their rivalry began in the sporting world–equivalent of the Jurassic period, and it would culminate when the teams meet tomorrow for the 100th time in 106 years. It will be the final piece in a century-sized collection of college football games, played between two perennially powerful opponents, and the renewal of the greatest rivalry in the world of sports.

How can this game make such a bold claim? Easily.

No other regularly scheduled game between any two teams in any sport is as consequential, as often. Since 1935, the year that Michigan and Ohio State moved their annual contest to the final week of the conference schedule, the Wolverines and the Buckeyes have decided the Big Ten championship between themselves—winner take all—19 times. Twenty-one other times, one of the teams going into the game had a shot for at least a share of the conference title. This means that on average, for two out of every three times that Ohio State and Michigan have faced off, the result has been huge. (Even the Yankees and the Red Sox have played some meaningless duds over the years.) And in the rare instance that one of the teams wasn't having a great season, that team relished playing the spoiler. In the last decade alone, one school has wrecked the other's championship hopes four different times.

And it's not just regional. Today the spotlight is on the Bowl Championship Series, and the OSU–UM game almost always shakes up the national standings. Since 1987, at least one (usually, both) of the teams has been ranked in the Top 15 of all Division I-A football teams in the country, when coming into their annual grudge match.

The best rivalry is one that is evenly matched, and this rivalry pretty much defines it. In the last 50 years, the

Michigan–Ohio State series has been deadlocked at 24–24–2. That's 24 wins by each team and 2 ties. You don't have to be a statistician to understand that this is not just evenly matched, it's an unambiguous dead heat.

While these statistics pertain to the outcome of the game, the rivalry has come to mean much more to both the players and the fans. Thanks to countless remarkable football games between these two huge schools, drawing hundreds of thousands of alumni and followers, the rivalry is now an enormous cultural event. Traditions have evolved specifically around this annual game. It is treated like a holiday, a family reunion, and the biggest party of the year, all rolled into one. It's so colossal, it doesn't even have to be mentioned specifically by name. Just say "the Game" in the Midwest or to either school's alumni or fans—or to any college football fan, for that matter—and everyone will know exactly what you're talking about.

This Game has taken root smack dab in the middle of the country, where football is actually more American than apple pie and young fans choose sides as soon as they're old enough to talk. The universities lie only 200 miles away from each other, and on that one particular Saturday near the end of November, friends, colleagues, neighbors, and even lovers can find themselves enemies for a day.

Since 1922, a mere 6,996,564 people have seen the Game in person. (The location alternates between Ann Arbor and Columbus each year.) It draws old friends and alumni back to the campus of their alma mater—to see the best game of the season and to party. And as new freshman classes arrive on both campuses new batches of fans claim their student tickets and circle the one game on the calendar that's an absolute can't-miss.

For fans who can't make the trip or aren't lucky enough

to get tickets to see the Game in person in either school's enormous stadium, there's always TV. The game airs nationally and is one of the highest-rated college football matchups of the year.

The action on the field is inevitably smashmouth, hard-hitting, heartpounding, highlight film–worthy college football played at the highest level. For the participants, the Game is the one they dream about while growing up, wanting nothing more than to play big-time college football. And long after they've left school, it's always the one they remember most vividly, and—win or lose—it's the one their college football careers are invariably measured by.

Tomorrow, now fewer than 12 hours away, the referee will blow a whistle and the annual slugfest will resume. For fans and players alike, hearts will relocate to throats, teeth will clench, palms will sweat, and voices will grow hoarse from yelling. In fact, the scene won't be dissimilar to the one inside Scorekeepers, which has become increasingly unbearable for any non-diehard. Even slipping outside into the night air isn't easy; you have to fight your way through the crowd and sidestep the feuds.

Back on the street, the scene has changed. A line has formed in front of the bar, composed of fans who are willing to stand in the freezing cold just for a taste of the excitement that's going on inside. Except one. A petite blonde in a big, puffy, white winter jacket stands near the door, waiting with the others but not nearly as cheerfully. The freezing air of the late Michigan night (by now, actually early morning) nips at her pink nose and ears. The sounds of arguments, boasts, cheers, and fight songs filter out of the bar and onto the sidewalk every time the door opens. She hears the excitement but just shrugs. She is impatient. She is cold.

"It's just a football game," she sighs, to no one in particular.

Just a football game? You've got to be kidding. This is a 100-yard war.

■   ■   ■

And it started, as wars often do, with a border skirmish.

First, take a look at a map. Any map of the continental United States will do. Now find Michigan. It's the state near the top, right of center and surrounded by a bunch of big blue lakes. You can't miss it; it actually looks a bit like a human hand, and the people who live there actually do use their own hands as rudimentary demonstration tools to explain to out-of-staters exactly where their home is. As in "Grand Rapids? It's over here," people will say, while pointing to the left side of their palms.

Now let your gaze fall slightly downward and to the right—catty-corner, actually (to use an expression that's popular in the region). See the block below Michigan and to the right? That's Ohio. It doesn't have a cute shape. It can't really be likened to any part of the human anatomy (except maybe the pancreas).

The two states were not always so clearly defined.

In 1787, a piece of paper called the Northwest Ordinance set the southern boundary of the area that would eventually become the Michigan Territory. It was defined by a line drawn due east from the bottom of Lake Michigan to Lake Erie. This seemed very basic and sensible, but you don't have to be a surveyor to understand that the accuracy of this border line depends on knowing exactly where those lakes lie. Well, in 1787, Lake Michigan—all 22,300 square miles of it—was misplaced, was thought to be a bit farther north than it actually is. As a result, the border line hit Lake Erie just north of the mouth of the Maumee River.

This didn't seem to be a problem until the 19th century, when a group of people living south of this line started calling that area part of the Ohio Territory. And when it came time to join the Union, the steadfast citizens of Ohio stuck with the old, inaccurate line that had been drawn by the Northwest Ordinance, and the territory officially became part of the United States of America on February 19, 1803.

A few years later, the folks living north of the new state of Ohio formally created the Michigan Territory, and they took a second look at that old border. A newly commissioned survey pushed Lake Michigan southward to where it rightfully belonged, and the redrawn line between Lakes Michigan and Erie put 468 square miles of land in question, including the mouth of this so-called Maumee River, which was being eyed as the future location for a port city to be named Toledo. The Michigan Territory then claimed this land for itself.

Nobody really cared about this claim until twenty-five years later, when Michigan petitioned the U.S. government to become a state and the issue of who actually owned the area called the "Toledo Strip" began to heat up. Michigan had quietly assumed control of the land, but Ohioans still felt it was rightfully theirs. Since Ohio was already a state at this time complete with representatives in Washington, it lobbied to block Michigan's acceptance into the Union until Congress acknowledged its version of the boundary.

In response to Ohio's defiance, the acting governor of the Michigan Territory, a brash young leader named Stevens T. Mason, advised the passage of a law that forbade any state to govern a piece of Michigan's territory. Ohio governor Robert Lucas then countered by mustering a volunteer force of about 600 men—fully armed and equipped. He marched into the disputed region, met no resistance, and set up a new county that he named after himself. At the same time, Mason brought about 1,200 men outside present-day Toledo and waited. The interstate one-up-manship was obvious as the Ohio legislature voted to approve a $300,000 military budget and the Michigan Territory countered with a budget of $315,000. Adding to the pressure cooker was a whole lot of hype, as reports from the period suggest that the entire country was wild with excitement over a possible clash between the two states. Even the pundits weighed in, as former president John Quincy Adams, now a representative of Massachusetts, remarked, in support of Michigan, "Never in the course of my life have I known a controversy of which all the right [is] so clearly on one side and all the power so overwhelmingly on the other."

During the summer of 1835, authorities from Michigan harassed Ohio supporters and arrested any land surveyors who attempted to go back in and redefine the border to their liking. The Ohioan force intermittently retaliated with a show of force and sent Michigan supporters fleeing into the woods.

The only real action came in the fall of 1835. The Michigan militia arrested a man named Major Benjamin Franklin Stickney and tied him to a horse for transport to the nearest court. His son Two Stickney (not to be confused with his older brother, who was actually named One Stickney), took offense at his father's treatment, and the militia tried to arrest him, too. In the scuffle, Two got out a pen knife and stabbed a deputy sheriff named Joseph Wood. It was just a flesh wound, but blood was spilled.

At this point, President Andrew Jackson did not want to hear any more reports of fighting in the hinterlands, so he offered a solution that was quick *and* political. Ohio, which already was a state and therefore had a valuable voting population, would get their way. (It was, after all, almost an election year.) The old inaccurate line would stand, and the Toledo Strip would remain in Ohio. As a sort of restitution, Michigan would be allowed to enter the Union, without this particular piece of land but with a huge piece of frozen tundra south of Lake Superior known as the Upper Peninsula.

Fair? At the time, it didn't appear so to the people of Michigan, and what became known as the Toledo War left a very bitter taste in the mouths of residents of both states. Michiganders felt that they'd been shafted, and Ohioans didn't like the way they were preyed upon. In fact, according to many historians, the people of Michigan (and later the University of Michigan football team) got the nickname Wolverines from Ohioans at this time.

The wolverine is a feisty 25-pound member of the weasel family ferocious enough to fight off bears and wolves that lived in the region at this time. Ohioans thought that Michiganders, like the animal, were pretty ruthless and aggressive. It was no term of endearment, but the nickname stuck, nonetheless. While the issue of the Toledo Strip was officially dead, interstate animosity had only just begun.

■   ■   ■

Sixty-two years later, the forces of Michigan and Ohio clashed again, but this time the disputed territory in question had hash marks. At first, the game didn't exactly resemble the one played today from Portland to Miami every fall weekend, but things were changing fast.

Football's earliest ancestor was a free-for-all played by the ancient Greeks, in which an unlimited number of players attempted to move a ball over a goal line by kicking, throwing, or running with it. The "sport" eventually evolved into the Brits' rugby. (A game that, in the United States at least, is probably best known for the shirts with wide stripes that share the name, rather than for its similarities to football.)

The version of football that first gained popularity in the United States was a mix of the British rugby and what Americans call soccer, and it also included a rule that allowed players to advance the ball by punching it with their fists. Odd, yes, but considered fun—especially by young men at college. Two universities in New Jersey, Rutgers and Princeton, played the first competitive inter-collegiate game of what they were calling "ballown" on November 6, 1869.

Harvard and Yale then played a seminal game on November 13, 1875. Featuring 11 men on a side, it more closely resembled modern football and was finally called football, although hyphenated as *foot-ball*—presumably so that it was clear that you'd need both a *foot* and a *ball* to play. Soon foot-ball clubs were popping up all over the place, including at the University of Michigan.

The school was one of the largest in the country at that time, although still very young by Harvard standards. UM was founded in Detroit in 1817 and was originally named Catholepistemiad of Michigania, before, thankfully, the name was changed. In 1837, it was moved to its permanent home in Ann Arbor.

Appropriately, this burgeoning university had its own football club. After students got bored of scrimmaging among themselves on campus for a few years, the club formally accepted a challenge from Racine College in Wisconsin, and the University of Michigan Wolverines played their first intercollegiate football game on May 30, 1879, at White Stocking Park in Chicago, Illinois.

That very first game was a defensive battle until Wolverine Irving Pond ran the ball into the end zone for the game's first and only touchdown. The team captain, Dave DeTar, added a field goal, but the victory was officially recorded as 1–0; the touchdown was worth 1 point, and the kick was kind of "extra point." Details, like scoring and rules, were still being worked out, but a dominant football program was born.

In 1870, the same year that Michigan played its first organized football game on campus, a new college almost exactly 200 miles due south of Ann Arbor, in the capital of Ohio, opened its doors for a small group of students. The Ohio Agricultural and Mechanical College, soon to be rechristened the Ohio State University, quickly expanded from its original student body of about two dozen, and in no time these male students were doing what male students of the day did: they were playing football.

In 1890, the OSU team competed in its first official intercollegiate game against Ohio Wesleyan University in Delaware, Ohio. About 700 people showed up to witness Ohio State win 20–14. A second Midwest athletic power was now on the map.

Once the calendar turned 1897, the world of college football was never the same. And yet by all accounts, it was a pretty ordinary year—as ordinary as life could be near the dawn of the 20th century. If you were looking for a gift for your sweetheart, you could pop into the local pharmacy and buy some chocolates, and it would have cost you about 60 cents a pound. If you wanted to be a gentleman and spend Saturday at the theater with your girl, you could take her to a matinee performance in Ann Arbor for a mere 25 cents. Cheap, perhaps, but you would have been forced to sit through Alexandre Dumas's *The Three Guardsmen*. This

Three Musketeers retread—think *Jaws 2*—was pretty much all the entertainment there was to choose from in Ann Arbor in October 1897. Still, life, for the most part, was good, and girlfriends and wives still had their men to themselves on Saturdays. That didn't last long.

By the time they squared off against each other, both the University of Michigan and the Ohio State University had been separately dabbling in the young sport of football for a while. UM had 18 years of playing experience and a combined record of 68–26–3, while OSU had been at it for only 7 years and was a more modest 28–27–3. Regardless of the dramatic difference in their records, the Wolverines reportedly took the first meeting against the Buckeyes seriously.

Two days before the game, Michigan's student newspaper, *The Michigan Daily*, printed a story that read "Saturday's game with the Ohio State University will be another close contest if the reports [sic] of their preliminary work is a criterion." That was fancy-pants 1897 language for "OSU's supposed to have a pretty good team." Football at this time was already being prominently covered by the school's paper, even getting front-page attention, but intercollegiate sports were still a relatively quaint endeavor. In fact, a tennis tournament scheduled for the same day was canceled because of a "dearth of tennis balls." Even a multibillion dollar industry like college sports had to start somewhere.

No one at Regents Field on October 16, 1897, could have possibly known that the first meeting between these two football teams would inaugurate a series of unforgettable games, one of the greatest rivalries in sports, and a century of drama that would play out over the next hundred years and beyond. But what the fans who packed into the 4-year-old athletic field down on South State Street did know was this: Michigan kicked Ohio State's ass.

Michigan's Frederic Hannan, primarily a fullback, kicked off, and the first Game was underway. (The squads were small—about 20 on a side—and kicking duties were shared by all.) The ball was downed on the Michigan 25 and Ohio State's quarterback Harry Saxby went two-and-out (there were only three total downs then) and he was forced to hand the ball over to the team's captain, Harry Hawkins, for a punt. The punt landed near midfield, and the Wolverines began their march. The backs James Hogg, George Stuart, and Hannan each found large holes in Ohio State's defense, and Michigan's very first drive against OSU culminated in a 10-yard run by Hannan into the end zone. Hogg kicked the extra point, and after 6 minutes the score was 6–0. (The forward pass would not be legal until 1906, and at this point, touchdowns were worth 4 points, extra kicks now 2 points, and field goals also 4 points.)

Before halftime, Stuart added three TDs, Hogg and Hazen Pingree one each, and Hogg kicked 5 successful extra points. The game was already in the bag at 34–0.

What must the Ohio State footballers have been thinking? They mustered absolutely no offense against the Wolverines, and any defense they threw at the opposing team was immediately overwhelmed. And when OSU came out in the second half, they were in for an even bigger surprise: disrespect.

Michigan not only took out their starting players but they proceeded to punt the ball on first down on just about every possession. The next day the newspaper justified Michigan's actions by saying they needed to give their defense some practice. Even if that were true, it was still impertinent. Michigan treated their opponent like a scrimmage squad, and they just handed OSU the ball back and dared them to try and do anything with it. Unfortunately, even with all the chances, OSU managed nothing more than a 5-yard gain in the rest of the game, and Michigan coasted on the points they accumulated in the first half. The game was called by the coaches before the allotted 20 minutes of the second half was even reached. Both sides had obviously seen enough. The final score was the same as the halftime tally: 34–0.

The best thing that the Ohio State newspaper, *The Lantern*, could say about the game was that it "was hard fought from start to finish and entirely free from slugging and objectionable features." Great, there was no dirty play, but what the 19th-century writer, who clearly had too much decorum, wanted to say was, Ohio State was pissed. They were 1–1 when their brand-new coach, Dave Edwards, brought his optimistic Buckeyes to Ann Arbor. They had promise, and they felt like they had a good shot at beating their northern neighbors, but they were embarrassed. And it only got worse. Ohio State went on to lose their next 6 games and finished the year a meager 1–7–1, the worst season of Buckeye football before or since. After only one year as coach, Edwards was dismissed. There was no doubt that the Buckeyes would remember the Wolverines, and it wouldn't be with warm and fuzzy thoughts.

Michigan, for its part, did nothing to help make the games between these two neighboring opponents into anything that remotely resembled friendly competition. Over the next 22 years, through 15 games, Michigan usually beat up on Ohio State, especially in 1902 (86–0), 1903 (36–0), and 1905 (40–0). The press had called the two squads enemies from their first meeting, and these lopsided victories could only have aggravated the sentiment—at least on the part of Ohio State.

It wasn't a blowout, though, that defined the fierce

competition that would become a hallmark of the Rivalry. On November 24, 1900, the universities met for the second time, again on Regents Field in Ann Arbor, only this time there was a lot more excitement in the stands, thanks to the 900 OSU supporters who had made the trip from Columbus to see two teams with identical 7–1 records square off.

The fans boarded special trains at 6:00 A.M. in Columbus and paid a $2.40 fare for the 400-mile round trip. According to the *Detroit Free Press*, "The whole university, co-eds and all, apparently followed the team into the enemy's country, and made a demonstration which was the feature of the game. They had songs and yells and, led on by official yell-masters, fairly took the breath of the home crowd away, for there has never been such a large number of outsiders at a game played at Ann Arbor." It was only 1900, and Ohio State versus Michigan was already not just any game.

Michigan's team was favored that miserable, snowy day, *largely* because its front line outweighed Ohio State's by 20 to 50 pounds per man. But this only underscored how, in the Rivalry, expectation and "favorite" status are usually less important than what's being served at the concession stand.

Ohio State actually outplayed Michigan that Saturday, gaining almost twice as many yards as the Wolverines did. Unfortunately, neither team could get the ball in the end zone of the snow-slicked field. In the first half, OSU's James Westwater and James McLaren both had gains of more than 20 yards, but the wet field and Michigan's defense put an end to what would wind up being the longest drive of the day. The game ended, and the final score was 0–0. It may not have been the most scintillating football to watch, but the undermanned, underappreciated, underweighted Buckeyes held their own against the Wolverines. The OSU supporters who had made the trip went home with smiles on their faces, presumably a fair share of whisky in their bellies and, most important, a moral victory against their newly minted rivals. The 1897 game was the first game, but the 1900 game was the first classic.

And at the start of every season thereafter, each team hopes that this season's Game—and their win—will make for yet another classic.

■   ■   ■

It's hard to look at a modern college football player—big, strong, athletic, sculpted by nutrition and training, and covered in pads made of synthetic materials that utilize the latest advances in materials science—and see even a shadow of that inchoate game, with its sweaters and bare heads and occasional deaths on the field—but it's in there. More than a hundred years have passed, and you probably couldn't find a single player on the 2003 University of Michigan or Ohio State football squads who could tell you what happened in either of the teams' first two matchups, but the legacy—an unwavering desire to beat their rival—has been passed on from player to player and from coach to coach. It's a lot like DNA. You can't see it, but it's in there. It's in their blood. And in the muggy heat of a midwestern summer, it's in their sweat, too.

Or perhaps that's just the acrid smell of the season's first practice.

In 2003, the Buckeyes hit the field for the very first time on a Wednesday morning, August 6. The team worked out at the Woody Hayes Athletic Center, a complex named for their immortal coach, who won 13 Big Ten championships and cultivated a tradition of winning that every OSU team is expected to live up to, year in and year out.

The general feeling was that the 2003 team should not disappoint. Expectations were high for both OSU and UM, as had been the norm for both programs for decades. And to reach their goals—to win the Big Ten conference, to play in the Rose Bowl, to win a national championship—there was, and always would be, one common obstacle: each other. In three and a half months, on the last day of the teams' 2003 regular college football season, Michigan and Ohio State would face off and if history was any indication, it would likely be winner take all—again.

Every player on the two squads knew this, from the redshirt freshmen to the few Heisman hopefuls. Every player who had ever worn a Wolverine or Buckeye jersey has known this since the day he arrived on campus, and usually years before, when he watched Michigan battle Ohio State at the stadiums or on TV. But before November 22 arrived, there was a lot of work to be done.

The Buckeyes came saddled with extra baggage in 2003—some of it good, some of it bad. To begin with, they were the reigning national champions. They came from almost nowhere the year before (their 2001 record was 7–5) and managed to finish 2002 a remarkable 14–0. They not only beat Michigan 14–9 in the annual slugfest—a tight contest that came down to the very last play of the game—but they played for the national championship in the Fiesta Bowl in Tempe, Arizona. And in another nail-biter, the Buckeyes beat Miami 31–24 in double overtime to become the first Ohio State team to win a national championship since 1968.

So, what would they do for an encore? Well, they'd go out there and try to win another one. But anyone could tell you that wasn't gonna be easy.

Head coach Jim Tressel started informing his troops in

the spring that they would have a big fat bull's eye on their backs come fall. But his team could do it. The Buckeyes could be the first team to repeat as national champions since the 1994–1995 Nebraska Cornhuskers. Why not? Ohio State had 18 returning starters, including a more-than-dependable quarterback named Craig Krenzel, who began the 2003 season with a 15–1 record as a starter.

In field houses across the country, the image of smiling Buckeyes kissing the championship trophy still lingered in the minds of opposing players and coaches, and OSU began the season ranked number 1 by several esteemed prognosticators, including *Sports Illustrated*, and was picked to repeat as champion. But expectations, coupled with the fact that everyone and his brother would be gunning for them, equals pressure. The players admitted that they felt it, but they planned to try to use that pressure to motivate themselves to work even harder—at least, that was the company line.

"We're going to have to step it up a notch if we want to have another great season," the 6-foot-4-inch, 300-pound senior center Alex Stepanovich told the media just prior to that first practice. "Everyone wants a piece of what we had last year and we want it again."

After the drills of the very first fall practice, lunch, and then showers, the players reassembled for the 2003 team photo and talked at length with the media for the first time that season. Most guys echoed Stepanovich's words, while trying to downplay the dreaded P word.

"There may be focus but no pressure," said senior safety Will Allen. And junior defensive end Simon Fraser added, "We're ready to take on the task. We're looking forward to it."

But there was a problem.

In fact, everyone was thinking about a certain 230-pound problem, even if they weren't talking about him. The focus of picture day was not on the players whose pictures were being taken; it was on the one guy whose picture was not being taken.

His name was Maurice Clarett. And along with a stingy defense, he had helped carry the Buckeyes to Arizona. A true freshman in 2002 (the first freshman to start for the Buckeyes at tailback since 1943), Clarett rushed for 1,237 yards and scored 16 TDs, even while missing 3 entire games and a large part of 2 others because of injury.

In the Fiesta Bowl, Clarett spun off a 5-yard TD run in the second OT that put the Buckeyes on top for good. And well before the last beer toasting the 2002 championship was chugged, OSU fans were dreaming of what a full season with Maurice Clarett might be like and about the very real possibility of another Heisman Trophy winner from Ohio State.

Then, over the summer, the wheels came off.

In fact, it all started with a car. Not just any car: a 2001 Chevrolet Monte Carlo with two TV monitors and an ass-kicking stereo in the trunk, along with 300 CDs, about $300 worth of clothing, and somewhere in the neighborhood of $800 in cash—allegedly. This dream ride was taken by Clarett to a workout at the very same Woody Hayes Athletic Center in April, was parked in the university lot, and was broken into. Clarett's car—well, not actually his car, but the car he was borrowing for an overnight test drive from the Car Store in Columbus—was looted of its rap star–worthy kitty. That much was fact. But the six-million-dollar question became: what was the true value of the stolen stuff?

That was what the police and the NCAA investigators wanted to know. When the details of the police report surfaced, the running back admitted to "exaggerating" the losses in the robbery. Clarett's motivations were unclear, but Tressel and OSU Director of Athletics Andy Geiger decided on July 29 that the furor surrounding the incident was enough to keep Clarett (for the time being) out of practice, workouts, and team meetings.

The running back already had a history of needling his coaches and fans. During the 2002 season, he told a writer from *ESPN the Magazine* that he would consider challenging the NFL's rule that a player must wait three years after high school before being eligible for the draft. And right before the Fiesta Bowl, he denounced Ohio State for not allowing (or paying for) him to fly home for a friend's funeral. He later accused school officials of lying, when they said he hadn't filled out the necessary application for emergency financial aid to pay for the flight. He even complained about play calling during the season. He gave 'em a lot of yards, but he also gave 'em some headaches.

When Coach Tressel began his press conference, at the end of a long day he knew exactly what the topic of conversation would be, and he allotted 20 minutes to answer the inevitable questions. In a nutshell: Coach Tressel was not sure how the NCAA would rule on the Clarett case. Yes, perhaps he could have handled the situation differently, although he wouldn't elaborate. And he had never seen the police report and did not know if it was accurate.

End of story? Not quite.

Clearly, this was something that would nag at the Buckeyes all year. And the big game against Michigan in three months was now buried somewhere in a big pile of crap. Coach Tressel was probably just praying that his team got to their first game against the University of Washington Huskies intact.

But if Tressel was looking for a little empathy, he could have always called University of Michigan head football coach Lloyd Carr.

On the field, in the weight room, at the training table, perhaps even in the library: these are places a coach would like to see his star cornerback and Big Ten preseason defensive player of the year. Probably topping the list of places a coach would not want to see that player is the chambers of Michigan 14th District judge John Collins. And that's too bad, because that's exactly where Wolverine star Marlin Jackson was on August 13, 2003. They had a conversation that included this disturbing question and answer:

> Collins: Did you punch him in the eye?
> Jackson: Yes.

They should have been talking about football. About how the number 7–ranked Wolverines had 15 returning starters from the previous year and how they had a proven core of offensive skill players that would give them one of the most dynamic offenses in college football. They could have talked about how Coach Carr was going to move Jackson from corner to safety, in order to get his 11 best athletes on the field at the same time.

They could have even talked about the Buckeyes. After all, OSU was voted number 1 in the conference at the Big Ten's annual media day in July, and the Wolverines were voted number 2—meaning, their November 22 showdown was already a hot topic of conversation in the preseason. But, instead, the talk was about a plea agreement. Coach Carr publicly stood by his man, but he could not have been pleased.

What Jackson pled guilty to was punching 26-year-old civil engineering student Shahin Farokhrny outside a party in Ann Arbor in June. According to Farokhrny, Jackson hit him with a glass—a felonious assault punishable by a maximum sentence of four years in prison. But Jackson wound up pleading guilty to just one count of aggravated assault, a much lesser crime, thanks to a request by the victim (a self-professed UM football fan). This was certainly a smudge on Michigan's preseason, but perhaps not a full stain.

If you take the Jackson situation out of the equation, there was a lot to be excited about when the Wolverines convened for their annual fan photo and media day at Michigan Stadium on August 9th.

Fifth-year senior quarterback John Navarre was smiling as he signed autographs in the sun and he had to be smiling on the inside too. During the off-season, Navarre and Heisman had been mentioned in the same breath, and with good reason. The QB had set school records for attempts, completions, and yards in 2002. With teammates like running back Chris Perry and wide receiver Braylon Edwards on his side of the ball, the Wolverines would attempt to put an end to the inconsistency that plagued them in 2002 (they finished the season 10–3) and would perhaps find themselves in the national championship picture come November.

The players knew they had a lot of talent, and they also know that talent alone would not get it done. "I really think that the only person that can beat us is ourselves," said senior wide receiver Calvin Bell to the media later that day. "If we can just execute, we'll be really good."

The 2003 season had not even begun, but the subject of the Ohio State game in a few months had already come up. Last year's Wolverine loss to the Buckeyes propelled OSU to the national championship game and a title. That loss was still on the minds of this year's Michigan players.

"That motivated me throughout the whole off-season," said Perry. "Everywhere you go you see the Ohio State championship T-shirts and commercials. So, of course, knowing that we had a really good chance to beat them and we let it slip away, it keeps the whole team motivated."

No Michigan team had lost three straight years to Ohio State since the early '60s—the mere mention of that fact could wipe the smile right off Navarre's face, even as he signed an autograph for another young Wolverine fan. The QB was dogged by questions about his ability to win big games since he first started for Michigan, and with an 0–2 record against Ohio State, he would have to brace himself for a hailstorm of criticism in the coming months. The game, scheduled for November 22, would likely be the biggest of his college career and would in essence define his legacy as a Michigan quarterback, a group that included well known names like Tom Brady, Elvis Grbac, Jim Harbaugh, and Brian Griese.

It was no different for any of the Wolverines and the Buckeyes. Every one of the guys, on both squads, knew deep down, even if he wouldn't say it publicly now, that the final game on the schedule was destined to be the biggest game of his life. And any doubters should brush up on their history—all 99 chapters of it.

2

BORN AND BRED

When Shawn Collier was just five years old, his future was as clear as the Ohio River in November. He was going to be a Buckeye fan. Actually, if you believe him, he was a fan from the day he "popped out of the womb." And, really, there is no reason not to believe Shawn. First, he seems to be a very likable and trustworthy kind of guy, and, second, but more important, his parents are Buckeye fans. As huge Buckeye devotees themselves, Columbus residents Herb and Olivia Collier were more likely to win the Ohio Mega Millions than not produce a ga-ga, worshipful Buckeye fan of a son. That's just how Buckeye fans come into existence: they are born and bred.

Shawn didn't see his beloved Buckeyes in person until he was five years old. His parents took him to see them play the Northwestern Wildcats, and if Shawn closes his eyes today, he can still picture the scene on Lane Avenue, outside Ohio Stadium. On Saturday mornings this crowded street is where tailgating and pregame partying reach a pinnacle—and it can make quite an impression on a young boy.

"I can remember the atmosphere," he said. "Of course, I was too young to partake, but I remember all the craziness. And when we finally got into the stadium, we sat near the student section and I told my parents, 'I'm going to sit there one day.'"

So what did a boy who was passionate about his football team, whose first words were allegedly "Go Bucks!" do once he got accepted to attend the Ohio State University and he became an official card-carrying member of the Buckeye Nation? He morphed from a run-of-the-mill fan into some kind of superfan.

Shawn does not just go to football games and root with 100,000 others; he is a member of Block O, OSU's official student fan club. But Shawn is not just a member; he is also one of the club's officers.

And there's more.

Shawn holds the distinction of being the chairman of the 2003 Beat Michigan Week committee, a group of students that plans activities the week of the Michigan game, with the goal of inspiring the student population and, ultimately, the football team to beat their rivals.

In April 2003, it began in earnest. When most students were beginning to forget about football and reprioritize their free time around playing video games, partying, and maybe even studying, Shawn was voluntarily locked in a nondescript conference room in the Ohio Union. Along with 50 or so other members of the committee, he was designing pep rallies, tug of wars, 5K runs, buffalo wing buffets—anything they could think of to make Beat Michigan Week a fun and celebratory event. And they didn't just meet one afternoon; they met every week that spring, took a break for the summer (remarkably), and then started up again weekly in the fall.

It may sound a little absurd, unless you've ever been to the campus of the Ohio State University in Columbus, Ohio. If you've seen firsthand the devotion that the people of Columbus have for the Buckeyes (or if you've felt it yourself), a school-sanctioned committee of students that would dedicate themselves to something as—for lack of a better word—frivolous as planning a week's worth of activities around a football game wouldn't seem strange at all. You'd probably expect it.

When you drive down High Street toward campus, you begin to get the picture. That's the main commercial drag that abuts Ohio State on the east side. It's got bookstores, fast-food joints, bars, banks, coffee shops, drugstores, clothing stores, and a landmark theater. In other words, it's like hundreds of other commercial strips that flank colleges across the country. Sort of.

This strip looks a little different. Hardly a moment passes when you don't spot someone walking down the street—perhaps a student, a faculty member, an OSU alumnus, or just a resident—wearing the colors of Ohio State: scarlet and gray. (These particular colors were chosen to represent the school by a committee of three students back in 1878. The reasons were sensible: they looked good together and they weren't being used by any other school.) On the OSU campus, supporters are always out in force, and it definitely doesn't have to be game day.

Physical evidence of an unwavering passion for the Buckeyes is all over Columbus. Signs on storefronts proclaim: "Go Bucks!" The big placards outside laundromats and fast-food restaurants that are normally reserved for store promotions and specials instead spell out predictions for the score of the upcoming game—usually, a forecast of some Buckeye shellacking or another. Buckeye Donuts, the campus purveyor of deep-fried dough treats for more than 30 years, has more Buckeye memorabilia than it does cream-filled pastries, and that's a lot.

Stores that in most cities might be considered sports-free zones don't exist here. The men and the women making the sandwiches in Subway on Olentangy River Road talk Buckeye football between building turkey subs. The guy working behind the counter at the minimart in the nearby Citgo station has some pretty passionate opinions about Tressel's game calling. And the antiquarian bookseller on East Arcadia closes shop early—the day *before* the game.

Even at a rundown little music shop on High Street, the town's obsession stares you in the face. It's a CD store that specializes in the kind of tunes the average music fan hasn't heard of (don't be caught asking for Britney Spears in here!), where the requisite too-cool-for-school clerks who can't be bothered with "pop music" work behind the counter. It's a store that wouldn't be out of place on a college campus; but not where you would expect to chat about BCS rankings and strength of schedule. But you'd be wrong.

Columbus is not obsessed; it's possessed.

Brad White, a bartender at the Varsity Club, a 44-year-old dirty, smoky paean of alcohol and all things Buckeye on Lane Avenue, succinctly described the Columbus he knows and loves. He actually read this on a T-shirt, and it's been used before, but there's no doubt the shirt fits: COLUMBUS IS A DRINKING TOWN WITH A FOOTBALL PROBLEM.

"Problem" might be a bit of an understatement. Brad and his friends who work at the Varsity Club have seen grown men pray, cry, bang on the bar door at 5 A.M., get drunk, scream at the top of their lungs, and act like assholes—all because of the Buckeyes.

It's hard to explain pure, unadulterated passion, but there are some clues about how it became so damn prevalent. To begin with, this college town isn't a college town. It's not even a town; it's a city. Columbus happens to be the capital of Ohio, as well as the state's largest city. Many out-of-staters will tell you that Cleveland is Ohio's largest city. Or perhaps Cincinnati is the big one. Maybe even Akron. Nope, it's Columbus, with a population of more than 700,000 people, spread over 210 square miles. It ranks as the 15th largest city in America (just behind Jacksonville, Florida, and in front of Louisville, Kentucky). It is also the media capital of Ohio, with a newspaper that has more than a million readers and nine commercial television stations.

Yet somehow, despite its population and media proliferation, for years Columbus managed to maintain the distinction of being the largest city in America without a professional sports franchise. That fact remained true until 2000, when the Columbus Blue Jackets started skating downtown. But can you really count an NHL expansion franchise? And it's not even worth mentioning the Major League Soccer franchise, is it?

The city didn't have a professional sports franchise, but it didn't matter, because Columbus already had what was basically the equivalent: the Buckeyes. Both the morning and the evening TV news programs in Columbus often lead with a Buckeye report (especially, close to game day). The team always gets front-page headlines; in fact, in the 1950s, a sports editor for a Columbus paper told a reporter that the Buckeyes were the most important news in the city. "We do not care what happens in the statehouse, courthouse, city hall, or any place else by comparison," the editor said. "Ohio State football comes first."

Not much has changed. As far as the people of Columbus are concerned, the OSU Buckeyes are their Yankees, their Green Bay Packers, and their Lakers rolled up into one scarlet-and-gray package. "In Columbus, things are intensified," said Buckeye play-by-play man Paul Keels, "because before Blue Jackets, Ohio State was the only game in town."

"What the hell else are you gonna do in the middle of fucking November," a former student said. "The mentality here is football." The Buckeyes are not just a way of life; they are *the* way of life.

"Even if I didn't go to Ohio State, I'd still be an Ohio State fan," said another supporter. "It's Ohio State football, then golf, then women. And God is up there, too."

The passion begins with the students of the Ohio State University, which just so happens to be a *really big* school. In 2003, there were 33,421 full-time undergraduate students enrolled at OSU, and 89 percent of them were from Ohio. (Think: born and bred.) An informal survey revealed that every single one of those students was a Buckeye fan. If you walk through campus, across the Oval (the big, green open space that sits in the center of campus), by the Ohio Union, or anywhere else, you will eavesdrop on conversations about the Buckeyes. In fact, instead of the customary student greeting of "Hey!" or "What's up?" you'll hear a lot of OSU students greet each other with "Hey, go Bucks!"

From the 1900 game against Michigan, when 900 supporters made the trip to Ann Arbor, to today's thriving Block O club—the biggest student organization on campus—the Buckeye Nation has been mobilized for over a hundred years, and it has raised being the fan of a football team to an art form.

The fiercely organized Block O group gathers on Friday nights before games to rehearse and run through their routines, from songs and cheers to stunt-card antics, where the entire Block O section—on cue—will spell out messages for the entire stadium to see ("Go Bucks," "Beat Iowa," "ESPN," etc.). On Saturdays, group members arrive at the game three hours before kickoff to allow time for face painting, maybe a little body painting, final rehearsals, and what can only be described as *frenzification*. Block O kids will tell you, they are not just watching the game; they are part of it. And they'd be right.

■   ■   ■

It is only 200 miles north of Columbus, but Ann Arbor, Michigan, feels very different. It's not just an American college town; it is arguably the prototypical American college town: an open-minded community where hippies, intellectuals, and fraternity brothers can sit side by side, drinking double-tall lattes in one of the city's innumerable coffee shops, while blissfully ignoring each other.

Over the years, Ann Arbor has garnered a reputation for being a bastion of liberalism. To back up this reputation, there have been numerous protests and political rallies, from antiwar to pro-abortion and anything in-between. Ann Arbor is also home to the infamous Hash Bash, an annual tribute to marijuana and its legalization, and a school year–ending ritual called the Naked Mile, which is self-explanatory. Ann Arbor is proud of its liberal tag.

This little city, with a population of 114,000, and the university it contains are basically one and the same. You are never more than a short bike ride away from Central Campus, and each draws its identity from the other. One

Michigan student who grew up in Columbus said, "The difference between Ann Arbor and Columbus is that Ann Arbor is mainly a campus town. In Columbus, the city dominates the campus. In Ann Arbor, the campus dominates the city." But there is another difference: on the whole, Ann Arbor is *not quite* as obsessed with its football team.

The drive into Ann Arbor from I-94 takes you up State Street and past the many practice fields and arenas that are clustered on the south side of campus. But as the sports-related buildings fade in your rearview mirror, so, too, does the presence of Michigan's enormous athletic program. If you were to stroll across the middle of the UM campus, through the large green space known as the Diag, you'd be more likely to hear someone attempt to incite students walking to class with the words, "JFK died for your parents' sins!" rather than "John Navarre cannot win the big game!" (For the record, both statements were heard on the Diag in the fall of 2003, the former much more frequently). Ghosts from Michigan football's legendary history do not constantly jump out at you from behind the campus's many maple trees. Although the Wolverines' influence is still strong, they just don't have the same kind of stranglehold over Ann Arbor that the Buckeyes do over Columbus. One Michigan grad student—a huge Wolverine fan—confirmed that most of his colleagues considered being a sports fan "uncool." "You're not supposed to have time for anything like that," he said.

The team's colors, maize and blue, are definitely prevalent, yet they do not blanket the area. They come out on game day, then mute and recede into the background during the week. The OSU student newspaper did not have to berate its fans for their lack of support the way the UM paper did in 2003. The *Michigan Daily* featured a "Hype-

Meter" that rated the crowd's performance each week in Michigan Stadium and often criticized the fans for their poor showing—the worst of which was likened to "sorority girls on cell phones." The staunchest supporters like to think that the lack of volume in Michigan Stadium is due to the huge bowl-like shape of the place, which is affectionately called the Big House. But people notice the strangely quiet crowd; even the players notice. During practice in the 2003 season, Wolverine star back Chris Perry even suggested that the university hand out paper cups with the bottoms cut out so that fans could use them as impromptu megaphones at the game. Silly, perhaps, but the man wanted to hear his fans when he was running with the football, and he deserved to.

This does not in any way mean that the Michigan Wolverines do not have an extremely large, passionate fan base. Just show up in Ann Arbor on game day, see the throngs of people, and you'll be more than convinced that people love their Wolverines. More than 100,000 fans have packed Michigan Stadium for every home game since 1975 (the longest such streak in college), and they include diehard alumni who return for elaborate tailgates. There are also millions of fans who watch the Wolverines on several nationally televised games each year. Wolverine football is huge.

Yet there are still differences between Michigan and Ohio State fans and the style in which they root for their teams. Several factors help to explain these differences. To begin with, the University of Michigan has an out-of-state student population that is almost three times the size of OSU's. A lot of students come to Ann Arbor already attached to a hometown team and plan to continue rooting for that team full time after graduation. Plus, just 45 miles

down the road is the city of Detroit, which has several professional sports franchises: the Pistons, the Lions, the Red
Wings, and the Tigers (although one could say that the
Lions and the Tigers are recently professional in name
only). That's a lot of action to distract southeastern Michigan sports fans.

Being such a close neighbor of a large city means that
Ann Arbor residents get their news and information from
out of town, and as a result, the Wolverines tend to get
lumped in with all the other teams. (Ann Arbor does have
its own newspaper, the *Ann Arbor News*, which has a circu-
lation of only about 60,000.) In addition, another big state
university—and a fellow Big Ten conference member—
Michigan State, is only 60 miles to the northwest, in East
Lansing. All of this contributes to the reason why you can
be a casual Wolverine fan, whereas being a casual Buckeye
fan is as feasible as being a half-virgin. You can live in Ann
Arbor and not be a Wolverine fan; in Columbus, you're
more likely to spot a rhino on the State House steps than a
non–Buckeye fan.

But the differences between the schools, the cities, and
the fans only feed the Rivalry. For many students, the competition has spread from what happens on the field to the
schools in general. It can be a losing battle when OSU fans
try to argue academic supremacy. In 2003, the *U.S. News
and World Report*, which does a popular ranking of schools,
listed the University of Michigan at number 25 among
national universities, whereas the Ohio State University
was ranked 60th. That's just the tip of the academic iceberg:
ninety-eight percent of UM's freshman class in 2003 had a
3.0 grade average or better in high school; at OSU, only 62
percent of incoming freshmen were in the 80th percentile
or better in their high school classes. The average SAT score

at UM ranges from 570 to 670 for the verbal test and from 610 to 720 in math. At OSU, the same averages are 520–620 for the verbal test and 540–650 in math. Ohio State is a major university, a prodigious place of higher learning and scholarly research, but Michigan can seem, well, more so.

Yet when it comes to having a good time, Ohio State is generally counted among the country's premier venues. *Playboy* magazine, the *U.S. News and World Report* of the party scene, ranked OSU number 12 on its 2003 list of the top party schools, while the University of Michigan did not even crack the list. Until the recent shutdowns, which were designed to clean up the south campus area, High Street was dotted with bars as far as the eye could see. And according to students, the closings have only forced students to be more creative, going to house parties and anywhere else where the alcohol is free flowing. "Yeah, OSU is becoming an academic university," sneered one former student sarcastically. "God forbid." But even mentioning OSU's supremacy on the good time front is splitting hairs, because, newsflash: Michigan students like to party, too. (Apologies to any parents who were not aware.)

A few facts, combined with widespread perceptions, lead to a healthy amount of stereotyping on both sides. OSU fans have labeled Michigan fans "stuck up," "arrogant," "entitled," and "snobs." And yet Michigan students will cop pretty freely to having a superiority complex about the school's academics. After all, a T-shirt that's popular on campus reads "Harvard: The Michigan of the East." On the other side of the coin, Michigan students call OSU fans "psychotic football freaks," "hicks," "rabid," "obnoxious," and "stupid." But at OSU, fans, for the most part, don't even care; their attitude is "Well, at least we'll have fun while we're in school."

The Michigan superiority complex also reveals itself in the stands. Michigan fans have been known to yell "safety school" at the opposing fans of pretty much every team they play in the Big Ten conference (except maybe Northwestern), even when playing those schools in other sports. And only nonconference opponents like Duke and Notre Dame, with their combined excellence in academics and athletics, seem to be considered on equal footing in the eyes of Michigan students.

The stereotypes also result in reams of jokes, like:

> **Q:** Why doesn't OSU have ice on the sidelines?
> **A:** The guy with the recipe graduated.

Or,

> **Q:** What do you call a good-looking girl on the University of Michigan campus?
> **A:** A visitor.

If you're a fan of the screw-in-a-light-bulb variety, there's always:

> **Q:** How many people from the University of Michigan does it take to screw in a lightbulb?
> **A:** Two—One to screw it in and one to brag about it.

And on the flip side:

> **Q:** How many people from the Ohio State University does it take to screw in a lightbulb?
> **A:** Two—One to do it and one to see if they beat Michigan's time.

There are many more, but the latter joke in particular brings up another common notion that's expressed by fans on both sides of the Rivalry: Ohio State is more obsessed with beating Michigan than Michigan is with beating Ohio State. The other professional teams in the area, the Big Ten school Michigan State nearby, and Michigan's supposed superiority complex all give credence to that theory, but there is still plenty of evidence to the contrary.

Block O member Pat Saad is a Michigan native. He grew up near Detroit but most of his family members are OSU alumni. He's seen the Rivalry from both sides and flat out disagrees with the characterization that Michigan fans don't care as much as Buckeye fans do.

"No way," he said. "I've had my car keyed in Michigan because I had Ohio State stuff on it. I've been booed and had stuff thrown at me. If I go to a mall in Michigan with Ohio State stuff on, I'm getting booed—even by people in wheelchairs."

Sometimes the most rabid fans are hard to pick out of the crowd. Take Luba Dub. At first glance, you wouldn't peg the Michigan student to be not only a passionate fan, but one prone to good old-fashioned nastiness. But you never can tell what lurks behind a girl's smile—even a big, sweet one.

"I don't think I've hated anyone as much as I hated the Buckeyes," Luba said, shortly before the 100th meeting between Michigan and Ohio State. Luba was a senior at the University of Michigan, and even though she is originally from Houston, Texas, the Wolverines had quickly taken root deep in her soul. The loss to the Buckeyes 2 years ago at Michigan Stadium was still fresh in her mind, even after 24 months had passed.

"The looks on the senior players' faces were just unbelievably sad," she recalled. "I was crushed. I remember it was a rainy day and we had so much hope going into the game. Even when there were a few seconds left, I was pleading 'There is still time.' When the clock ran out, I couldn't believe we lost to the Buckeyes."

And even worse, it happened again the following year, but Luba—like many Michigan students—was now looking for a bit of redemption. "This year I'm feeling it," she said. "I have no doubt we are going to kick their butts. I have no doubt that they are going to lose. It's the gut feeling I have." And on the off chance that the Wolverines didn't win, Luba had already supplied herself with some preemptive comforting thoughts. "If we do lose against them, I'll think at least we're smarter than them. Yeah, they'll work for us some day."

It's moved beyond the gridiron. The Rivalry is now between the two student bodies of two huge midwestern universities that are only a three-and-a-half-hour drive apart. "Everybody has to hate somebody," said one fan in Columbus. Thanks to all the hard-fought games on the gridiron, the history, the proximity, and these differences, Michigan and Ohio have suitably chosen each other as the enemy.

And it's hardly a recent phenomenon.

■   ■   ■

In 1928, Ohio governor Vic Donahey referred to Michigan and Ohio State as "historic rivals" and mentioned the "long struggle for athletic supremacy between these two neighboring states." And it turns out that Ohio State and Michigan fans just didn't like each other from square one. Then, sometime during the '20s, someone from Columbus wrote a song to express how a lot of fans were feeling. Well, "wrote" is a stretch. The way the story goes is that the song just sort of spontaneously evolved.

It was a few hours before the Game one year in Columbus, and fans had gathered in a downtown hotel, some buying and selling tickets, some making bets, and just a few imbibing an early morning libation—it was, after all, the roaring '20s. One fan, who very likely had been partaking of said libation, walked across the hotel lobby and shouted: "We don't give a damn for the whole state of Michigan!" A band in the lobby stopped playing Ohio fight songs to the gathering crowd and broke into a tune called, "The Old Gray Mare." The boisterous crowd sang along, "Oh, we don't give a damn for the whole state of Michigan, we're from O-HI-O." Eighty years later, it's an OSU favorite, and the Buckeyes don't even have to be playing the Wolverines for fans to start singing it.

The years passed, but the Rivalry only grew. Even before World War II, the Michigan–Ohio State game was one of the biggest sporting events in the country, and the surrounding fan frenzy was already making headlines. Before the 1934 game in Columbus, the city was gripped by a Beat Michigan Week precursor, and the *Ohio State University Monthly* (OSU's alumni magazine) noted a "week of celebration." By Friday, fraternities and sororities, overcome with school pride, were decorating their houses with "all sorts of weird designs," and students took to the streets in a pregame frenzy.

More than 10,000 people gathered at Fifteenth Avenue and High Street to line up behind the OSU marching band. The crowd sang the fight song "Buckeye Battle Cry" ("Smash through to victory / We cheer you as we go / Our honor defend / We will fight to the end / for O-HI-O") and made their way to a field near the stadium. There, students erected a huge bonfire, using old boxes, tree stumps, telephone poles, and every combustible item imaginable. The blaze rose skyward in a triangle of fire, as the crowd roared its approval. It was a huge spectacle in an era not generally known for spectacle—after all, men did not even leave the house without their hats. But this throng was possessed.

In the 37 years since the first matchup, Ohio State had not yet managed a really convincing defeat of Michigan, which was again the defending national champion. The next afternoon, though, after the students' spirited rally, the Buckeyes finally handed the Wolverines their asses on a platter with a 34–0 wallop. (The only thing Michigan could be proud of that day was the fact that a future president of the United States of America named Gerald Ford was playing center. He was even named the team's most valuable player that year.)

After the game, the party really began. A horde of students took to the field and quickly made their way toward the south goal post, surrounding it and pulling it down. The ensuing celebration lasted well into the night. Long before Woody and Bo, long before ESPN, long before people on Internet message boards were arguing which was the greatest rivalry in sports, this one was already the real deal. And the team spirit only seemed to breed hostility.

The next year, mounting aggression between Wolverine and Buckeye fans reached a dangerous level when the game shifted to Ann Arbor. The Buckeyes were in the midst of another strong season (OSU finished 7–1–0 and shared the Big Ten championship with Minnesota), and fans were looking forward to once again smacking the Wolverines around—this time, on the enemy's home turf. They were hoping for a victory at least equal to the one Minnesota pulled off against Michigan earlier that season (40–0), and an incredible 20,000 Buckeye fans made the trip to Ann Arbor to help their team get the job done.

They came pretty darn close to seeing the shellacking

they'd hoped for. The final score was 38–0, and OSU put on a clinic, even scoring a touchdown on what today might be called a triple flea flicker—not by design, but the play did include one forward pass, two laterals. With the second victory against the Wolverines in two years, the fans were ready to celebrate—even on the road. OSU supporters stormed the field, looking to tear down the goal posts in Michigan Stadium and haul them back to Columbus as trophies. Michigan fans, angry from a bitter loss, made it their business to stop them. The opposing teams' fans clashed first at the north goal post, then at the south goal post, and, finally, in the middle of the field. The fight reportedly lasted an hour, and many fans stayed to watch— either while waiting for traffic leaving Ann Arbor to ease up or perhaps for their own enjoyment. And the visiting marauders actually managed to bring one of the posts down but could not get it out of the stadium.

The extended melee was pretty rough, resulting in a lot of black eyes and cut lips, while one man was reportedly knocked unconscious and a second one had six of his teeth kicked in. If that kind of bitter brawl happened today following a football game, it would result in the use of tear gas, riot police, and rubber bullets; perhaps even the National Guard would be summoned.

■ ■ ■

Almost 70 years later, fans are still spilling blood for the Rivalry.

In a room that looked a lot like a mobile hospital, 10 to 15 people were laid out on gurneys, and most of them were not moving. In a businesslike fashion, nurses with white coats and sterile rubber gloves swabbed skin and inserted needles into outstretched, limp arms. Volunteers helped people on and off the tables, and some stumbled as if they were going to pass out.

What looked like a horror show was really for a good cause. The University of Michigan versus the Ohio State University Blood Battle has become an annual tradition, alongside the Game, and after 22 years, it is now the largest blood drive in the region. Both schools took part in the campus-wide drive before the 100th game, and after the pints were tallied, the school that donated the most blood was to be given a trophy during the game. Channeling the natural rivalry between the students into a good cause, the Red Cross and the two schools' chapters of the coed service fraternity Alpha Phi Omega were urging students to donate their much-needed life juice.

Linking a blood drive with the Game is a novel way to use the competitive spirit for a good cause, but it is a competition, nonetheless. Even while working the room, some of the volunteers at the 2003 drive got in some good trash talking.

"It's the armpit of America," Kelly Clement said, unprovoked and matter-of-factly, about the city from whence the Buckeyes came. "You know, Michigan is the hand and Columbus is below, like the armpit." Kelly was a member of Alpha Phi Omega and a huge Wolverine fan since she saw her first game at age 12. In-between seeing to the comfort of would-be blood givers, she offered her thoughts about the enemy from the south.

The conceit of a rivalry blood drive was working; many donors showed up because they wanted to beat Ohio State's butt. "They want to kill OSU," Kelly confirmed. "We murdered 'em last year in the Blood Battle, and I want to beat them again." It was some violent-sounding talk from a woman who was planning to become a nurse, but it reflected how Michigan students felt just before game day. After two straight losses, revenge was in the air.

Unfortunately, there was a dirty little secret about the Blood Battle: whoever donated more blood actually ended up losing the Game. Recently, word of this so-called curse had made the rounds. "It's really hurt us this year," confirmed a senior named Kat Lesko, who was one of the event's chairpersons. "A lot of people, including the entire marching band, refused to donate because they want to win the game." Then she tried to justify it. "The curse hasn't happened every year—just the past 10." Try telling that to fans who have been looking forward all year long to winning this one game. Helping a good cause is one thing, but not if it jinxes the Game.

Still, plenty of nonsuperstitious fans were on hand to make a donation—and to talk Michigan football. Many of the donors suggested that just as it is in Ohio, Wolverine fandom is a birthright passed from generation to generation. As students rose from their gurneys and ambled over to the snack table to stuff their faces with Oreos and apple juice, almost all of them said that they'd grown up as Wolverine fans, and they reminisced about going to games as kids with their families. (Of course, the Michiganders pointed to the corresponding spot on their palms to indicate exactly where their hometown was.) Many students even suggested that the football team was the main thing that brought them to Ann Arbor. So much for academic excellence.

As long as these kids have been Michigan football fans, they've been taught to dislike all things scarlet and gray by parents, older brothers and sisters, friends, and even teachers. A Michigan sophomore named Heather Wilkins first realized just how big Michigan versus Ohio State was while in seventh grade at Shumate Middle School in Gibraltar, Michigan (a town just south of Detroit on Lake Erie—in other words, slightly below the thumb). Her teacher, Mr. Krolack, was an Ohio State fan, and he rubbed a lot of kids the wrong way. Gibraltar is only about 45 miles from the Ohio border. Like many border towns, it has split allegiances, so there were some OSU fans, but Mr. Krolack's openly anti-Michigan stance angered the Michigan fan majority. He even had the nerve to award extra credit whenever Ohio State won. Heather already knew where she stood. "I just remember not liking that teacher very much."

Kaitlin Holloway could relate to Heather's story—as much as a Wolverine fan and a Buckeye fan can relate about anything. Kaitlin is a very young-looking high school sophomore who has already been bitten by the tenacious Buckeye spirit bug. College was still a few years away, but she acted like nothing in the world was more important than the Ohio State Buckeyes.

Kaitlin stood just inside the entrance of the Dreese Laboratories building on OSU's campus early on a Sunday morning, wearing a homemade T-shirt on which she had written, Dave Letterman-style, the "Top 10 Reasons to Love Columbus, OH." The reasons, scrawled on the back of her shirt in her own girlish handwriting, included "Cuz Jim Tressel is way cooler than Lloyd Carr" and "Town-wide attitude of Muck Fichigan." She was already an active participant in the Rivalry, and although she couldn't articulate why ("It's just fun," she said), she was devoted.

Kaitlin woke up at dawn to root for some of her friends who were participating, along with about 500 others, in the Beat Michigan 5K. This was the inaugural event of Beat Michigan Week on the Ohio State campus—Shawn Collier's baby. As the participants (students and nonstudents alike) filled out their entry forms and did stretches, Buckeye patriotism hung thick in the air. "It's a great way to support the team," grad student Tammy Ortman said shortly before the race began.

From the students who showed up wearing "Fuck Michigan" T-shirts to the guy who claimed to have a birthmark on his ass that looked just like a Buckeye (never confirmed), these fans were getting pumped. By the time the runners gathered at the starting line, they were rarin' to go—and to start the clock on the most anticipated and most spirited week of the year.

The runners had Shawn and his diligence to thank. That five-year-old-boy-turned-superfan was the guiding force behind the months of planning that went into Beat Michigan Week. He helped to bring these fans together in a communal show of support, of charity (money was raised for a local food pantry), and in service of what Shawn labeled "faith."

"Being a Buckeye fan for all of my life, going through tough losses, tough seasons, heartbreaking games, ridicule of fans, ridicule of sportswriters . . . there can only be one thing that keeps you hanging on: faith." He compared being a Buckeye fan to believing in a religion, and seeing these spirited fans in the early morning light made it appear as if he was on to something.

"Why go out of my way to do things I'm not even getting paid for?" Shawn said rhetorically, after the race. "It's for the love of it all. Whether it's through seeing everyone else enjoy something I helped to create, or by a Buckeye victory, or by simply something I'll smile about 20 years down the road—that's why I do it. And, go Bucks! Beat Michigan!"

Amen, brother.

3

COLD WAR

Michigan fans were beaming. It was only September 13, but the Wolverines had just passed their first real test of the 2003 season with flying colors.

This time, the kids in the student section were celebrating loud and early. They began to sing that ubiquitous Michigan fight song, raising their fists in unison and bouncing up and down on the long metal bleachers. The Big House was unusually loud because a NCAA-record 111,726 football fans had not short-changed anyone in the cheering department this time. While the final seconds of the game ticked away, some players, including cornerback Jeremy LeSueur, made their way to the student section to celebrate with the Blue Nation. But before he got across the field to slap a few high-fives and get congratulatory pats on the back, LeSueur first turned to look at the scoreboard one more time.

Yup, it was still there: Michigan 38. Notre Dame 0.

It was a pretty good rout. In fact, it was the largest margin of victory the Wolverines had ever managed against the Fighting Irish and the first shutout against that other storied football program since 1902. Notre Dame happens to have a pretty good rivalry going with Michigan, too. As the winningest program in Division I-A college football history, the Wolverines have picked up a few enemies along the way. By putting the hurt on Notre Dame in the middle of September, the Wolverines signaled that 2003 really might be a season to remember.

It also looked like the start of a special season for running back Chris Perry. After two years of battling injuries and struggling for playing time, Perry considered leaving UM. In fact, Coach Carr knew that his back was unhappy and at one point was ready to show him the door.

"'You can leave,' that's how he said it," Perry recalled. "I don't think he was bluffing, but if he was, I didn't call it."

Good thing for the back—and a good thing for Wolverine fans. After a decent year in 2002, while both he and his game matured, Perry came out at the beginning of the 2003 season like he had something to prove. Not the fastest back in college football, Perry learned to use his vision and dexterity to find holes and make big plays. He also had good hands and was on the receiving end of the ball quite a bit, while not being afraid to make a big block or two as well. He helped the Wolverines dominate their first two opponents, Central Michigan and Houston, by a combined score of 95–10, and Perry contributed 4 touchdowns and 416 yards. For an encore against Notre Dame, the shifty runner dodged for 133 yards and scored 3 TDs on 31 carries; he also caught 4 passes, including 1 for a touchdown.

If there was any doubt at the beginning of the season, Perry and the Wolverines were now squarely in the national championship picture. The Marlin Jackson incident was no longer a topic of conversation (after being benched for one game, Jackson was now contributing again on defense), and at 3–0, the Wolverines jumped from number 5 to number 3 in the AP poll. The hype was building—and so was the Wolverines' confidence.

"Our goal is to go undefeated and to win a championship," said LeSueur, the unabashed scoreboard gazer. "We work hard during the summer to do that. This team as a unit is very close, and when we go out and perform like we can, we don't feel we can be beaten."

Well, what a difference a week makes.

The following Monday at a press luncheon, just one week and two days after annihilating Notre Dame, LeSueur and his teammates were chirping a slightly different tune. "We're out for a Big Ten championship," the corner told the reporters, who had gathered, two days after the Wolverines were shocked by the Oregon Ducks on the road at a noisy Autzen Stadium. "We want to win the *rest* of our games." The pledge to win them all and go undefeated was extinct.

LeSueur did his part against Oregon. In the first quarter, the defensive specialist returned a blocked field goal 78 yards for a touchdown, but it was downhill for Michigan from that point on. Special teams' disasters hurt them; these included two missed extra points, one UM punt returned for a touchdown, another one blocked and returned for a touchdown, and a fumble on the snap of a fake punt attempt. While the number 22–ranked Ducks played a tough game in front of a record home crowd, it was the "mighty" Wolverines who waddled through another dispiriting road loss. For the fourth straight year, UM lost a nonconference game away from Michigan Stadium.

And once again, post-game criticism was directed at their quarterback, a fifth-year senior who had taken snaps for three of those previous nonconference losses and who now, for the umpteenth time, was accused of not delivering the big play when his team needed him most. It was a bitter pill to swallow for John Navarre, who threw for 360 yards and 3 TDs and was starting to shoot up the all-time Michigan leader board. But in the fourth quarter, when the Wolverines were engineering a comeback, he threw a costly interception, and after recovering an onside kick, Navarre could not get the ball into the hands of his corps of athletic receivers.

Navarre already knew what the questions would be. He'd been hearing them for three years now. And after the Oregon game, he decided that he just didn't want to talk about it anymore. The Michigan captain did something very un-Wolverinelike (the players are instructed on the proper way to deal with the media): he ducked out of the locker room and boarded the team bus without talking to reporters. The Michigan PR people claimed responsibility for the defiant mute act, citing a mix-up, and finally got him off the bus to answer a few questions. But John Navarre was not enjoying it.

By Monday, the quarterback had calmed down and was able to offer an honest critique of his game. "I think sometimes I forced some balls," he said, "especially on first-down situations where maybe a throw-away or a scramble would have been a better play."

Coach Carr was still trying to protect his quarterback, perhaps because he knew there was a lot of season left and he needed a confident John Navarre in order to continue competing for the Big Ten championship. He did it by mentioning the crown on the field of Autzen Stadium, the area of the field between the hash marks that is built a little higher than the sidelines for drainage purposes. The coach estimated it was 8 to 10 inches higher than Michigan Stadium's. "When you've been around football as long as I have," Carr said, "you know that in the old fields, there's a big crown, and that affects the throws to the sidelines particularly, and I think that affected John. We haven't played on a field with a crown like that. We don't make excuses, but I'm making one for him, because I don't think it's an excuse; it's the truth."

Crowns? Old fields? Michigan fans weren't buying it. The media certainly didn't buy it.

"I'm worried about the Michigan players getting too caught up in their press clippings," said the 2003 sports editor of the *Michigan Daily*, J. Brady McCollough. "I heard stories about players at parties toasting to the Sugar Bowl and then going and losing to Oregon the next week."

Whatever the reason, the team's quest for a second national championship in six years looked like it was over. Now a Big Ten title would have to be enough. Still, no small accomplishment. But the nemesis from Columbus still remained the class of the conference—for now.

■   ■   ■

Everybody said the scarlet and gray were doing it with smoke and mirrors early in 2003, and when the Buckeyes traveled to Madison to play the University of Wisconsin Badgers on October 11, it started to look like everybody might have been right.

Wisconsin's backup quarterback Matt Schabert dropped back to pass and did something the Badgers hadn't done all game: he looked up into the cloudy night sky and sought his star receiver, Lee Evans. With 5:20 remaining in a tie game, Schabert hit Evans (who had beat the Buckeyes' All–Big Ten cornerback Chris Gamble), in stride, to complete a 79-yard touchdown play. The Badgers, in front of a ravenous home crowd at the always-loud Camp Randall Stadium, held OSU in check the rest of the game and, just like that, they ended the Buckeyes' nation-best 19-game winning streak.

You could say it was bound to happen. OSU was tiptoeing through their post–national championship season as if they were a team that was still possessed by the same benevolent football gods that allowed them to beat Miami in the Fiesta Bowl. Those gods allowed OSU to eke out a 16–13 victory in the second game of the '03 season against an unranked San Diego State. Then the deities reappeared the following week and presided over an overtime goal line stand that meant a victory, but another close call against number 24–ranked North Carolina State. And then, yet again, it took a last-second interception to ice a victory against Bowling Green in the fourth game of the season. Now, there's luck, and then there's whatever crazy voodoo the Buckeyes had on their side.

You could also chalk it up to good coaching, and the Buckeyes certainly had that. Before being hired by OSU in 2001, Jim Tressel coached at Youngstown State for 15 seasons, where he led the Penguins to four Division I-AA national championships and earned a reputation as a coach who places tantamount importance on field position, defense—and doing just enough to win games. At OSU, the same formula translated into success and that monster 2002 season—even if it meant that watching OSU football games was a lot like watching paint dry.

"He's very, very, *very* conservative," one Bucknut said.

"That's why people say OSU's lucky. And they can be, they play a lot of close games. But the thing about OSU is you have to go 60 minutes to beat them."

Buckeye radio play-by-play man Paul Keels agreed. "One of the clichés that Tressel uses is 'win the surest way,' but it's not always that pleasing to the eye."

Five games into the season, the Buckeyes were still undefeated, but they were also still searching for a consistent offense. OSU's football team was ranked third best in the country coming into their game against Wisconsin, and they were riding the country's longest win streak at 19 games, but they were averaging only 298.4 total yards of offense per game. That was good enough for 105th best among the 117 Division I-A teams.

It was easy to try to pin the blame on Clarett. Sure, OSU's star running back had been suspended (after Clarett was charged with a misdemeanor, Geiger suspended him for the entire season), and he had already begun legal proceedings to fight the NFL's mandatory three-year, post–high school waiting period before entering the draft, but according to players and coaches, the Buckeye approach to offense was never about just one player. Still, there appeared to be a missing weapon in Coach Tressel's arsenal. And even with a healthy, cleared Clarett on the team, he would never have been on the field when Wisconsin's Lee Evans made that one big catch.

Regardless, all of those close, gut-wrenching games had to be taking their toll on the Buckeyes. And if you wanted to look for any visible signs of frustration, you wouldn't have to look any farther than that third quarter against Wisconsin. The only reason Badger backup quarterback Schabert, who had just two touchdown passes in his entire collegiate career, was even in the game was that OSU linebacker Robert Reynolds exercised his own inner frustrations on the throat of starting Badger QB Jim Sorgi. Under a big pileup, Reynolds intentionally pushed his hand hard into Sorgi's throat, and the QB had to leave the game after he experienced difficulty breathing. Perhaps Reynolds and some of his teammates were a little tightly wound.

"I lost my poise and there is no excuse for that," Reynolds said later. "That is certainly not characteristic of Ohio State football. I take full responsibility for my action. As a senior, I have a responsibility to set a better example."

An apology would not take back the winning touchdown; it would not bring back an undefeated season, a clean run to a back-to-back championship bid, or any of that ol' voodoo. The smoke and mirrors were gone, and Michigan and Ohio State had both hit the first bumps in the season's long road to their ultimate clash. The promise of a magical 100th showdown that would be equal to all those historic battles was now up in the air—way up in the air. Just like that pass to Evans.

■　■　■

And just like the extra point attempt by Ohio State's quarterback Meyers Clark on November 13, 1926.

The QB—who also handled the kicking duties—was snapped the ball by the center and as a "drop kicker," he attempted to put it through the uprights the way a punter would. He tossed the ball in front of his foot and swept his strong leg across his body until it made contact with the leather. The ball then ricocheted off Clark's foot and cut through the unseasonably warm November air in a perfect line toward the center of the goal posts. The 90,411 fans (the largest crowd ever to attend a football game at OSU, until that point), who were packed into every nook and cranny of the university's grand four-year-old stadium were breathless, as the Buckeyes were on a verge of a late-game tie with the mighty Wolverines.

Even at the first hint of dawn, it had looked as if it would be a magical day.

From all over Ohio, people descended on the state capital. There were so many out-of-town visitors that Columbus police had to enlist soldiers from nearby Fort Hayes to help them handle the unprecedented crowds. Thousands camped overnight for a block of extra tickets that went on sale the morning of the game, and many of those who could not get a seat stormed the gates anyway. Others scaled fences to get in, and there were more than a few broken arms and legs. Once inside, fans were treated to the sight of a huge banner, stretching the entire length of the field, that urged the home team to BEAT MICHIGAN! in big red letters.

Adding to a somewhat chaotic scene were pregame "aerial bombs" (think really big fireworks), set off under the supervision of the OSU military department. They were supposed to launch over the stadium walls, excite the big crowd, and land innocently outside. An errant bomb landed in the crowd in the south stands and exploded, injuring two sisters, one of whom was badly burned and spent time in the hospital. (OSU was kind enough to pay her medical expenses and awarded the woman $5,000 for personal injuries.)

Bomb or no bomb, drama was flying through the air. Ohio State was sporting a gaudy undefeated 6–0 record, while Michigan was a respectable 5–1, and the Wolverines had swept the last four clashes between the two rivals.

Another compelling story line revolved around the two teams' captains: OSU's Marty Karow and UM's Benny Friedman. Both were Cleveland natives who'd first battled each other on the gridiron as members of rival high schools and then three previous times during their college careers, while in Columbus and Ann Arbor, respectively.

The first points of the 1926 game came after Friedman (the traitor from Cleveland) fumbled a fair catch punt return, and OSU recovered on Michigan's 11-yard line. The play resulted in a field goal, thanks to Clark's sure foot.

The next score would have been reshown hourly on *SportsCenter* if it had happened during the current highlight-reel-frenzy gaze of modern college sports. OSU's Robin Bell dropped back as if to punt, caught the Michigan secondary off guard, and lofted the ball 40 yards in the air. Clark had lined up to the left, behind Michigan's halfback, and he took off at full speed down the field. As the ball came hurtling toward him, Clark left his feet in an uncontrolled, full-tilt leap, barely catching the ball on his outstretched fingertips. He then dragged two Michigan defenders to the 2-yard line before finally being brought down. It was the longest pass in Ohio Stadium history, and the Buckeyes' Karow quickly ran the ball in for the TD. Clark hit the point after, and OSU led 10–0.

The huge crowd was ecstatic.

OSU had scored 10 points in the first 12 minutes of the game, and the Wolverines took a much-needed timeout. During the break, Michigan fullback Wally Weber turned to three-time All-American end Bennie Oosterbaan and said, "Ben, at this rate they're going to beat us 40–0." Oosterbaan was not concerned. "Dammit, Wally, we haven't had the ball yet," he shot back.

Now on offense, Michigan began to chip away. Friedman

hit Oosterbaan on a pass to OSU's 21-yard line. Then, on fourth down with four yards to go, the Wolverines lined up like they were going to kick a field goal, and the two again connected for a touchdown. The fake worked perfectly.

The Wolverines now had the Buckeyes playing a guessing game. With 30 seconds left in the half and the ball on Ohio State's 43-yard line, Michigan again lined up as if they were going to kick a field goal. This time, Oosterbaan walked over and whispered something to Friedman, and the Buckeyes thought the fake was on again. The defense dropped back again, thinking pass, and without any rush from the confused Buckeyes, Friedman split the uprights. Call it a *fake* fake. The game was tied.

The third quarter was a scoreless battle, and then in the fourth, Michigan got the break they were looking for. Like any great football game—and the best rivalry games—it came down to a split-second decision, this time by OSU's Elmer Marek. As the quarter came to an end, UM's Louie Gilbert kicked a low punt that seemed to be headed for the end zone. It took a funny bounce, and Marek made the fateful decision to try to recover the ball near the 5-yard line, rather than let it reach the end zone. He streaked to the ball, bobbled it, and it wound up in the arms of Michigan guard Sid Dewey. As the fourth quarter opened, the Wolverines scored another touchdown and were now up 17–10.

The hometown fans would not let the Buckeyes quit. Buoyed by the monumental crowd, OSU went back on the attack. They marched down field and completed a flawless drive to the end zone, capped by Byron Eby's short run uncontested from just outside the goal line. Clark was now dog-tired from marching his team down the field, but he had been OSU's successful kicker all day—money in the bank—and so he took the snap and attempted to tie the game from the 15-yard line.

This was the fateful ball that went sailing through the air, but when it came down, it was short of the crossbar by inches. The crowd was stunned. Almost immediately, tears began to stream down the QB's face, and as he walked to the sidelines, he threw himself on the ground in despair. Friedman then made an interception, to beat his rival captain and ice another Michigan–Ohio State thriller.

Goats and heroes: they both tend to rear their heads in important games, and the 99 meetings between Michigan and Ohio State have been riddled with both of them. In 1926, Clark wound up the goat when he muffed that kick, and for his play, Friedman was the hero.

In 1939, UM's Fred Trosko got to be both—in one game.

The Flint, Michigan, native was having a bad year. He'd made a lot of mistakes for the Wolverines, and his coach knew it. Before the OSU game, Fritz Crisler called the 154-pound halfback into his room at the Barton Hills Country Club, where the Wolverines at that time stayed the nights before games. "Freddie, I still have supreme confidence in you," Crisler reportedly told the senior (reminiscent of Carr's words of encouragement to his QB in 2003).

It's hard to imagine what Crisler must have been thinking, then, when Trosko fumbled on a Michigan first down and gave the ball to the Buckeyes, who scored the game's first touchdown. And then, only three minutes later, a long pass by Trosko was intercepted by OSU's John Hallabrin and run back to the 20, leading to another Buckeye score. It was 14–0, thanks solely to Trosko's two costly mistakes. The coach's endorsement of his player appeared to help no one.

But the Wolverines were not going to lie down—especially if Tom Harmon had anything to say about it. Tom Harmon was the greatest football player the University of Michigan has ever seen. He wasn't just a prolific passer. Harmon was a powerful rusher. He was an incredible kicker. He was an accomplished punter. And—for good measure— he was a ferocious defensive back. He was a two-time All-American and the Wolverines' first Heisman Trophy winner. He probably would have driven the team bus if Coach Crisler had asked him to.

Harmon would also contribute the greatest single player performance in the history of the Rivalry. In 1940, Harmon completed 11 of 12 passes for 151 yards and 2 touchdowns, ran for 139 yards and another 2 touchdowns, intercepted 3 passes, averaged 50 yards a punt, and kicked 4 extra points, as Michigan beat OSU, 40–0. He was so good, he even received a standing ovation from the Ohio Stadium crowd. Now *that's* respect. After playing football at Michigan, Harmon became a popular broadcaster and paved the way for many ex-athletes to jump to the airwaves. Harmon is also the father of actor Mark Harmon. All-American? You could say so.

In the second quarter of the '39 game, the Michigan powerhouse hit Joe Rogers for a 44-yard completion and followed it up with a TD pass to Forest Evashevski. Harmon then single-handedly tied the game by carrying the ball into the end zone from the OSU 16-yard line and nailing the extra point.

Still, the Buckeyes had more than just a slim chance to get back in and win the game. They returned the kickoff 57 yards and were on the Michigan 11 faster than Buckeye fans could sing "Carmen Ohio." But OSU's Hallabrin fumbled, and the Wolverines' Bob Westfall quickly recovered the loose ball. Still, Michigan could not convert on offense, and the two teams traded punts until OSU began another big drive. This time, OSU made it to the 38 before coughing up another fumble, again recovered by Westfall.

Harmon once again marched his team down field, and with 50 seconds left, they were at OSU's 24-yard line. It was fourth down, and the game was on the line. In a moment so perfect it couldn't have been scripted, Crisler was faced with a decision. So who does he turn to, to try and win the game? His best player, or the man whose confidence he tried desperately to reinflate just 12 hours earlier and who had already cost them dearly?

Trosko, of all people, trotted back into the game, knelt behind the center, and took the snap, as Harmon ran up as if to kick the field goal. OSU charged the ball, desperate to try and block it, but the oval remained in Trosko's slippery hands. He then got to his feet, ran toward the sideline, and raced untouched into the end zone for a touchdown. This time, as Trosko left the field, Michigan Stadium erupted in applause. Like the plot of a bad science fiction movie, a goat was genetically altered and a football hero emerged.

OSU still won the Big Ten championship, following Northwestern's tie of heavily favored Iowa, but the title was more than just a little bittersweet. Even when you win a championship, if you lose to Michigan, there is no celebrating in Columbus.

But OSU's luck would quickly change, and the football-crazed fans of Columbus would have a lot to celebrate. The 1942 season was a memorable one for the Buckeyes. OSU was undefeated and captured a conference and national championship, after dispensing with the Wolverines 21–7. But it was the 1944 game that became a permanent part of Rivalry lore.

As World War II raged, college football programs were a

shadow of their former selves, with teams populated mostly by freshmen too young to be drafted and older players too weak to be soldiers. Still, the '44 game was between two very good football teams (OSU was 8–0 and UM was 8–1), and the winner would once again walk away with the conference championship.

Looking for a distraction from war news, 71,958 people came to Ohio Stadium on November 25 and saw a football game for the ages—a see-saw ground battle that could be considered yet another blueprint for the entire war.

This time, it was OSU that had the Heisman Trophy winner on their side, and his name was Leslie Horvath. An unlikely football hero, Horvath was rail-thin but possessed amazing speed. But after leading Ohio State to a championship in '42, Horvath quit football and enrolled in the dentistry school. Coach Carroll Widdoes convinced Horvath to come back and play an extra season, which he was still eligible for, thanks to special wartime rules.

It was Horvath's 18-yard punt return in the first quarter that set up an eventual score, when Oliver Cline punched through the Michigan line and scored a TD with 1:42 left. After a missed conversion, the Buckeyes were up 6–0.

Michigan was getting nowhere fast, and as halftime approached, the Wolverines hadn't moved the ball beyond OSU's 45-yard line. That changed when UM's Ralph Chubb intercepted a Horvath pass and ran it to the 25. Just 22 seconds before the half, Michigan broke through and took the lead 7–6.

The Wolverines came out driving in the second half, but their efforts were quickly cut short by a Donald Lund fumble that was recovered by Gordon Appleby. Still, Ohio gave the ball back, but another fumble, this time by Chubb, and another recovery by Appleby, and the Bucks finally scored when Horvath ran the ball in from the 1-yard line. The point after was blocked, but OSU led 12–7 as the third quarter ticked away.

In the fourth, though, the Wolverine defense stopped the Bucks on the 16 and marched 84 yards the other way for a score, the point after, and a 14–12 lead.

Then it was decision time. There is a certain person on the same side of the field as the players, who does not suit up, does not get dirty, and does not get bruised, but who can be just as instrumental in the game's outcome. On this particular day, that person's name was Fritz Crisler. The Michigan coach felt that the Wolverines needed more than a 2-point cushion against the mighty Buckeyes. He elected to have his team gamble with an on-sides kick, and the ball went out of bounds at OSU's 49-yard line.

The good field position was enough to inspire the Buckeyes. They moved the ball up field, driving for more than 5 minutes with an aggressive ground attack that landed them on the 1-yard line. It was Les Horvath who plowed in for the TD. OSU missed the extra point, but they now led 18–14.

The 71,958 in Ohio Stadium went crazy. The home team had again wrestled the lead, and the game's final hero, Dick Flanagan, sealed the victory with an interception. OSU won the conference championship, and Horvath became the Rivalry's second Heisman Trophy winner.

For all their delirium after that game, Buckeye supporters were probably pretty glad to see the 1940s pass by the wayside. OSU was just 2–6–2 against their hated rivals and was outscored in those 10 games 232–85.

As the annual contest entered a new decade—its seventh— it seemed as if it would be hard to match the excitement that recent Michigan–Ohio State games had generated. Not a chance. Even if there was a remote possibility that the Rivalry's best days were past, Mother Nature stepped in to declare that the best was yet to come.

■ ■ ■

The night before the game, it just seemed like it would be cold—really cold. And football players are used to the hard sting of the leather on cold, chapped hands. Or the way solid frozen turf punishes knees and backsides. So, it was with normal game-time trepidation that Michigan and Ohio State players awoke on November 23, 1950.

For the Buckeyes, it was a slightly more restful sleep. They were 6–2–0 that season (and had even spent some time at the number 1 spot in the national AP football poll) and were playing at home and facing a much weaker Wolverine squad, which had managed only 4 wins. Even with the mismatched records, both teams arrived at Ohio Stadium with a shot at the Big Ten championship, and the Wolverines held onto a slim hope of earning a trip to the Rose Bowl (OSU could not go to Pasadena, due to a no-repeat rule enacted by the conference committee).

But at daybreak, all that was an afterthought. Columbus and the rest of northern and central Ohio woke up under a heavy blanket of snow, and it was still falling—fast. Out of nowhere, the region was gripped by the worst blizzard anyone had witnessed in 37 years. The temperature was hovering around 5 degrees, and the winds were swirling at nearly 40 miles per hour. Not a particularly great day for football or even to try to get to a football game.

By early morning, traffic was almost at a standstill, and trains were delayed more than two hours. The Michigan team slowly made its way from Toledo, where they stayed the night before, and as game time approached, the two athletic directors, Michigan's Fritz Crisler (now AD) and Ohio's Dick Larkins, had a decision to make. Crisler reportedly favored playing the game, despite the bad weather. Some people thought he believed that the messy weather might favor the underdog Wolverines and that he supposedly convinced Larkins to play, citing the potential disaster of trying to refund more than 87,000 ticket buyers. The OSU chief bowed to the pressure. Unable to get in touch with the conference commissioner, he decided on his own that the game would be played.

Into the stadium trickled fans toting blankets, layers of clothing, multiple pairs of gloves, ear muffs, and even cardboard boxes with holes cut out of them to slip over their heads to keep their faces warm. The chief groundskeeper, Ralph Guarasci, and his makeshift crew (consisting of several hundred volunteers, including local Boy Scout troops) desperately tried to clear the snow off the field and remove the frozen tarpaulin. They started clearing the field at noon, and in many cases, the tarp was just ripped off in strips. After a 2-hour-and-20-minute delay, the field was as good as it was going to get, and the players went through some quick warm-ups (if you could possibly call them that).

During the pregame workout, Michigan assistant coach Dick Kempthorn saw that UM back Chuck Ortmann was having trouble handling the snap because of the frigid temperatures, and he gave Ortmann a brand-new pair of deerskin gloves he had bought in Colorado. Ortmann gladly wore them in the game, where holding onto the ball would become paramount.

The official attendance was said to be 50,503, but photographs and eyewitnesses confirm that this figure was grossly exaggerated. A sparse crowd watched what would be hard-pressed to be called football, but it was compelling, nonetheless.

Traditional football plays just did not work. Formations and designed plays were useless on the snow-white turf, passes sailed high over receivers' heads in the swirling winds, and making cuts and running routs in the snow were almost impossible. On top of that, finding the goal line, the side lines, or even the yard markers was an adventure. Volunteers were stationed around the field with brooms to help the officials when it was time to measure for a first down. "Having the ball today is a liability," said Michigan's Oosterbaan.

Instead, punting the ball became the name of the game. The two teams combined for 45 kickaways, by far a conference record.

Michigan's second of many punts that day was blocked, and OSU's Bob Momsen recovered the ball at the 8-yard line. OSU then turned to their star Vic Janowicz, the Buckeyes' second Heisman Trophy winner, and the man many consider to be the greatest athlete to ever play football at Ohio State. In the tradition of the utilitarian way that football was played in 1950, Janowicz did it all: passing, running, blocking, punting, kicking, and playing safety. And he did it all extremely well.

In the snow, however, nothing worked. Janowicz tried a run around the right side of the Wolverines' defense and was getting nowhere fast. He then stopped and spun his body completely around, in an attempt to go the opposite direction. It was useless and Janowicz began to run away from the line of scrimmage, while being pursued aggressively by the defense. In desperation, he then just lofted the ball to the back of the end zone. No receiver was even close to the ball, and intentional grounding was called.

The play symbolized the futility that both teams faced all afternoon.

Back at the 34, the Buckeyes ran again but were stopped for another loss before Janowicz finally found a receiver. The 13-yard completion to Tom Watson was the longest gain of the day.

OSU coach Wes Fesler decided that this might be his team's best shot of the day at scoring and opted to kick the field goal immediately. With a vicious wind still circling, snow falling, and the uprights almost completely hidden from view, Janowicz lined up for the kick. Somehow, he put the ball through the uprights and gave the Buckeyes a 3–0 lead. The 27-yard kick into a driving snowstorm is still considered one of the greatest feats in Ohio State football history.

"When he kicked the ball, it went up in a cloud of snow," former OSU sports information director Marv Homan recalled. "It just disappeared."

The referees seemed to see it; it was just too bad that score didn't hold up.

Predictably, the game became mostly a battle of field position. Later in the first quarter, Janowicz attempted a punt (on first down!) and Michigan captain Allen Wahl charged in and blocked it. When the ball bounced out of the end zone, the Wolverines were awarded a safety, and the game was now 3–2.

But the controversial turning point of the game came near the end of the second quarter. OSU had the ball on third down on their 13, with 47 seconds left in the half. Since everyone on the field and in the stadium was slowly freezing to death, OSU coach Wes Fesler instructed Janowicz to just punt the ball away.

After the snap, Michigan's Tony Momsen charged the

line of scrimmage and miraculously blocked the ball off his chest. He followed the bouncing oval into the end zone and fell on top of it in a snow sandwich. The ball squibbed away, but he reached out with one hand while face-down in the snow and finally corralled the football. After the touchdown and the extra point, the Wolverines had the lead, 9–3.

Momsen was the brother of OSU's Bob Momsen, and the boys from Toledo were, along with the snow, the story of the day. They wound up on either side of the Rivalry, thanks to a sibling rivalry. Tony first chose to play football at Michigan, and later Bob decided to attend OSU so that he no longer had to be in his brother's shadow, as he'd been during their years together at Libbey High School. And like a cruel joke, even after recovering a blocked punt himself, Bob wound up in his brother's shadow, in the annals of football history, thanks to Tony's historic touchdown.

"It was a big play at the time," Bob said years later, "but I thought we were going to come back and win it in the second half."

Almost immediately, grumblings started in the sparsely populated grandstand, and Fesler's decision to punt the ball was more than a little controversial. Had the OSU coach run just two plays, it is possible that the Buckeyes would have used the remaining time on the clock, and they could have retreated to the warmth of the dressing room with a 3–2 lead. In his defense, Fesler later said that running two plays would not take "enough time to close out the end of the period. So rather than take a chance of anything happening, I wanted to get the ball out of there. That's why I ordered the punt."

Perhaps even more amazing than Momsen's blocked punt was the fact that both teams' marching bands performed their scheduled halftime shows. Instruments had to be treated with alcohol to keep the valves from freezing. It's hard to imagine that anyone left in the crowd paid any attention, but the bands slipped and slogged through their routines, nonetheless.

The second half of what quickly became known as "The Snow Bowl" was just a punt-fest. The weather got worse, and the players on the field were almost impossible to see from the press box. Down on the field, it wasn't much better. On Michigan's first possession, they fumbled the ball, and OSU recovered at the 30-yard line, but the Wolverines quickly intercepted Janowicz, and the threat was neutralized. Moving the ball was basically impossible, and neither team did it—for the rest of the game.

With two minutes remaining, the players got the news of an impossible upset in Evanston, where Northwestern beat Illinois. As a result, Michigan, if they could hold on, would improbably win the conference and a trip to the Rose Bowl—without ever getting a first down. It happened.

The statistics were freakish. Michigan gained a net total 27 yards on the ground, and OSU gained 16. Michigan threw 9 passes and completed none. OSU threw 18 and completed 3 for 25 yards. Both teams combined for those 45 punts and 10 fumbles.

A disappointed Buckeye team was in shock after a strange end to what was now a failure of a season. Many of the players retreated to the locker room, with tears already frozen to their cheeks. "It's like a nightmare," said OSU's Sonny Gandee, bloody from a cleat to the chin, right after the game. "It couldn't have happened, and you're going to wake up and find it was a bad dream."

The nightmare continued for the city of Columbus and for fans trying to get home. Cars were stranded, and runways were closed. Deliveries were canceled, and many restaurants began to run out of food. The university didn't resume classes again until the following Thursday.

But all of that paled in comparison to losing to a Michigan team that everyone knew was much weaker than the Buckeyes. The talk in town continued to revolve around Fesler and his decision to punt that ball right before halftime. (AD Larkins and his decision to play the game in the first place took a lot of heat as well.) It didn't help Fesler's case that in four years, the OSU coach had not beaten his northern rival. The fans and the press set their targets on the coach, and Fesler bowed to the pressure and quit a couple of weeks after the Snow Bowl.

Anger and disappointment blanketed Columbus like the dirty snow left by the blizzard, but shortly after it all melted away, Ohio State had a new coach, and beating Michigan became not just an annual goal but appeared to be the program's and its eccentric new leader's sole reason for being.

4

TWO MEN AND
A RIVALRY

It was a freezing-cold February night, and the portly head coach snoozed in the passenger seat of an automobile speeding down a Michigan highway. The driver was a man named Ed Ferkany. He'd been an assistant coach at Ohio State for only one month, but he'd accompanied his boss on a recruiting trip. It was all part of the job.

Something suddenly made the driver glance down at the fuel gauge. It was getting dangerously close to "empty." They would need to pull over and get gas. He had to wake his boss.

"Nah, keep going," grunted the coach.

So they drove on, even passing a gas station. Ferkany was getting worried, but another service station's lights loomed in the distance. So he asked his boss one more time, and this time the coach's response was unambiguous.

"No, goddammit!" he growled. "We do not pull in and fill up. And I'll tell you exactly why we don't. It's because I don't buy one goddam drop of gas in the state of Michigan!

We'll coast and push this goddam car to the Ohio line before I give this state a nickel of my money!"

The story has to be a fake.

It sounds exactly like a legend that has been passed down over the years, exaggerated, embellished, overblown—anything to perpetuate the myth. Sure, many popular variations are told around campus, including one that has the coach pushing his car seven miles to the state line after running out of gas, but the story is as real as the walls of Ohio Stadium itself.

Wayne Woodrow Hayes, the legendary OSU head coach, refused to buy gas in the home state of his biggest rival. Not only that, he couldn't even bring himself to say "Michigan." He referred to the state from which his greatest competitor came only as "the place up north."

It's an extraordinary tale, but fitting, because the man everyone called Woody was no ordinary football coach.

The record stands alone. In 28 seasons as the head coach of the Ohio State Buckeyes, Hayes's teams went 205–61–10, while winning 13 Big Ten championships and 5 national championships. He took the Buckeyes to 8 Rose Bowls and won 4 of them. Plus, he coached 2 Heisman Trophy winners and 56 All-Americans. He is the eighth-winningest NCAA Division I-A football coach of all time and can easily be spoken of in the same breath as immortals like Paul "Bear" Bryant, Knute Rockne, and Glenn "Pop" Warner.

But with the wins came a larger-than-life personality, not to mention a wicked temper.

During his sometimes-volatile tenure as OSU's coach, Hayes ripped up his own hat, threw his wallet, threw his attaché case, stomped on his own watch, crushed his own glasses (until his hands bled), threw down markers on the field, threw water coolers, threw coffee, threw play cards, threw telephones . . . Basically, if it wasn't nailed down, Hayes probably threw it. In general, he threw more fits than could ever be properly cataloged.

And in what has to stand at the height of a temper-laced career, in a state of unadulterated rage, Hayes once even punched himself in the face—with both fists, cutting his cheek with his own 1968 championship ring. What drove the coach to literally beat himself up? Not much. One of his players accidentally got injured in practice, but among his many eccentricities, Hayes loathed injuries. He apparently had a fetish about injury prevention, even making his players do special neck exercises to help prevent injury.

Blow-ups were frequent and fiery. Players, refs, coaches, and the media—no one was immune to the coach's verbal wrath and occasional physical assault. A good knock on the shoulder pads was Hayes's preferred way to get a football player's undivided attention.

And yet this ornery, unpredictable man was—and is—the icon of Ohio State football and, by extension, the city of Columbus. Everywhere you turn, you'll still see his famous visage: a paunchy man in a white short-sleeved shirt—which he wore for almost every game day, no matter how cold it was—with glasses and a hat emblazoned with a single block letter "O" perched on his head. You'll still see it in bars, restaurants, stores, and coffee shops; on bill-boards; and on the big electronic scoreboard at Ohio Stadium. The multitude of Woody Hayes images around town can make Columbus resemble a strange country where the dictator is a fat football coach. There is even a Woody look-alike who skulks around the stadium and poses for pictures. Woody Hayes is still—and always will be—king.

But beyond the cult of personality and unpredictability, the real reason that Woody Hayes is revered as a deity in Columbus is his unrelenting desire to win football games. Nothing else was even remotely important in comparison. Hayes made winning paramount, he would accept nothing less, and his attitude helped transform OSU into a veritable winning machine.

His approach to the game of football was, in a word, *basic*. He wasn't known as a great tactician. But what he lacked in playmaking skills, he made up for with his attention to detail and motivational skills. His pregame and half-time speeches were legendary for their evocation of military might—his hero was, perhaps unsurprisingly, General George Patton—and for making his players believe they were invincible.

On the field, Hayes was hopelessly dedicated to the running game and famously referred to his own brand of football as "three yards and a cloud of dust." He loathed to pass the ball and once said, "There are three things that can happen when you pass, and two of them ain't good." And when there were critics—and there were always critics—he didn't care. "I'm not trying to win a popularity poll," Woody said. "I'm trying to win football games."

But to get that far, to even be in a position to not buy gas in Michigan, blow up at one of his players, or generally be a cantankerous SOB, Hayes had to be given enough rope to stick around for a while and run the program the way he wanted to run it, and that's something that wasn't particularly easy for OSU coaches to do. In fact, the university had a reputation for loving and leaving its coaches, like a bored john. OSU was referred to in the press as a "graveyard of coaches."

And without fail, the one thing that could send even the most qualified field practitioner to the boneyard with a shovel to start digging his own grave was losing to Michigan.

Even from the very beginning, it wasn't tolerated.

■　■　■

It may have taken Ohio State 15 tries to notch their first victory against the Wolverines, but once the Buckeyes got a taste, they didn't want to stop lining up at the buffet.

The man who first led them over Michigan was Dr. John W. Wilce, who began coaching the Buckeyes in 1913. And with the help of his All-American Chic Harley (OSU's first truly immortal footballer), the Buckeyes finally vanquished their already "ancient foe" 13–3 on October 25, 1919, in front of 27,000 football fans at Ferry Field in Ann Arbor. Harley scored on a 42-yard touchdown run, kicked an extra point, intercepted 4 passes, and punted 11 times, including a 60-yarder. The *Ohio State University Monthly* described the game as "perhaps the biggest game of all Ohio State athletics to date" and worried, for good reason, that they would "run on for page after page in superlatives." Following the victory was "the biggest night's celebration Columbus had ever seen."

Together, Harley and Wilce were the toast of the town, and OSU football was now officially big time. Unfortunately, 1919 was also Harley's final year of eligibility, and the good doctor (who also continued to practice medicine on the side) was the one who had to stick around and listen to the invariable cries of "Beat Michigan," which seemed to reach a fever pitch overnight.

As was bound to happen, the Wilcemen (the team was

nicknamed after their coach) hit a bump in the road. And worst of all, it began amid the fanfare of the dedication of their brand-new stadium.

In 1922, the $1.5 million, two-tier, concrete structure that could hold 65,000 fans was officially opened for use. It was called Ohio Stadium, but the grand structure was nicknamed "The House That Harley Built," for the excitement that their former star generated.

But on their day to shine in front of Columbus and the entire college football–loving world in the newest, greatest example of athletic architecture in the country, the Buckeyes got their butt kicked—by Michigan.

There was plenty of pomp that day, plenty of circumstance, but no OSU offense. The final score was Michigan 19, Ohio State 0. And this celebrated setback was only the beginning.

Ohio State also lost the next 5 battles with Michigan, and their coach was on the chopping block. People in Columbus were happy to have Wilce be their doctor but not their football coach. He saved them from undergoing any more dispiriting losses to Michigan by retiring his post after the 1928 season.

Next!

The person who slipped into Wilce's not-so-comfortable shoes was one of his own assistants, Sam Willaman, who had the unfortunate nickname "Sad Sam." Willaman was a winning coach (26–10–5), but the Big Ten title eluded him, as did victories against the Wolverines. Remarkably, Willaman lost only two games in his final two seasons at OSU; unfortunately, they were both to Michigan. Not one to shy away from controversy, the OSU student paper called publicly for a coaching change. Willaman spared everyone further heartbreak, and Sad Sam sadly called it quits.

Next!

The subsequent coach to walk through OSU's revolving door was a real doozy—and just what the program needed. This new coach made his presence felt the second he arrived.

"My name's Schmidt," the tall, cocky new leader told his team on the practice field in the fall of 1934. "I'm the new football coach here," he growled in his trademark southern drawl. "This thing is a football," he told his boys, while clutching the pigskin. "At one time, it was used here at Ohio State to place behind opponents' goal lines, for which Ohio State was credited with six points. I understand that usage has been sort of overlooked here in recent years. That's not funny. It's tragic. For your information, I'm figuring on reviving the old custom. And one more thing, I want you to remember it from now on: we're going to beat Michigan this year. Yes, beat Michigan. Why not? Those guys put their pants on one leg at a time, the same as you do."

His full name was Francis A. Schmidt, and he came from Texas, where they apparently did things a bit more demonstratively than in central Ohio. But Schmidt seemed to have the mouth, and also the track record, to inspire his new team. He had already won two Southwest Conference titles in five seasons with Texas Christian University, where he had compiled an impressive .868 winning percentage. His style of play was referred to as "razzle dazzle," and his offenses used several different formations (then mostly unheard of), and contained more than 300 plays. Many of those plays consisted of several laterals behind the line of scrimmage—highlight film–type stuff, which he was constantly diagramming and showing off while using his favorite expression, "Lookee here."

But what really got the OSU fans excited were those decisive words about Michigan—and Schmidt's ability to put his money where his mouth was. That first year as coach, Schmidt and his Buckeyes blasted the Wolverines 34–0, and fans poured onto the field at Ohio Stadium and tore down the goal posts for the first time in Ohio State history.

That win against Michigan created such a buzz that some supporters didn't want it to end, so they founded a club to keep the celebration going. But these weren't crazy college students, flush with extra allowances from their parents and free time. They were Ohio businessmen and VIPs, who joined together on April 17, 1935, to officially start the Ohio Pants Club.

Named after Schmidt's immortal words about Michigan's typical dressing habits, these fat-cat boosters decided that they would honor the Buckeyes who achieved the historic win and beat their rival by giving them their own special banquet and presenting each player and coach with a miniature metal pair of golden football pants engraved with the date of the conquest and the winning score. The doling out of "golden pants" after beating Michigan is a practice that continues to this day.

(In fact, a mini-scandal erupted in September 2003 when a pair of the tiny pants commemorating the 2002 Buckeye win over Michigan popped up, of all places, on the Internet auction site eBay. Fortunately, the item was quickly taken offline before anyone found out who the seller was—or before the university or the NCAA could take action. Not only was selling the pants an affront to Buckeye fans every-where, but if the item had actually been put up for auction by a player, it could have been considered a violation of the NCAA's rules against obtaining improper benefits.)

Schmidt did the job of beating Michigan, and he did it well. In fact, he pummeled the Wolverines for four straight years, shutting them out four times. And the people of Columbus were, not surprisingly, very happy (in Ann Arbor, it was an altogether different story). But all good things must come to an end, and it wasn't long before everybody's favorite Texan was himself thrown from the bucking bull that is Buckeye football. Those four straight wins were followed by three straight losses, and the grumblings were audible—from the fans, the press, and the players. Like other coaches before him, Schmidt quit just before he probably would have been fired.

Next!

Into the void stepped an Ohio native and a wunderkind who had made Missillon Washington High School (south of Akron) into a football factory. His high-schoolers won a record 56 games and 6 straight championships. Sure, at 32 years of age, he was still a baby by coaching standards, but Paul Brown was a winner and therefore was selected to be the next OSU coach—a job he performed admirably, leading the Buckeyes to their first national championship.

Unfortunately for Buckeye fans, Paul Brown left OSU to enlist in the Navy. And although everyone assumed he'd be back, Brown was lured away by the pros and signed a contract in 1945 to coach the All-American Football Conference's Cleveland team (eventually named for him and later folded into the NFL). He also founded the Cincinnati Bengals, and along the way Brown revolutionized coaching and the game of football.

Paul Brown was the first coach to use playbooks and the first to use film to study his players and his plays. He instituted the face mask, the full-time coaching staff, the draw play, play calling from the sideline using a messenger, the radio helmet allowing coaches to talk to quarterbacks on the field, and the use of the 40-yard dash as a measuring stick of a player's skill (that was about the length of a punt, so he timed players running the distance to see who could cover kicks).

Brown was also the progenitor of the so-called West Coast offense—the system that emphasizes short and medium-range passing and the man in motion—that is so prevalent in the NFL today. The common misconception is that Bill Walsh and the San Francisco 49ers developed it, but it was actually instituted while Walsh was an assistant under Brown in Cincinnati and Walsh later took it with him when he went out west.

Who knows what would have happened if Paul Brown, the future football trendsetter, had returned to OSU.

Next!

Carroll Widdoes was up. And after his stirring win over Michigan with Heisman-winner Les Horvath in 1944, he lost to UM in 1945 and opted out of the pressure cooker, asking for his old job of assistant coach back.

Next!

Paul Bixler, another assistant who was promoted to head coach, lasted only one season. He lost to Michigan 58–6. (If that's not the equivalent of signing your own death certificate in Columbus, then nothing is.)

Next!

Not able to bring Paul Brown back, OSU hired Wes Fesler—the very same Wes Fesler who later made the controversial choice to punt the ball before halftime in the Snow Bowl.

Next!

"I didn't come here for the security. I came here for the opportunity," Woody Hayes said in an early press conference, after being hired, as a virtual unknown, to coach the Buckeyes. Hayes was, of course, no shrinking violet, and, as it turned out, he was just what was needed to bury the epithet "graveyard of coaches" for the time being.

His new offense (or lack of offense) took some getting used to, but Woody proved himself capable of handling the team up north. From 1951 to 1968 Woody beat his nemesis a respectable 12 times. But by 1969, that turbulent and emblematic year in American history, Woody finally met his match. This was the year that the Michigan–Ohio State football rivalry entered what was without a doubt its golden era—a period during which not only the passion for the game but the level of play reached a staggering plateau. This stretch of games between the two football teams consisted of such intense battles, with such enormous implications, that the period is commonly and accurately referred to as the 10-Year War.

But before you can have a war, you need two generals— two larger-than-life personalities who drive their respective troops. OSU obviously had its general, and now it was Michigan's turn to find a leader who could match him.

Yet not in a million years could Woody Hayes have conceived that he would be the person most instrumental in creating his bitterest rival. That he would be the one to personally tutor the man who would one day become the sole reason for the biggest disappointment in Hayes's life. Sophocles? Shakespeare? George Lucas? None of them could spin a yarn this good. But it happened, and the ball was set in motion the day that Glen Edward "Bo" Schembechler went off to play football at Miami University of Ohio.

He wasn't particularly big and he wasn't particularly strong, yet a kid nicknamed Bo was recruited by Miami University of Ohio to be an offensive tackle. He was playing football and school was paid for, so the young player couldn't be happier. Schembechler was in his junior year and feeling comfortable when a new coach named Woody Hayes took over the program.

Schembechler had the same reaction most players had when they first met Woody. "I despised him," Schembechler said. "Most of us did."

But that initial feeling receded pretty quickly, and Schembechler warmed to the intense coach who liked to talk about military history. So much so, that when Schembechler graduated from Miami, he got a job with Hayes, who had since moved on to OSU. Schembechler became a graduate assistant to the coach for one year, gaining access to the inner circle—and to Hayes's unique mind, and the many variations of the off-tackle play. Schembechler then left for the military and when he returned, he got his first full-time coaching job in 1954 at Presbyterian College in South Carolina. Schembechler then went to Bowling Green University and later was hired as an assistant at Northwestern. In 1958, when Hayes had an opening in his staff, he called his old player Bo.

For five years, Bo coached alongside Hayes—and fought with Hayes. One time, the two headstrong coaches sparred about something or other in the staff room, and as they yelled, they kicked chairs at each other—lots of chairs. According to Schembechler, Hayes fired him in a rage and later rehired him on more than one occasion. Perhaps this was an early clue that both men were a little too similar than either of them cared to admit.

Also intense, also a devout worshiper at the altar of

winning, Schembechler hoped to become the head of a major college program himself. But for the moment, he was stuck behind the most successful coach in Ohio State history. He knew he'd have to move on to realize his dream. So, when his alma mater called, Schembechler didn't have a choice.

Bo told Woody that he wanted to take the job, but Hayes asked him to stay, going so far as to tell Schembechler he would be the next coach of OSU after Woody retired in, by his own estimation, 3 to 5 years. Schembechler wasn't prepared to wait even that long, and it turned out to be a pretty wise decision. Hayes remained at the helm of the Buckeyes for another 16 years.

Bo got his first high-profile head-coaching job at Miami of Ohio, and he made the most of it, winning 2 championships in 6 seasons and compiling a 40–17–3 record. People noticed, including the University of Michigan's brand-new athletic director Don Canham, who was looking to hire a new Wolverine head coach.

In early 1969, Canham met with Bo and, after 15 minutes, knew that Schembechler was the man to take over coaching duties for the Michigan Wolverines—a program that already had a legacy of some pretty astounding coaches.

Including an eccentric legend by the name of Fielding Yost.

■   ■   ■

When most people who were associated with collegiate sports were still trying to figure out where the young sport of football was really going (the forward pass wasn't even legal yet), Yost was already obsessed. And when he arrived in Ann Arbor in 1901, Yost became the reason why the University of Michigan immediately transformed into a national football powerhouse.

Fielding H. Yost had barely turned 30 when he took over the Wolverines, but he already had a lifetime of experience. A coaching vagabond, Yost had been responsible for 4 winning seasons at 4 different schools in 4 years. But the man they called "Hurry Up" (because he always told his players to do just that in practice) just up and left after his 1897 Ohio Wesleyan team went 7–1–1, after his '98 Nebraska team went 7–1–1, then after his '99 Kansas Jayhawks went 10–0, and finally after his '00 Stanford team went 7–2–1.

The football tactician with a lawyer-trained mind (he got a law degree from the University of West Virginia) was a larger-than-life character who believed in a sound diet as much as he did in a solid defense and once supposedly benched a player for eating a slice of pie. But his eccentricities finally found him a permanent home in Ann Arbor, where he coached the Wolverines for 25 seasons. His record for that quarter century of coaching was 165–29–10, a remarkable .851 winning percentage, still in the Top 10 of all NCAA Division I-A coaches.

And Yost started things off on a colossal footing. His inaugural 1901 Wolverine squad was a perfect 10–0, scoring 550 points and allowing opponents none. The Wolverines then beat Stanford in the very first Rose Bowl, another shutout, and were Michigan's first national championship team.

A tough act to follow, but Yost's sophomore season was almost as brilliant, and the next and the next, until before long, his Wolverines had gone 56 games without a loss (easily still a school record that will never be broken) between 1901 and 1905 and won 4 national championships. During this time, the Wolverine squads got the nickname "Point-A-Minute" team for averaging 49 points per game (almost equal to the number of minutes on the game clock). For a period of time, Yost's Wolverines were basically invincible.

And if you're looking for the origin of Michigan football "arrogance," you don't have to look much farther than Fielding Yost. The coach once commented about Michigan's famed fight song "The Victors," written by a UM student, Louis Elbel, "I reckon it's a good thing Louis Elbel was a *Meechigan* [thanks to his southern accent, he always said it that way] student when he wrote that song. If he'd been at any other Big Ten school, they wouldn't have had much chance to use it, y'know?"

But even a run as brilliant as Yost's had to end. Other teams in the Midwest eventually learned the benefit of training, discipline, and a little creative playmaking (not to mention recruiting). And when it was all said and done, even "Hurry Up" Yost lost a couple of games to Ohio State. In fact, 1921's 14–0 drubbing by the Buckeyes put the once-invincible Yost squarely in the hot seat. The *Michigan Daily* even ran a letter to the editor with the headline "Yost Has Seen His Day." So the man who basically built Michigan athletics, later built Michigan Stadium (even built Michigan's 18-hole golf course), and built a program with a legacy of winning was eventually sold out by fans after a loss to Ohio State. Yost finally resigned his post and became the school's athletic director.

Michigan's next great coach also put an eternal stamp on the program—this time, physically. His name was Herbert O. Crisler, but everyone called him "Fritz," and you can't help but think of him even when you look at the Michigan Wolverines in 2003—they're still wearing his helmet.

Fritz Crisler was recruited to help inflate what had

become a sagging Michigan football program. For four years before Crisler showed up, the Wolverines had been a very un-Wolverinelike 10–22. It was time for a ringer.

Crisler had the credentials. He was an assistant in Chicago to Amos Alonzo Stagg, a legendary coach who is credited with such football innovations as the man in motion and the end around play. (Incidentally, it was also Stagg's brainstorm that basketball should be played five-on-five.) Crisler later became coach and athletic director at the University of Minnesota, before being named head coach at Princeton—when Princeton was a national powerhouse—and accumulating a gaudy 35–9–5 record. It took UM officials two meetings and a promise that he'd eventually be named AD to reel him in.

Out of the chute, Crisler beat OSU 18–0, and it was the first Wolverine win over the Buckeyes in five years. The *Detroit Free Press* reported, "Today's triumph was so welcome to those fans who have followed Michigan closely in the last five years that many of the exuberant ones in attendance tore up a Buckeye goal post in a wild melee after the game."

Fritz was home. But even though he was at the helm of the Wolverines for 10 years and accumulated an impressive .816 winning percentage—second in school history only to Yost's—Fritz Crisler will always be remembered for *the helmet*.

The helmet's maize stripes and the crown shaped into a slightly winged design are still synonymous with the Michigan Wolverines today. It's the first image many Wolverine fans remember from watching their team on TV as kids, and, of course, it gets under the skin of opponents—and their fans.

"The helmet?" said one longtime OSU supporter. "Everyone thinks that helmet is so unique. That helmet is the ugliest helmet that was ever put on the face of the Earth."

While it still gets style points (or the lack thereof), its origin was a little more utilitarian. Crisler brought the design with him from Princeton, where he was experimenting with ways to help his quarterback spot receivers down field. At the time, the design traced the way the structural pieces of the leather helmet were sewn together, but even when synthetics were used to form the helmet out of a single piece of material, the markings remained. Today you can buy a souvenir Michigan Wolverines helmet bank, mailbox, or Christmas ornament. Fritz would be proud.

Crisler also did a rare thing as a head coach: he went out on top. An undefeated season, a Rose Bowl win, and a national championship were his parting gifts to fans in 1947, as he moved behind a desk and became Michigan's athletic director.

The next two Wolverine coaches, Bennie Oosterbaan and Bump Elliott, were both former players. Although they had their ups and downs, athletic director Don Canham inherited a world in 1968 where coaching was much more than a vanity position. Former players were nice to have around, but veteran, professional coaching talents had become paramount. After all, OSU had Woody. Now UM needed someone—maybe even someone a little Woody-like.

■   ■   ■

Schembechler roared.

It was only August. It was only practice, but the rookie coach was screaming like a banshee. "When are you going to get that 270 pounds of lard moving?" he screamed face-to-face with some lineman—a big guy, but, presumably, one with feelings.

Schembechler was attempting to make his rookie coaching presence felt early—and so far, it seemed to be working. Players who had been around the year before saw a marked difference from his predecessor Elliott, a man who was frequently described as quiet and well-mannered.

In contrast, Schembechler put his team through punishing practices that stunned a lot of the returning players. He rode his team hard, but he knew what it would take to put the program back on the map. Like any good coach, he also knew that half the battle was mental, and at the beginning of the season, he left a bit of motivation in the locker room by hanging a sign that read: "Those who stay will be champions."

"He's rough, and he knows every earthy word in the book," one player said. "He's like an animal; he wants us to be like animals," said another. And, finally, another remarked, "He's what we need here."

Why not? Quiet was definitely a thing of the past. After all, this was late summer 1969. A couple of months later, Michigan Stadium, normally reserved for protests against pass interference calls and holding penalties, would become ground zero for expanding protests against the Vietnam War. October 15 was dubbed Moratorium Day across the nation, and on the Michigan campus antiwar sentiment was extremely popular. Twenty thousand people massed in the stadium to show their support and listen to pacifist speeches by the likes of Michigan senator Philip Hart and the founder of Students for a Democratic Society, Tom Hayden. Students were angry.

And while they were ticking off things in the world to be up in arms about, don't be surprised that a few mentioned the Buckeyes and that irascible Woody Hayes. This isn't to say that an actual war is even remotely in the same universe as a football game, but college students live in an insular world, by definition, and UM football was a large part of the fabric of university life. So, on the topic of Things That Annoyed University of Michigan Students in 1969, the Buckeyes were definitely near the top of the list. And the 1968 game had everything to do with it.

A drubbing is one thing, but Woody saw the bleeding gash across the belly of the Wolverine squad late in a game, and he dumped a shaker of salt right into the wound. The '68 game was supposed to be a classic. OSU was ranked number 2, and UM was right there at number 4, with, per usual, the Big Ten championship, a Rose Bowl berth, and a possible national championship all on the line.

Bump Elliott's Wolverines scored first, but then it got away from them. The Buckeyes and an amazing crop of players being called the "Super Sophomores" steamrolled the Wolverines on their way to a national championship. But even the end of the blowout was not without excitement. With the scoreboard reading 44–14 and with 3:30 left in the fourth quarter, Michigan had the ball, but it was immediately picked off by OSU. The Buckeyes then faced a third-and-one situation on Michigan's 2-yard line, and OSU backup fullback Paul Huff couldn't get a first down or the touchdown. So Woody, apparently not satisfied with the 44 points his team had already amassed, went back to his star runner Jim Otis, who was already out of the game and resting after scoring 3 touchdowns, to get the Buckeyes to an even 50. Then he went from getting what might be considered insurance to a total slicing of the jugular.

With the Buckeyes "holding on" to a 36-point lead, Hayes went for 2 more. When asked after the game why he went for 2, Hayes reportedly replied, "Because I couldn't go for 3." The conversion failed, but the coach might as well have gotten down on his hands and knees and personally written *"Take that, Michigan fans!"* in block letters across the Diag.

The 1969 Wolverines didn't talk about the loss, but that 2-point attempt was on everybody's mind. "I don't know why he did that," said Jim Mandich, Michigan's star tight end, shortly before the '69 rematch. "If he was trying to rub it in—to make the defeat seem worse—then I don't have any respect for him. It certainly wasn't necessary. We weren't going to come roaring back to beat him. But I'll tell you this, we haven't forgotten."

Even with the "revenge factor," not many people gave the '69 Wolverine squad a snowball's chance in hell of actually getting the redemption they craved. In the ensuing year, OSU had only gotten better. By November, Woody Hayes's Buckeyes were not only ranked number 1 in the country but were being hailed as perhaps the greatest team in college football history. They were a juggernaut. By the time they arrived in Ann Arbor, they'd already won 22 consecutive games and had a season average of 46 points and 512 yards per game. After trouncing Purdue, the Boilermakers' coach told the press, "Nobody has a better defense—unless maybe the Minnesota Vikings." (The Vikings that year dominated the NFL, going 12–2.) The clippings were clear: be afraid, be very afraid.

In Ann Arbor that season, Schembechler was doing an admirable job for a rookie coach. The Wolverines were 7–2 and ranked 12th in the country. After some missteps, Schembechler and his new authoritative regime had finally righted the ship. Against their last four opponents, the Wolverines won by an average score of 45–6.

But as the 66th meeting between Michigan and Ohio State approached, the Wolverines were officially put at

17-point underdogs. And yet the rookie coach was part of the minority that believed his Wolverines could slay Woody's Goliath. He told the *Daily*, "Ohio State is beatable" and noted that the revenge factor gave the Wolverines "every incentive to win." As a subtle reminder, Schembechler had "50–14" stenciled on the scarlet-and-white jerseys worn by the scout team during the week's practices. None of the coaches mentioned it, but the players got the message. As another not-so-subtle reminder of who they were gunning for, Schembechler had photos of the complementary Ohio State player taped to each of his players' lockers. Perhaps the pupil had learned a thing or two about motivation from the teacher.

When the teams started warming up on that cold November day, it was Woody's turn to play mental games, but the target was his old assistant. When Schembechler got his team out on the field, his players noticed that Woody and his squad were already warming up—on Michigan's side of the field. The rookie coach was thrown for a loop, but he went right up to his mentor and asked him to kindly move his players to their side of the field. Woody grudgingly moved his team.

"I know it wasn't Woody's first time in Michigan Stadium," Bo joked later on. "But that stimulated a lot of enthusiasm in the tunnel for our team."

"We were trying to psych out one another," Woody said. "He's not above that, nor am I."

A remarkable 103,538 fans packed into Michigan's enormous bowl—the largest crowd that had ever assembled to watch a college football game, to that point—and with palpable anticipation watched the spectacle about to unfold on the turf. Most fans stood, restless. And on the field, standing across from each other, were two men, one the proven field general, the other his protégé—both about to be tested, at the onset of a war.

Ohio State won the toss, elected to receive, and when Pontiac, Michigan, native Dana Coin's foot impacted the leather football, *the* Game was on. The boot sailed 53 yards in the air and landed in the hands of Tom Campana, who made a nice return, scampering through the Michigan coverage and barreling all the way to the 44-yard line.

Into the game then trotted OSU's quarterback Rex Kern. Now a junior, the Lancaster, Ohio, native—a fiery red-head—was the team's leader, and he'd proved to Hayes that he could carry the Buckeyes in a big spot all by himself. As a sophomore, in just his second game taking snaps, he faced a fourth-and-10 against SMU, and while Woody was trying to get his punter in the game, Kern ran a play himself and wound up gaining 16 yards and a first down. The win that day started OSU's impeccable streak and gave Hayes supreme faith in his QB. He proved this by even allowing Kern to pass the ball from time to time.

Kern came out of the chute looking like he was going to do just that. He dropped back, made a quick pump fake, and started up field. Michigan was caught off guard, and the scrambling quarterback made it all the way to the 30 before tiptoeing out of bounds.

Next, it was back to the script. OSU lined up in what Woody Hayes called the "Old Button Shoe," a tight T-formation with a full house backfield. From there, it was textbook "three yards and a cloud of dust" all the way. Kern pitched the ball to Jim Otis, and he was off and running, getting 7 yards. Then he got 3. Then he got 1. Then he got 7. In a few brief minutes, the Buckeyes were on the Wolverines' 11-yard line, facing a fourth-and-two.

An old aphorism is often associated with football: *You*

dance with who brung you. And on cue, Kern gave the ball once again to Otis, who smashed over the middle, looking for that first down he had reached countless times in the last two seasons. But surging forward to stop him, wearing maize and blue, was a young man named Henry Hill, a walk-on from Detroit who was playing middle guard for Schembechler. The two players clashed above the fray, and after the officials came out for a look, they signaled that Otis was still short of the first down. Hill got his first of a game-high 13 tackles, and Michigan had stopped the mighty Bucks' initial charge. Some of the Michigan players—pumped tighter than a new bicycle wheel—jumped in the air in excitement over the big play. The crowd erupted, and from the very first series, it looked like something magical might actually be flitting about in the crisp November air.

Although not yet.

Ohio State scored on their next possession. Larry Zelina returned a punt past midfield, Kern completed a pass to Stan White, and the Buckeyes were already knocking on the door. Then Otis nailed it shut with a short touchdown run. OSU missed the extra point, but when a team averages 46 points a game, you can't worry too much when they flub the point after. Hayes and Co. were back in business.

Surprisingly, it was Michigan QB Don Moorehead's arm that put the Wolverines right back in the game. Like Hayes, Schembechler has always been known as a coach who likes to keep the ball on the ground (after all, he learned that from Woody), but lo and behold, the ball was moving down the field, through the air. In no time, Michigan fullback Garvie Craw blasted through a hole in the defensive line and into the end zone. Schembechler had called for the off-tackle play "Dark 26"—it was the same play that had made

Woody Hayes's career, and now it was being used successfully against him by his pupil. The irony was delicious, and
after the extra point, the Wolverines took the lead. It was
the first time the Buckeyes had been behind in a game all
season.

It wouldn't last long, however. Kern hit White on a
22-yard TD pass, and this time OSU made the point
after, but a Michigan penalty moved the ball half the
distance to the goal, and Hayes figured he might as well
accept the penalty and try for 2. Kern was sacked, and the
Buckeyes had to settle for a 12–7 lead 8 seconds into the
second quarter.

The Wolverines continued their high-flying ways, and,
backed by a boisterous home crowd, they marched the
ball right back down the field, and Craw busted another
short run into the end zone. Michigan was again in front,
14–12.

After Ohio State went three and out, Barry Pierson
fielded the punt at the 37 and—in one of the biggest runs
in Michigan football history—took it straight up the field,
breaking tackles left and right, before being brought down
60 yards later at the OSU 3. Moorehead ran it in himself,
two plays later, and, suddenly, Goliath was looking smaller
and smaller. On their next scoring drive, Michigan had to
settle for a field goal (after a touchdown was called back,
thanks to an illegal procedure penalty), but before the half,
the Wolverines were leading 24–12.

Already, they had shocked the world. No other team had
scored more than 21 points on the Buckeyes all year. The
Wolverines floated into the locker room on a cloud, accompanied by the deafening roar of the crowd. Inside the inner
sanctum, the players sat in stunned silence until defensive
coordinator Jim Young broke the quiet by pounding on the

chalkboard and yelling, "No more, damn it, they will not score anymore!"

Young, a normally reserved coach, was prophetic. The Michigan defense—or, more specifically, Barry Pierson— took over the second half of the game. The 178-pound defensive back intercepted three passes in the second half and gave what Schembechler called "one of the greatest performances I have ever seen in a single game."

The defensive line had been instrumental in shutting down OSU's running game (building on that first big stop by Hill), and it forced Hayes to do what he loathed most, pass the ball. As the coach himself probably would have predicted, the results were disastrous. He pulled his QB (who, it turned out, was having a flare-up of chronic back spasms before the game) and put in second stringer Ron Maciejowski late in the fourth quarter. Pierson picked him off, too.

As the clock ticked away, Michigan players and fans began to realize that what they had dreamed about for a year was now remarkably becoming a reality. The Michigan fans in the crowd began singing "Good-bye, Woody. Good-bye" and chanting "We're number 1!" And when the game finally ended, the celebration—of what was immediately called, on the field, on the TV broadcast, and eventually in the papers, one of the greatest upsets of all time—began.

It was chaos on the field, as fans spilled onto the turf and players mobbed their rookie coach and hoisted him onto their shoulders. Woody did the right thing and tried to shake hands with Bo, but the pandemonium on the field blocked his path.

It was the pupil's turn to celebrate, while the teacher beat a retreat.

Kern said later that it was as if Schembechler was in the

huddle with the Buckeyes, anticipating their every move. The truth was, the rookie coach was not a magician, but he was a man who had thought about this game since the day he was hired at Michigan. In a post-game interview, Schembechler said that his game plan was simply to concede Otis his yards but concentrate on denying Kern's ability to move the ball, both on the ground and in the air. After that opening play, the Wolverine defense was able to do just that.

It was enough to make Hayes doubt his own game plan—a conservative style that had worked 22 games in a row but suddenly seemed like not enough.

"One of [Woody's] downfalls was he would outthink himself," OSU's two-time All-American linebacker Jim Stillwagon said later, "and I think he did that in that game. Woody was predictable when it was close. Bo knew Woody's mind-set, too. He knew we would run right and run left. He stacked those tackles in there on the line of scrimmage."

"Bo came in knowing what Woody would do," the defensive star Pierson said years later. "And the Buckeyes were true to form. We put them in a bind, forcing them to pass, and that wasn't in their books. It backfired on them."

After the game, Hayes was, not surprisingly, not very talkative. The coach opened the visitors' locker room door for all of 90 seconds and offered only a few words to the throngs of press stationed outside: "All good things must come to an end, and that's what happened today. We just got outplayed, outpunched, and outcoached. Our offense in the second half was miserable, and we made every mistake you could possibly make. I've talked to the reporters and now we've got to leave."

Inside the locker room, the coach didn't have much else to say to his team—a squad that he later said was the greatest he'd ever coached—but he told them one more thing: "We will start preparing for those guys on the way back home." And that's exactly what they did.

■ ■ ■

For both teams, the next nine years were like a single game season. Between 1969 and 1978, the Game decided the Big Ten championship 9 out of 10 times. The two schools dominated the conference to such a degree that it was nicknamed the "Big 2 and the Little 8." Of course, every year it was Woody versus Bo. And the gamesmanship only got more intense.

The '69 loss infuriated Hayes, and avenging that loss became his obsession for the next 12 months. At the beginning of the season, a custom-stitched rug was placed outside the Buckeyes' dressing room:

"1969
MICH 24
OSU 12
1970
MICH
OSU"

He passed his obsession to his team. "I've been thinking about Michigan every morning when I got up for a whole year," said Kern. And by the time the week of the big game rolled around, Hayes's normally intense practices got even more extreme, as the coach played his patented psychological games.

Offensive lineman Tom Deleone remembered one incident at Thursday's practice, when the offense was huddled up around Woody, and the coach suddenly got down on his knees. He then began to crawl around on the ground and touch all the players' feet.

"I want to feel your feet to see if you're ready," he said. After touching them all, he pronounced his offense "ready to play."

Remarkably, he was right.

Coming into the 1970 Game, both teams were undefeated and untied for the first time in the history of the series. Ohio State was ranked number 1, and Michigan was right behind at number 2. Michigan's Lance Scheffer fumbled the opening kickoff, and the Wolverines never regained their poise. The first battle between undefeated titans ended 20–9, and Hayes had his revenge.

"It was our biggest victory," said Woody. "It was the biggest because it makes up for what happened to us last year. The players were hurt. They promised me all along they were going to play their greatest game today—and they did. Going to the Rose Bowl wasn't the main thought on their minds—it was avenging last year's loss." When the Rose Bowl had been superseded by beating Michigan, you knew the coach really had a one-track mind. It didn't matter what kind of year they'd had, or who had won the previous game, beating Michigan was Woody's primary objective.

Even in a rare down year for the Bucks, Woody wanted that game more than anything. In 1971, Michigan had already won the Big Ten and had locked up the Rose Bowl bid, but you never would have known it if you'd seen Woody Hayes throwing a tantrum for the ages on the sidelines.

It *was* a big play. It came with 1:25 left in the game and Michigan clinging to a 10–7 lead. OSU attempted a desperation pass, and Michigan's Tom Darden went over the back of the intended receiver, Dick Wakefield, to make the pick. No interference was called.

In disgust, Woody grabbed a down marker and tried to break it before throwing it, javelin style, onto the field. He then took the first down marker and ripped off its bright orange encasement. After that, he stormed onto the field and yelled at the officials when his team didn't get the controversial pass interference call. It took two assistant coaches and two players to forcibly remove him from the field. After the game, he said he was sorry for the outburst, but later, after reviewing the film, he rescinded his apology.

The two coaches had raised the football drama from high art almost to high camp. Paranoia reached a level that would even make the era's Cold War participants shiver. Woody always whispered in the locker room when he visited Michigan Stadium because he was afraid Bo had the place bugged. Bo once saw a cameraman taking pictures of one of his team's practices, and he had the film confiscated. He was afraid that pictures of UM formations would get back to Woody.

Another year, Woody was watching a film of a Michigan game and noticed that the team up north was wearing a type of shoe he'd never seen before. Worried that Michigan might garner some kind of an edge on the field, Woody found out exactly what kind of shoes they were and got his team the exact same ones.

Another time, he thought that Bo was trying to psych out his team, but not with shoes, with boobs. On a trip to Ann Arbor, Hayes ordered all the waitresses to leave the dining area during the team's breakfast. He was sure that the comely servers had been hired by Bo to distract his team from the task at hand.

Woody even pulled his mind games on the referees. A

Wolverine fan remembered a story told to him by Michigan alumni Gerald Ford's brother (who actually refereed a couple of the Games). The refs were walking down the tunnel to the stadium when Woody grabbed them and pulled them into the locker room. Before they even realized what was going on, Hayes started showing the refs photographs from past games of Michigan guys doing illegal things on the field against Ohio State guys. "The message to the referees that day," said UM fan Don Ianitelli, "was 'Watch those Michigan guys!'"

"Woody would get you ready [for Michigan] all year," said his former superstar Archie Griffin. "We used to say that Michigan was a separate season, a season in itself. He prepared for Michigan all year. Spring practice we'd be getting ready for Michigan defense. It was a constant preparation for *that* game—the whole season every Monday."

Archie would know.

He is the only man who is perhaps as synonymous with Ohio State football as Woody Hayes. Griffin was instrumental in many of Ohio State's big wins in the '70s. Griffin is the only college football player ever to win two Heisman Trophies, and his success was staggering. At OSU he amassed 5,589 yards (a school record) and 26 touchdowns and averaged 6.13 yards per carry. He holds NCAA records for 34 career 100-yard games and a streak of 31 straight regular season games of 100 yards or more.

Archie was also a local boy. He was the fourth of eight children, the first born to his parents in Columbus after they moved from West Virginia to escape poverty. The elder Griffin worked three jobs and wanted his kids to participate in sports, in order to "learn discipline and teamwork."

By age 9, Archie Griffin was too big to play football with kids his own age, so he joined a team of 12- to 15-year-olds.

He mostly sat on the bench, but "it gave me a whole lot of confidence playing with guys older," Griffin said.

A few years later, he became a fullback when his coach was looking for volunteers to play the position, and he took off immediately. While playing at Eastmoor High School, Griffin anchored two City League championship teams, made the All-City League team his junior and senior years, and was named All-Ohio and shared state Back of the Year honors his senior year. He was also an excellent student, and it was only a matter of time before college recruiters came knocking. But would the big school in town be interested?

"When I came out of high school, they didn't have many kids from right here in Columbus on the team," said Griffin. "I had been told Coach Hayes was reluctant to recruit kids from Columbus because when you weren't playing, a lot of people from Columbus were always in your ear. So I wasn't sure he was going to recruit me."

In the meantime, Griffin applied and was accepted at Northwestern, the Naval Academy, and (yes!) Michigan. And it was the "school up north" that made overtures about getting Griffin to play for their football team.

"I was really honored that Michigan was showing interest in me," said Griffin. OSU assistant Chuck Stobart, who had been an assistant under Schembechler and later became an assistant at OSU, told Griffin that Michigan's interest finally made Woody notice the local boy. "Chuck used to say OSU didn't start recruiting you real hard until we started to recruit you [at Michigan]."

Whatever made the old coach come to his senses, Woody finally went after the back, but offered no guarantees. "If you're good enough, you'll play," was all he told Griffin, and the back finally chose to stay in Columbus so that his parents could watch him play football. And on that simple decision, the Rivalry's momentum swung. Of his impressive college statistics, Griffin is most proud of one figure: 3–0–1. It's his career record against the Wolverines.

Archie Griffin still loves to talk about his old coach and his unconventional methods. "He spoke of how terrible Michigan was, and how bad they were, and how they'd do things to try to get an advantage and the whole works. And he had us believing that Michigan was the worst team that you could possibly ever want to play against, and he had you feeling like you wanted to kill them. And I remember the end of his talk, at the end of his talk as I looked around that room, I saw tears coming out of my teammates' eyes. He said, you know, 'This is not a game, this is war.'"

And that war got increasingly intense.

Sometimes the two coaches' obsession with beating each other even seemed to affect the way they managed the game on the field. Never was this more apparent than in the 1972 showdown. Michigan trailed 14–11 in the fourth quarter of a game that featured two incredible goal-line stands by the OSU defense and key gains by freshman back Archie Griffin. But this nail-biter will always be remembered for Bo's fourth-quarter decision not to kick a field goal.

The Wolverines intercepted an errant Ohio State pass to land on the Buckeyes' 29-yard line. They got the ball to the 5 and had a first down and goal to go. UM's Harry Banks's three carries got Michigan within inches of the goal line (Michigan actually argued, to no avail, that he'd crossed the plane), and it set up a fourth and goal–ball game on the line. Instead of opting to kick the easy field goal and tie the game with nine minutes to play, Schembechler had his quarterback Dennis Franklin attempt a sneak, and the play was snuffed. Game over.

Incredibly, a tie would have given Michigan a share of the title and a ticket to Pasadena. But it wouldn't have given Bo an outright victory over Woody. "Woody and Bo were fierce competitors," said Griffin. "Instead of Bo going for a field goal, he was going to try for a touchdown, and our defense was going to be there to stop them. But that's what made the thing so exciting."

In 1973, neither coach could get a leg up. They both came into the game undefeated, and that's the way they remained after it was over. In the first half, OSU had the offense. Griffin's 59 yards in a first-half drive led to a Blair Conway field goal, and then it was Archie plugging away for another 41 yards in 5 carries on a different drive that led to a Pete Johnson run into the end zone. The Buckeyes, who had only allowed four touchdowns all year, led 10–0 at the half.

The Wolverines took the kickoff and drove all the way to OSU's 22, before quarterback Dennis Franklin was picked off by OSU's Neil Colzie in the end zone. The game's second-biggest play came later in the third quarter, when OSU was on Michigan's 42 and went for it on fourth-and-two. QB Cornelius Greene tried to make the first down himself and came up short. Hayes claimed after the game that he had called for an option, with Archie carrying.

Suddenly, Michigan was back in the game and with good field position got a quick field goal. On their next possession, the Wolverines came back down the field after a short punt and wound up with fourth-and-inches on OSU's 10-yard line. Franklin faked a handoff to fullback Ed Shuttlesworth, ran to the right, and scored the game-tying TD standing up.

The game was knotted, and it stayed that way (the first tie in the series since 1949). The only other memorable play was a painful one for the Wolverines and Franklin, who broke his collarbone after being hit while releasing the ball. Not only was UM without its starting QB, but the play cost them a trip to the Rose Bowl.

The Big Ten had finally done away with the no-repeat rule, and the Rose Bowl bid would go to the winner of the conference, no matter what happened. The only problem was, thanks to their 10–10 game, Michigan and Ohio State were tied for the title. It was determined that a vote by the athletic directors would break the tie, and it looked like Michigan was the favorite. Bo was in a good mood after the game and confident that because his team dominated statistically, they would be chosen. (UM had more total yards, 303–234; more first downs, 16–9; and was 7-for-12 passing, while OSU was 0-for-4.)

But the ADs went with Ohio State by a 6–4 vote, and it was widely believed that the Big Ten, after three straight losses in Pasadena, wanted to go with the team they thought had the best chance to win the game. Without Franklin, UM was at a deficit. Schembechler went crazy. The coach was about to tape his weekly TV show when he got the news. He walked away from the press and went into the studio and took his frustration out on a lot of innocent furniture. "Goddamn it! Goddamn it!" he roared. "I want to know what happened here!"

It was all just part of the Game.

Fans definitely appreciated the histrionics. Just mention Michigan versus Ohio State today, and the first words that 9 out of 10 fans utter are "Woody versus Bo," always accompanied by a smile.

Even without the breadth of media coverage that the game garners today, every year the press hyped the story of the two great coaches battling each other for all the marbles. Drew Montag, a UM graduate in the '70s, remembered how the students also focused on the ongoing battle between the two idiosyncratic personalities. "It wasn't just beat Ohio State back then," said Montag, who still owns a vintage "Crack Woody's Nuts" T-shirt that he bought in Ann Arbor while in school. "It was always 'Beat Woody!'" around campus, "not Beat Ohio State."

Michigan's legendary radio announcer Bob Ufer helped to perpetuate the mythic battle by firing up the *Meechigan* fans—as he famously pronounced the name of the school in an homage to Fielding Yost—and taunting the Buckeyes. Ufer would scream hysterically in the booth whenever the Wolverines came up big against the Buckeyes, and after one big game he recited a now-infamous poem that ended: "Twenty-two Michigan Wolverines put on gloves of gray / And as the organ played 'The Victors,' they laid Woody Hayes away." The eccentric announcer even had a miniature casket with a dummy of Woody with him inside the broadcast booth.

Unfortunately, it was Woody's passion for winning and his particular obsession with beating "the team up north" that may have led to his ultimate downfall. By the end of the decade, Bo was getting the best of Woody, and the Wolverines went into the '78 game having won two in a row against the Buckeyes. With the dependable QB Rick Leach still wearing maize and blue (he started a NCAA-record 48 games for the Wolverines), UM beat OSU 14–3.

The 65-year-old Hayes (in his 28th season as Ohio State's head coach) was predictably unhappy after the game. A reporter asked the coach about his team's next game, the Gator Bowl in Jacksonville, Florida. For the man who had led OSU to eight Rose Bowls, he did not want to talk about any Gator Bowls. "We'll get to that in due time," he said. "I hope we don't have to go down there too early."

You can't blame Woody for not wanting to go to Florida—especially in retrospect. In the final minutes of the game, the Buckeyes trailed Clemson 17–15 and were on the Tigers' 24-yard line when OSU quarterback Art Schlichter's pass was intercepted by Charlie Bauman. Schlichter tackled Bauman out of bounds on Ohio State's sideline, and Hayes came running over to the Clemson defender and—on national television—punched him in the chin. Woody was given an ultimatum by OSU brass, and he resigned the next day, never coaching again.

The eccentric coach had snapped.

He never apologized for his actions and offered no explanation. Two weeks later he said, "I have a temper. I've had it all my life. I have a lot of regrets, but we all do. Do you expect me to go around crying over spilled milk?"

Around the country, Hayes was reduced to a caricature, but his players and fans knew Woody as a much more complex man than he was portrayed to be, and men like Griffin are still fiercely loyal to him 25 years later.

"Just like my father, not a day goes by I don't think of [Hayes]," said Griffin. "Regardless of what anyone says about him, the man was outstanding. I say that from first-hand experience and love of the man."

For their personalities and for their passion, Woody Hayes and Bo Schembechler were as big a part of the Rivalry as the football played on the field. Fans across the country responded to two feisty, old-school tacticians who just loved to go at it, year after year. Bo said later of that 10-year period: "If that was war, sign me up forever."

■　　■　　■

Following in the footsteps of Woody and Bo are two guys named Jim and Lloyd.

The coaches of the 2003 Wolverines and Buckeyes already know what it's like to be in those same trenches. Their mentors and the 10-Year-War haunt their every move. Tressel grew up in a suburb outside of Cleveland, worshiping Buckeyes like Kern and their field general Woody Hayes. And he'd clearly learned a thing or two about showmanship from the Fat Man.

Just hours after his first 2001 news conference in Columbus, he made his way to an Ohio State–Michigan basketball game at OSU's Schottenstein Center. At halftime, in front of a crowd of more than 18,000 fans, Tressel took the microphone, strolled to midcourt, and said, "I promise you'll be proud of our young people in the classroom, in the community, and, most especially, in 310 days in Ann Arbor, Michigan, on the football field."

Needless to say, the crowd went nuts.

And up north, Carr can't escape the shadow of his predecessor. After all, his office is in Schembechler Hall. He was mentored by the legendary coach as one of his assistants from 1980 to 1989, but that didn't automatically make them best buds.

"Like everyone else," Carr said, "I was awed by him, scared by him." Now that Carr is the Wolverines' top man, he and the coach have a healthy respect. "We talk pretty regularly," the current coach said. "He comes out to watch practice occasionally. He's been not only my mentor, but one of my very best friends."

In 2003, Carr faced a situation that no Michigan coach had faced since 1962 B.S. (before Schembechler)—possible back-to-back-to-back losses to the Buckeyes. When asked about Carr's job security, Bo—who still has his own office on campus, a right he earned by winning a school-record 194 games as Michigan's head coach—chuckled and said,

"Lloyd Carr is as secure as any football coach in America." The 74-year-old added, "Anybody takes issue with that, they'll have to go through me."

The press was hounding Bo the week before the 100th meeting between Michigan and Ohio State, and he did a lot of reminiscing. The more he talked about the old days, the more playful he became. It was obvious that he was enjoying the attention, as well as the chance to rehash all the old stories. He told a room full of reporters that he missed his old mentor, who died in 1987. "I enjoyed it a lot with Woody," Bo said, harking back to their 10-Year-War. "He was doing his thing and I was doing my thing." He then added, "It would be nice if he were here today to talk to you as well."

Good thing he wasn't; none of the chairs had been nailed down.

5

BOYS TO MEN

Bright floodlights illuminated the football field in Columbus, Ohio. A running back stood slightly crouched, in the set position. As he exhaled, small clouds were visible in the bitterly cold air. A quarterback stood behind the offensive line, barking a quick count before the ball was snapped by the center. The QB stepped back, then turned, and handed the ball off to the lone back.

Nothing fancy.

The back took the ball, cradled it delicately in his bare hands, and looked up field, searching for his hole. As soon as he saw the daylight he was looking for, he accelerated before smashing into a tackle, spinning, stumbling, ultimately regaining his balance, and then surging forward a couple more yards before being dragged down by two more tackles.

Three yards and a cloud of dust, indeed.

The twisting back could very well have been Archie Griffin scampering to collect a few more of the 111 yards he accumulated on November 23, 1974. It was Griffin's performance that day—well on his way to his first Heisman Trophy—that was responsible for OSU's 12–10 victory over Michigan in another amazing battle between the two teams coached by Woody Hayes and Bo Schembechler.

The victory was sealed by Czechoslovakian walk-on kicker Tom Klaban's four field goals. Klaban, who with his family escaped from communist East Germany 10 years earlier, still holds the record for most field goals by a single kicker in the more than 100-year history of the Michigan–Ohio State rivalry. But, remarkably, it wasn't even Klaban who got the most headlines that day.

Down 12–10, Michigan still had a pretty good chance to win the game and preserve an undefeated season. With 18 seconds left on the game clock, the Michigan offense was camped on the 23-yard line, and Mike Lantry was setting up to kick the winning field goal.

The pressure rested squarely on the shoulders of Lantry—again. He had missed two field goals late in the game the previous year, in the infamous 10–10 tie. But this time the ball had plenty of distance, sailing toward the uprights and seemingly through. The UM contingent in Ohio Stadium was roaring; the fans thought their Wolverines had done it. But the officials still hadn't made the call. The Buckeyes on the field were signaling no good, and after a delay, the officials signaled the same. The kick had sailed wide to the left by an estimated 18 inches. Ohio State won yet another stunner.

But this wasn't *that* game. It wasn't Griffin who'd made that surge to pick up a few extra yards.

In fact, this football field on a frigid November night in Columbus wasn't even the one in Ohio Stadium. It was about 29 years later and 13 miles away at Dublin Scioto

High School. The Independence High School 76ers were squaring off against the Brookhaven High School Bearcats in the Division II Regional Finals.

Small potatoes? Not in Ohio.

Even at this level, football is an obsession. The state of Ohio has a lot of talent and a lot of fans. Both were apparent to anyone who tried to even get near this game. Well after the opening kick, cars continued to creep slowly along Sawmill Road, approaching the field. Traffic was at a virtual standstill. Impatient fans sat in idling vehicles, with heaters turned up, waiting their turn to enter the already jammed grassy field that was now an overflow parking lot.

And although the temperature barely threatened to crack 30 degrees, the bleachers were crowded. (Most of the empty space was later occupied by fans who were waiting in line at the concession stand to buy hot cocoa.) Cheerleaders huddled close together, attempting to stay warm in their skimpy outfits, and the band did their best to look spirited, even as some musicians revealed their discomfort by blowing on their hands between fight songs.

And down on the field, those players, in familiar football garb—big shoulder pads, helmets, and pad-laden pants—looked, well, they looked a lot like the guys who play on Saturdays just 13 miles away. It wasn't until one's eyes scanned farther down the sidelines and saw some of the smaller and a couple of—diplomatically speaking—less fit players did it finally become clear that most of these guys were not future All-Americans.

But that one running back—he clearly had skills. His explosive quickness almost startled the opposing defense, even though they were clearly keyed in to him more than any other player on the field. And his final numbers on the day—224 yards rushing, including a 35-yard touchdown—

were statistical evidence that he'd outclassed almost every player on the field.

Ohio State's coaches sure hoped so.

Independence High School senior Erik Haw will be a Buckeye in 2004. Months before this game, before he received that hand-off from quarterback John McDonald and broke a tackle to give the 76ers an extra couple of yards in what was ultimately a losing effort against Brookhaven, he'd already given his verbal commitment to attend the Ohio State University. The local boy had made good, and now the big school wanted him. It sure sounded a lot like Archie Griffin.

During his junior year, Haw rushed for 1,271 yards and scored 14 touchdowns, but in the heartland, where an inordinate number of boys grow up dreaming of playing on the biggest fields, that was not even enough to raise eyebrows of Big Ten and Big East recruiters.

Until he ran for them.

Haw was also a track star at Independence High. During the summer of 2003, he was invited to the football camps that were run by Ohio State, Notre Dame, and Michigan to look at potential recruits. The camps give would-be prospects a chance to work out for coaches, and Haw knew going in that he had to do something special to raise eyebrows. At the Ohio State camp, the 5-foot-11-inch, 208-pound back got his chance at running the 40-yard dash (a major barometer for recruits) right after fellow Ohio prospect Tony Pittman.

Pittman, going into his senior year at Akron's Buchtel High School, was the kind of player that almost every Division I-A coach *had* heard of. A blue chip prospect who had legitimate interest from several schools, thanks to 2,325 yards running and 35 touchdowns his junior year. At camp, he was clocked running the 40 at 4.39 seconds, but that time was academic. He had already been offered, and had verbally accepted, a scholarship to OSU. For Pittman, like so many recruits, it was either Michigan or Ohio. Ohio liked him, and he decided to go with the closer school.

Things weren't easy for Haw, but coming into the summer of '03, he was a young man with a plan. "I was working out three times a day, just waiting for the football camps to come around so I could showcase my speed," he said. Now his dream of playing for the hometown Buckeyes could actually become a reality, if he could—in his own words—"do twice as good [as Pittman]."

Haw reached deep, gave everything he had, and ran for the men with the whistles and the watches who literally held his future in their hands. And he rocked it. Haw sprinted 40 yards in 4.21 seconds. Now Haw was on the radar—smack dab in the middle of it.

He made equally solid runs at the Notre Dame and Michigan camps, and in no time the dam burst and interest poured in. Cincinnati offered a scholarship. So did Bowling Green, Toledo, Akron, Kentucky, Louisville, and, yes, Michigan.

"Things are just happening a lot faster than we thought they would," his mother, Cornelia, said.

Even with the stack of offers, Erik knew where he wanted to be in the fall of '04. The same school where his mother got a degree and where he could study his already chosen field, pharmaceuticals. And a place where one day maybe he, too, could lead his team into field goal range and ice their bitter rival. That place, of course, was Ohio State University.

This field at Dublin Scioto High School was just another, more secluded, battleground in the war.

When most people think the season ends for schools like

Michigan and Ohio State, in a sense it's only just beginning. Recruiting is college football's second—and arguably
equally important—season. And when it involves the
teams, it involves the fans.

In today's Wi-fied, Web world, recruiting is followed
almost as closely by a rabid core of fans as the regular
season is. A number of Web sites and magazines report on
high school prospects, summer camp performances,
campus visits, the general interest that teams express, verbal commitments, and, ultimately, signings.

"I'm obsessed with the recruiting process," admitted one
Buckeye fan. "The day after the national championship, I
started focusing on recruiting." It's not as sexy, but for the
fantasy sports-obsessed type, it's something to do—and it's
a lot easier than talking to girls.

"There definitely are fanatics," confirmed Michael Spath,
an editor and writer for the *Wolverine*, a tabloid that focuses
on recruiting in print and online. "To get a magazine that
comes in your mail once a week, that's a fan,
but to join a web site and pay, you have to be a little bit
more than a fan. We put up 5 to 8 stories a day. You can read
about Michigan every day of the year, except maybe Christmas—we try and take that day off. The recruiting fuels it.
During the season, people are less focused on recruiting, but
the rest of the year attention turns to football recruiting."

Michigan and Ohio State fans can follow the travails of
two extremely successful programs that continue to be two
of the top teams in the nation every year because they have
the same success in recruiting. (Recruiting classes are ranked
just as the teams are during the year, and both schools are
consistently Top Ten recruiters, just as they are Top Ten per-
formers.) Only a handful of blue chip prospects are out
there, and the competition to get them is pretty intense.

So, if you have two perennially competitive football pro-grams that draw 100,000 fans to their houses every week and get plenty of national TV exposure, how is a young stud prospect, especially one from the region, to choose?

It depends. Some stay close to home and go to the schools they've been rooting for since they were kids. The Ohioans generally flock to their state school. Of the 114 guys on the 2003 OSU roster, only 26 were from somewhere other than the friendly confines of the Buckeye State. Only one member of the OSU football team was from Michigan, and he just happened to be their quarterback. Michigan, the state, is not as talent-rich as Ohio is, and the university has traditionally cast the recruiting net wider. On the Wolverines' 2003 roster, there were 108 players, and more than half were from somewhere other than Michigan, including a handful of Ohio natives.

But it doesn't matter. OSU can be successful by recruiting mostly in the state because of the predominance of talent that exists in Ohio, while Michigan doesn't have a problem recruiting in other parts of the country because of the team's national popularity, combined with a far-flung net-work of alumni.

Other kids look to the individual programs and how their personal goals mesh and, of course, how successful they are at sending players to the NFL. Quarterback prospect Chad Henne from West Lawn, Pennsylvania, couldn't help but notice that NFL QBs like Super Bowl MVP Tom Brady, Todd Collins, Jim Harbaugh, Brian Griese, and Elvis Grbac were all Michigan graduates. Henne, one of the nation's top quarterback prospects in 2003, signed a letter of intent to go to Michigan in February 2003 and said, "I think it's the Michigan tradition," in reference to the success the school's quarterbacks have had in the NFL.

Sometimes the recruiting process is more surreal than matter-of-fact. In one instance, it may have even been a bucket full of fish that landed the big recruit. In 1998, one-time Buckeye assistant Lee Owens recalled a fishing trip on Lake Michigan that was arranged to hook up OSU coach John Cooper and St. Vincent–St. Mary high school coach Jimmy Meyer, the idea being that if Coach Meyer became more familiar with Coach Cooper, he might convince the Sandusky, Ohio, star lineman Orlando Pace—who was also considering Michigan—to attend Ohio State.

While everyone stared at still lines, Cooper was hauling in fish like they were running from the law. Everyone was in awe of the display, and, according to Owens, Cooper earned the Sandusky coach's respect that afternoon, and maybe he bent the recruit's ear a little bit. "I'm not going to say Orlando chose [OSU] over Michigan because of the impression Coach made on those coaches," he said, "but I'm sure it didn't hurt us a bit."

And guess what else hooks 'em? Yup, the Game helps, too.

"The biggest thing is not who wins the Game but the Game itself," said Spath. "Recruits will tell you they want to one day beat Michigan. Or they want to beat Ohio State. It's a huge selling point."

When it comes time for an official visit (according to NCAA rules, each recruit is allowed one official visit at five different schools), prospective players will arrive in town on a Friday, meet a current football player who will act as their chaperone, hang out in the dorms, see campus life, tour the facilities, eat in the town's fanciest restaurants, see games (if football season is over, probably a basketball game), and generally get the royal treatment.

In early 2004, these visits were put under the microscope when University of Miami recruit Willie Williams published a diary of his recruiting-trip adventures in the *Miami Herald*. He recounted first-class suites, police escorts, and exorbitant surf-and-turf dinners. The NCAA was quick to point out that the rule states that schools may entertain recruits "at a scale comparable to that of normal student life."

Much more foul was the scandal that came out of Colorado soon after the Williams story. Three women filed a lawsuit against the University of Colorado, claiming that they were raped by football players or recruits in 2001. It was abundantly clear that recruiting visits nationwide warranted further investigation.

Ohio State didn't even have to resort to any kind of hard sell to reel in their local prospect.

"It's where I wanted to go; I wanted to be a Buckeye," Haw said. "I'm relieved. But at the same time, I know it's going to be another challenge." He was already versed in the sound bite. It's hard to believe that Haw was still just a kid, a high school senior—only 17 years old.

Strip away the enormity of college football, the billions of dollars spent and generated by the big schools, the millions of fans, the TV contracts, the merchandise sales . . . Strip it all away, and in many cases, what you have are players who until a few months ago were living at home under their parents' roofs. The players on the field on Saturdays in front of 100,000 fans were just recently high school kids; now, in the blink of an eye, they are the proverbial big men on campus. In the spotlight. In the papers. On *SportsCenter*. And when they get on campus and get thrust into that limelight, they all respond in different ways.

A rare few, you could say, were born to be there.

■ ■ ■

Bo Schembechler walked into his office one day and saw a 10-year-old kid sitting in his chair, leaning back with his feet up on the coach's desk. Schembechler—a man known for the more-than-occasional sideline temper tantrum— looked at the boy and growled, "How are you, Jim Harbaugh?"

Any boy in his right mind would have made a mad dash for the playground. But this particular boy didn't even move his feet. "Okay. How you doin', Bo?" he shot back.

Damn, that kid was cocky. And by the time he was old enough to run around a football field, he had every right to be. Jim Harbaugh grew up with football. His father, Jack, was an assistant under Bo, later a head coach at Western Michigan, and then the head coach of the Western Kentucky University Hilltoppers for 14 years.

As a 13-year-old, Harbaugh even made the trip with his dad and the Wolverines to the 1977 Rose Bowl—and the big game made an impression. Jim went into his dad's room on that trip and told him (rather poetically, for a barely teenage kid), "I want to be on the field in the Rose Bowl someday when the sun drops behind the mountains in the second half."

That was a lot of talk by a kid who was just passing through puberty, but when Jim showed up as a freshman quarterback at the University of Michigan, he had to prove to fans and players that he wasn't there just because of his family connections to the Wolverines' head coach.

It didn't take long.

By his junior year, Harbaugh led the Wolverines to a Big Ten championship and was the nation's most efficient passer, completing 145 of 227 attempts. The following year, he amassed a then school record, 2,729 yards in the air.

But the moment that defined Harbaugh's career at

Michigan and became etched in the permanent history of the Rivalry happened not on the field but at a routine press conference. The Monday before 1986's Game, the Michigan QB faithfully fielded questions from the media and instead of offering the usual saccharine "I respect the other team"–type quote, the normally soft-spoken quarterback suddenly channeled that inner cocky kid—the one who left his feet up on Bo's desk.

Harbaugh told a roomful of reporters who were probably dozing off, "I guarantee we will beat Ohio State and be in Pasadena New Year's Day. People might not give us a snow-ball's chance in hell to beat them in Columbus, but we're going to. We don't care where we play the game. I hate to say it, but we could play in the parking lot. We could play at 12 noon or midnight. We're going to be jacked up and we're going to win."

Now, that, sports fans, is what's known as bulletin board material!

During the ensuing week, if Harbaugh and his own mother had walked into the OSU practice facility, she would have lost track of him, there were so many pictures of the QB festooned around the place. And each had the "guarantee" scrawled right over it.

OSU had their rallying cry, but their coach (and Woody Hayes's successor) Earle Bruce was careful not to put too much emphasis on Harbaugh's dis of his team. "One thing about football, and this is neither to Jim Harbaugh's credit or discredit, the game is played on the football field," he said. "It is not won by talking."

Schembechler did his best to laugh it off. "I'd be more upset if he'd said we'd lose," the coach said. "He's 22 years old, so he can say whatever he wants."

For a game that usually generates more than enough

buzz on its own, Harbaugh managed to make the glare of the spotlight appear just a little bit brighter for the 83rd face-off between the two rivals. It was a game that featured the teams ranked number 6 (Michigan) and number 7 (Ohio State) in the nation, playing for the Big Ten championship (an OSU loss would still give the Buckeyes a tie for the conference) and a trip to Pasadena (after a lull, it was the first time since 1980 that the Rose Bowl bid would go to the winner of the game).

But, really, what it came down to was: Would Harbaugh be a prophet or a blabbermouth? Almost all of the 90,674 fans who packed Ohio Stadium on November 22, 1986, were hoping for the latter, and they were pretty vocal about it, as "Harbaugh sucks!" chants went up around Ohio Stadium.

And they continued when the Buckeyes' Jamie Holland returned the opening kickoff 47 yards, and 10 plays later, OSU quarterback Jim Karsatos hit Ohio State's athletic receiver Cris Carter in the end zone for a quick 7–0 lead.

Harbaugh sucks!

Michigan squeaked out a field goal, and then OSU, on their next possession, scored a touchdown in only three plays, with a big 32-yard pass from Karsatos to Everett Ross and a 46-yard scoring run by Vince Workman.

Harbaugh sucks!

Following another field goal, the Wolverines were down 14–6 by halftime. "I knew if I made that kind of statement," Harbaugh said after the game, "I would have to back it up. I made sure I wasn't going to leave nothing on the field."

In the second half, the quarterback finally delivered. The Wolverines received the kickoff and marched 83 yards in 14 plays, finishing with a 4-yard run by back Jamie Morris. Following a Buckeye field goal, it was Harbaugh and

Morris again who moved the ball down the field and into the end zone. (On that day, the 5-foot-7-inch Morris compiled 216 yards on the ground—at the time, a Rivalry record.)

Silence from the crowd.

In the fourth quarter, the Michigan offense continued to dominate. The Wolverines made it a 26–17 game, following a big play from Harbaugh, who delivered a 23-yard screen pass to Bob Perryman. "I can't recall [a game with] so many points, so many yards and so many big plays," Schembechler said later, and he was talking about both sides.

The Buckeyes came roaring back again after blocking a Michigan field goal attempt. From 27 yards out, Karsatos lobbed the perfect pass to Carter in the end zone, and the All-American wideout (a school-record 164 receptions and 27 TDs in his OSU career) made an acrobatic pick off the fringe of the turf to bring the Buckeyes back within 2 points.

Then, suddenly, the focus of the game had shifted. Harbaugh had done his part, with 19 completions and 261 yards passing—all he could do to guarantee the guarantee. Now the game was tight, and the attention turned to Buckeye coach Earle Bruce and his late-game play calling.

Bruce was in a tough spot.

Well, if you think about it, he'd been in a tough spot since 1979, the year he was asked to do the impossible: replace Woody Hayes. And yet Bruce proved himself more than capable on the field, going 11–1 in his first season and coming within 1 point of a national championship. The Buckeyes remained consistent under Bruce, with six straight 9–3 seasons and, more important, a .500 record against Michigan. Still, in the rabid pressure cooker of Columbus, Bruce somehow managed to remain an unpopular coach.

"Why Earle has a problem with popularity I have never quite understood, because everybody who knows him likes him," said OSU athletic director Rick Bay. "Maybe he needs to get out more."

He didn't exactly have what anyone would call a magnetic personality. He didn't give the best quotes to the media or know the best quips. But in Buckeye land, winning is still everything . . . especially in that big annual game against Michigan. The Buckeyes started 1986 0–2 for the first time since 1894, but after 9 straight redemptive victories, Bruce was 3 points from another big win over Michigan and, perhaps, a full pardon from his critics.

Trailing by 2 points, the Buckeyes were on the Wolverine 36-yard line, with 1:32 remaining in the ballgame. With a third-and-10, Bruce called for a pass, and Karsatos hit Carter on a button-hook, but it would net the Buckeyes only 8 yards. "The play depends on coverage," Bruce said afterward. "It *could* go 10 yards."

It didn't.

Now it was fourth-and-two and Bruce summoned freshman kicker Matt Frantz to attempt a 45-yard game-winning field goal. The thing is, Matt Frantz had never hit a 45-yard field goal—let alone, one into a 10-mile-per-hour wind. There was still time to go for the first down, maybe burn a little clock and put Frantz into a much more comfortable position to make the winning kick.

Buckeye kicking coach Randy Hart gave Bruce assurance that Frantz had the foot to make it. And, it turns out, distance wasn't the problem. Frantz's ball climbed high and far toward the uprights, and even the young kicker thought he'd nailed it. "I thought it was good when I got my leg into it," he said afterward. "But it was a little bit to the left."

Just like that, OSU's dreams of an undisputed title and a trip west were dashed. "This is the worst feeling I've ever had," OSU's fiery linebacker Chris Spielman (who contributed to a monster 29 tackles on that day—still a Rivalry record) said afterward. "It's gonna take me a while to get over it."

His coach, who'd made the controversial play call, was equally distraught. "It's such a tough game to lose. You don't like to lose to Michigan, especially in Ohio Stadium. You don't get over it for a while."

Meanwhile, Harbaugh, a.k.a. the Guarantor, was on top of the world, and he had helped Schembechler notch a school-record 166th win as the Wolverine coach. After the game, the coach said about the guarantee, "I'd have said it myself if I had any guts."

If he'd had any guts, he probably would have kicked that cocky little son of a gun out of his chair, too.

■   ■   ■

Emotion. *It* drives the Game. Forget records. Forget championships and Rose Bowl bids. Sometimes it's just about pure emotion, and there was a ton of it in the Ohio State practice facility the Monday of Michigan week, a year after the devastating loss in the "Guarantee Game."

With the full team gathered round, Coach Bruce told his team that he had an announcement to make. "I have been let go by the university," Bruce said. He did not bother to hold back the tears running down his face. But in the wake of the sudden bad news, he tried to make sure his team remained focused on beating Michigan on Saturday.

"This is the most important game in your entire life. The school up north is good, but they're not great." At this point, the tears were streaming, and the coach's face was turning red.

"Strap on your helmets, boys," he continued, "because there is no game like this one, and we'll be flying around the field and cracking heads. This will be the hardest-hitting game of your lives. We are going to go up to Michigan, and we are going to kick their ass!"

It was the start of a very emotional week for Bruce, who had been fired as head coach of the Buckeyes with one game still remaining on the schedule and with a remarkable cumulative record of 80–26–1—the best in the conference over the last nine years. And even worse was the fact that Bruce had never been given a concrete reason for his firing.

There was plenty of speculation around Columbus as to why Bruce was let go: his lack of personality; his fondness for playing the ponies (an affection, it turned out, that he shared with OSU's starting QB from 1978–1981, Art Schlichter); the dip in the performance of the Buckeyes, who finished 6–4–1 in 1987; and, the most credible, the fact that he just was not and never would be Woody Hayes.

Regardless of the reason, Bruce's players felt that he got a raw deal, and they rallied around their coach. Tackle Joe Staysniak bought white headbands for the entire team, with the name EARLE printed on them. After warm-ups, the Buckeyes removed their helmets and revealed their custom headgear. It was a symbol of solidarity and support for their lame duck coach.

Unfortunately, on the football field they quickly fell in a hole, 13–0.

But the score, for a moment, was beside the point. On this day, it was clearer than ever: the Game is a thing unto itself. The 1987 Michigan–Ohio State game proved that you can throw everything you know away when that game starts. Throw away the records. Throw away the headlines. The Game is simply the biggest event of the year for both teams, no matter what. There was no better proof than the intensity that still surrounded a game in which both teams had no shot at a championship and in which one of those teams was led by a lame duck coach. Even after one team fell into a 13-point hole early on, they both still played as if it were the biggest game of their lives, and more than 100,000 fans were still on hand to hang onto every last play.

As if to underline the point, the action really began to pick up in the second quarter. Ohio State's defense made a big play by recovering a Jerrod Bunch fumble on the Buckeye 39-yard line. OSU then moved the ball down the field, and with 1:36 remaining in the half, quarterback Tom Tupa hit Everett Ross on a 4-yard pass, and Bruce's boys were finally on the board.

Still, the Wolverines went into the locker room dominating the game statistically and confident about their now 7-point lead. At the same time, OSU's players made their way to the locker room, still sorting through their emotional baggage. But it was during that break that they finally decided to channel their feelings into football.

"We didn't make a lot of adjustments [at halftime]," said Spielman. "We didn't have to. Someone mentioned that we had 30 minutes of our football season remaining. No one needed to say anything more."

On the Buckeyes' first possession after the half, Tupa dropped back to his own 30-yard line, looked deep, and saw Everett Ross well covered down field. He switched gears and tossed the ball to tailback Carlos Snow 5 yards from the line of scrimmage. Snow then outran Michigan's John Milligan and faked out Doug Mallory before running 70 yards into the end zone. OSU added to their lead midway through the third when Tupa ran it in from a yard out, but OSU missed the point after.

After a Snow fumble, Michigan tied the game 20–20. But with 5:18 left in the game, OSU moved into field-goal range, and for the second year in a row, Bruce turned to Matt Frantz to try to steal one from the Wolverines. He'd disappointed his teammates in '86, but Frantz, like the rest of the team, was focused on getting a big win for his coach. During the week, Frantz had told the press, prophetically, "The coach told us not to talk about his situation, but I'll have plenty to say about it soon. Ask me after I kick the winning field goal against Michigan." He called his 26-yarder, and he nailed it. Flying high on pure emotion and adrenalin, Spielman and the rest of the Buckeye defense squashed any Wolverine attempt at scoring the rest of the way.

After the game, several players hoisted Bruce on their shoulders and marched him around the field. It was the most bittersweet victory in the history of the epic Rivalry.

■　　■　　■

But not every story has a happy ending. Not every college football player can successfully play the part of an emotional leader, like a Harbaugh or a Spielman. Remember, these are still young men being asked to simultaneously grow up and perform on one of the biggest stages in sports. They don't all rise to the challenge.

Art Schlichter was just not prepared for the accolades, the pressure, and the stardom. Schlichter's name resurfaced when Bruce was fired in 1987. There was a lot of speculation that his lenient treatment of the Buckeye quarterback during the early '80s led to the coach's eventual ousting. Even the governor of Ohio, Richard Celeste, told the press that Bruce was fired partly because of his handling of the QB. (He later backpedaled and said that his comment was purely "speculation.")

But it was Schlichter's life story that had the arc of an after-school special. He was the fallen archetype: the football hero with a troubling secret that, eventually, he could no longer hide.

A high school phenomenon whom Coach Hayes had personally recruited, Schlichter brought (of all things!) a successful passing game to Ohio State football. He started as a freshman and began a streak of 48 straight games, taking snaps as quarterback for the Buckeyes. By his senior year, Schlichter set OSU records for passing yardage, touchdown passes, and total offense, while leading the Buckeyes to two Big Ten championships. He even dated a cheerleader. On paper, life could not be better for Art Schlichter.

The 1981 game against Michigan, in particular, may have been Schlichter's most memorable moment as a Buckeye. Michigan had started that season ranked number 1 in the country, but after a couple of blind-siding losses, the Wolverines were desperately trying to hang onto a shot at a shared Big Ten title when they faced the 7–3 Buckeyes.

Anthony Carter started things off in dazzling fashion for the Wolverines, returning the kickoff 52 yards. (Carter was an electric receiver for UM, who over his career at Michigan averaged less than 4 catches per game—thanks, in large part, to Schembechler's conservative offense—but still managed to score 37 touchdowns. Basically, he made every catch a highlight film–worthy reception that meant something.)

Unfortunately, UM quarterback Steve Smith killed the

first drive with an interception. On Michigan's next possession, they managed a field goal, thanks to the strong foot of
Ann Arbor's own Ali Haji-Sheikh. When OSU got the ball,
Schlichter connected on a few passes, and the OSU running
game brought the Buckeyes within inches of the goal line.
Then the QB snuck the ball over the end zone and gave the
scarlet and gray a 7–3 half-time lead.

In the third quarter, Michigan had a third-and-two at
the Buckeye 6, but Smith was sacked by John Gayle for a
loss, and the Wolverines had to settle for another Haji-
Sheikh field goal. Following an interception, the Wolverines scored once again, thanks to Haji-Sheikh. It was good
enough for a 9–7 lead, and Michigan looked to be back in
control.

But then momentum shifted again—fast. Smith threw
another costly interception at the goal line and gave the
ball back to Schlichter, who completed a remarkable, scrambling, off-balance pass on third-and-eight at OSU 33. The
drive stayed alive, thanks to a second big third down play
(this time, goal to go). Schlichter rolled right, looked to the
end zone, and, without seeing an open man, ran for the sidelines. He got just enough of a block to sneak into the corner
of the end zone, right next to the orange pylon.

Schlichter's second touchdown, with only 2:50 left to
play, gave the Buckeyes a 14–9 lead and an eventual upset
in Ann Arbor, knocking UM out of the Rose Bowl and earning a piece of the Big Ten title. Schlichter's teammates
hoisted the quarterback onto their shoulders and carried
him off the field.

At that point, the made-for-TV movie would have slowed
the image of the smiling Schlichter and begun playing the
dramatic orchestral music. Few of Schlichter's Buckeye
teammates knew at the time that Art had a secret life of

gambling. It turned out that he was an addict, and making bets was the only thing he could do to keep the mounting pressures of being a big-time quarterback at bay. Schlichter was a regular at the local track, and by his junior year, he was betting through a bookie on various sports. Not exactly the hobbies of a team leader or a role model.

The QB was able to shield his habit from most of the world while at OSU, although Coach Bruce reportedly knew and even ran into Schlichter at the local track they both frequented. It wasn't until Schlichter became a pro that his troubles surfaced, after he got into some legal trouble and eventually wound up at a psychiatric hospital to treat his addiction. In no time, Schlichter went from being an all-time Buckeye hero to an afterthought whose name is always accompanied by a nod of the head and three little words, "What a shame"—even in Columbus, where they don't easily let go of football heroes.

Of course, there are too many cases where the dark secrets of troubled college football players come to light a lot sooner. If you scan the headlines in any sports section, you're sure to find them. Wolverine Marlin Jackson's arrest in 2003 was fairly well-publicized, but less well-known outside the state was the story of Kelly Baraka. The football player was one of the country's top running back prospects in 2001, but two successive arrests on marijuana possession charges (which led to four nights in a Kalamazoo, Michigan, jail cell) left Baraka on the sidelines. Coach Carr finally dismissed Baraka from the Michigan football team for "undisclosed reasons." And the prospect eventually left UM and wound up playing football at Joliet Junior College. Although it was only 250 miles from Michigan Stadium, it might as well have been on Mars.

Sometimes players get a chance to redeem themselves

after a moment of poor judgment. The UM cornerback Jeremy LeSueur, who became a star in 2003, had to re-earn the trust of coaches and teammates after a 2001 arrest for soliciting a prostitute.

"You learn how fast things can turn, good or bad," LeSueur said. "It might take just a second to get into something but forever to get out or be able to come back. You just have to watch your step."

In Ohio, the athletic department's PR machine had to douse the fires that raged all year over the situation involving Clarett, but Ohio State sports information director Steve Snapp and his staff already had plenty of practice in that department.

Prospective starting linebacker Marco Cooper was suspended from school in April 2002 after being arrested for drug and firearm possession (he watched the national championship game from prison). Wide receiver Angelo Chattams was arrested for theft of golf equipment in July 2002. In October 2002, backup middle linebacker Fred Pagac Jr. was arrested on a disorderly conduct charge. And those are just a few examples of recent arrests and team-rule violations under Tressel's three-year watch.

Even on the eve of the 2003 game against Michigan, some OSU players found themselves in hot water. Starting wide receiver Santonio Holmes and kick returner Troy Smith were charged the Thursday before the Game with misdemeanor disorderly conduct for their roles in an altercation that happened early Sunday morning outside a school dorm. Making a decision about how to punish players is not something any OSU coach wants on his plate during Michigan Week.

The sad reality, found throughout the NCAA, is that police reports are nearly as common as stat sheets, and probation for players and programs has become just another part of the game. The biggest games, like Michigan versus Ohio State, only add to the enormous pressures that players face and the intensity under which they are scrutinized.

The troubled OSU running back Clarett eventually pleaded guilty to a lesser charge of failing to aid a law enforcement agent and was guaranteed no jail time. And even though he continued his suit against the NFL, the Clarett camp kept alive the possibility, for the time being, of returning to the Buckeyes in 2004. "I look forward to shifting all of my attention back to my studies and the team at the Ohio State University," he said in a January 2004 statement. Fans, for one thing, can be pretty fickle about players who get in trouble. The attitude is really what-have-you-done-for-me-lately on the field. LeSueur, once a laughingstock, was now revered, and although "Fuck Clarett" shirts were being sold outside Ohio Stadium in '03, one Buckeye fan said, point-blank, "If he comes back to play here and he performs, he'll be loved."

Now, in a way, it was Erik Haw's turn to prove that he was more than a high school kid who could run 40 yards really fast. He had to prove that he's up for the challenge of playing in front of 100,000 people and the millions more watching on TV every Saturday. How would he respond? Maybe one day he'd lead Ohio State in a victory in the Game. Or maybe he'd pick up some bad habits and even wind up in jail. He could end up as a punchline or he could be a school hero . . . even an immortal, like his heir apparent Archie Griffin.

At that moment, he was probably just happy. Happy to be given a chance to one day soon participate in the biggest rivalry in college football—a rivalry that was steamrolling toward a storybook 100th edition.

Carriages and wagons supplement the seating in 1901 at the very first UM–OSU game in Columbus. Fans couldn't have been happy with the outcome: Michigan 21, Ohio State 0.

By 1927, the venues were a little larger; 84,401 spectators were on hand to dedicate the brand-new Michigan Stadium in Ann Arbor and watch another UM victory over OSU.

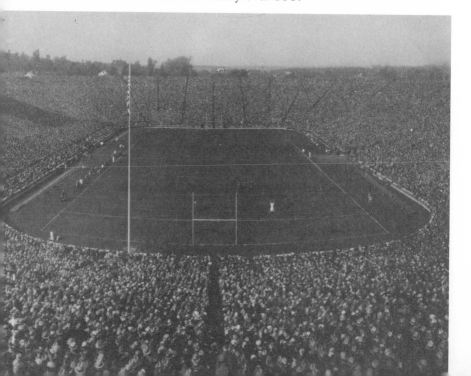

Fans and players alike suffer through 1950's legendary Snow Bowl
in Columbus.

The Buckeye faithful celebrate on the field of Ohio Stadium after a
21–7 win in the Game in 1954.

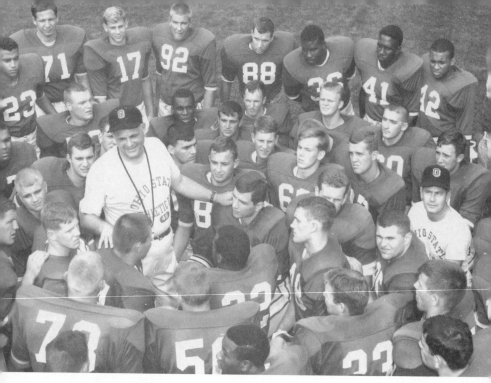

The man they called Woody commands the attention of his troops
in the early sixties.

Bo and Woody in a rare moment of calm during their ten-year war.

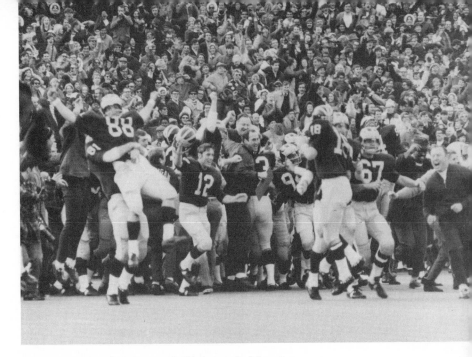

The Wolverines celebrate 1969's improbable win.

Michigan's Tom Darden
goes over the back of
OSU's Dick Wakefield to
make an interception in
1971. No interference
was called and Woody
had a mini meltdown.

A sign held by a statue of former OSU president William Oxley outside the main library proclaims what everyone on campus was thinking in the fall of 1976.

This sentiment has been around for quite a while, as this fan from the seventies shows.

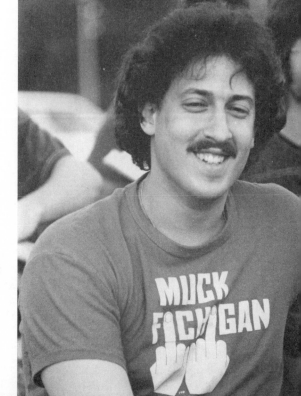

Archie Griffin (far left) runs the ball in OSU's 14–11 win in 1972, which was memorable for Bo's fourth-and-goal play call late in the game.

The Buckeyes paid tribute to their embattled coach, Earle Bruce, and then delivered him a victory in 1987.

OSU quarterback Bobby Hoying evades UM's Jason Horn in 1992. Ohio State tied Michigan 13–13, but the Ohio State University president still called it "one of our biggest victories."

Michigan's Tim Biakabutuka couldn't be stopped in 1995, single-handedly ruining the Buckeyes' undefeated season.

The 235-member Michigan Marching Band takes the field before the 100th Game.

The Wolverines in the tunnel, getting ready to take the field to play Ohio State for the 100th time.

"How you do against Ohio State is a big part of any career here," said John Navarre, seen here preparing to take a snap in the biggest game of his life.

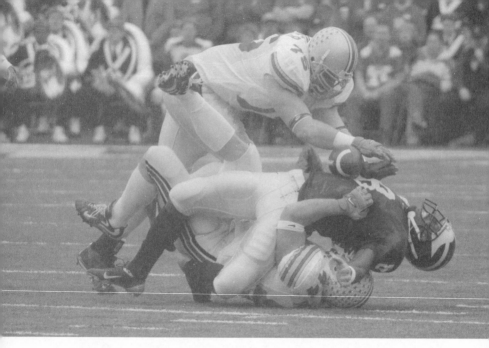

Michigan receiver Jason Avant gets twisted under OSU's Robert Reynolds. As one fan said, "This is going to be a tough, hard-hitting game just like the tradition of the previous 99 meetings."

After a victory in the 100th Game, Wolverine fans celebrate a Big Ten championship on the field in the Big House.

6

BROKEN HEARTS AND BALLOONING WALLETS

It's really difficult to watch a grown man cry.

Thankfully, Mike didn't exactly let the tears fly, but he came pretty close. In lieu of bawling like a baby, he opted instead for yet another Miller Lite and tried his best to enjoy the exceptionally convivial atmosphere in the Buckeye Hall of Fame.

This Columbus bar, a few miles from campus, is a literal shrine to the Buckeyes. Imagine a cross between a museum and a T.G.I. Fridays, decorated exclusively in scarlet and gray, and you'll be picturing the Buckeye Hall of Fame. It's a colossal-sized joint that would make a Times Square theme restaurant blush. Once you leave your car with the valet and step inside, you can shop for Ohio State slippers, stroll the OSU All-American Walk of Fame, inspect one of Archie Griffith's Heisman trophies, have your picture taken with the 2002 national championship trophy, or—if you're feeling really bad about the state of the Bucks—you might even order a Wolverine Death. The drink special is a mix of

Jagermeister, amaretto, and orange juice, with a splash of grenadine. Mike didn't opt for the Wolverine Death, but he was wishing for its outcome, nonetheless.

"It brings tears to my eyes," said the diehard, recalling one of his most painful memories as a lifelong Buckeye fan. "OSU was 10–0. I was living in New Jersey at the time, but OSU kicked everybody's ass that year. And Michigan was having one of its worst years in a while. So I came into town for what in my mind was going to be the coronation! Michigan was going to get the ass-kicking that they were due, and it would seal our undefeated regular season and a chance to play for the national championship.

"We're up at halftime, of course, I'm still talking shit. I think OSU was up 9–0. Long story short, they lost 13–9— in Columbus. I came all the way from New Jersey to see a Michigan ass kicking that would allow us to walk into the national championship game. And even though UM was having a bad year, Michigan fucking won!"

This now extremely agitated fan was talking about the 1996 Ohio State–Michigan game, but he could have been talking about 1990. Heck, he could have been talking about '92 or '93 or especially '95. In total, the '90s were not kind to the Buckeyes and their ardent supporters. And if you were to ask any of the numerous fans hanging out at the Buckeye Hall of Fame, drinking beer and eating chicken wings, they would shake their heads and probably mumble basically the same thing that Mike said next: "John Cooper, man. He just couldn't win that fucking game."

■   ■   ■

After Earle Bruce was shown the headbands and then shown the door, OSU brought in a 50-year-old Tennessee native named John Cooper to be their new head coach. Cooper's previous job was at Arizona State, where in 1987 he led the Sun Devils to their first Rose Bowl and a 22–15 win over Michigan. There is no better way to make your résumé stand out from the others piled on the desk of an OSU athletic director than a big win over the Wolverines. Cooper, who had no previous associations with Ohio or Ohio college sports, got the state's biggest sports-related job.

And so began one of the most exasperating periods in Ohio State football history.

After first taking over the team in 1988, Cooper's Buckeyes struggled. Not until 1989 did they come into the Game with a shot at a championship, but the favored Wolverines won 28–18 in a close contest that ended with a late Michigan interception and a touchdown. The Buckeyes were down by only 3 points, with 3:42 to go and the ball on their own 34. On a second-and-12, Buckeye quarterback Greg Frey was picked off by Wolverine defensive back Todd Plate, and the contest was over.

The next year, a Rose Bowl trip for OSU was a long shot but still a possibility. If Minnesota beat Iowa and OSU beat Michigan, then the Buckeyes would earn a trip west. Minnesota did its part by upsetting Iowa, and Cooper's team was on the threshold, tied with the Wolverines 13–13 late in the fourth quarter with a fourth down and inches on their own 29. Kicking the ball away probably would have guaranteed a tie and therefore no Rose Bowl bid for the Buckeyes. Cooper called for a play named "Base 4," an option play to the right that would give Frey the choice of dumping the ball to his tight end or running it himself. Frey followed his fullback Scottie Graham into the line of scrimmage and, with no room to move, looked to run up field. Michigan nosetackle T. J. Osman made a gallant play from his back and tied up Frey. Chris Hutchinson helped wrap him up, and before the Buckeye QB knew what hit him, the Wolverines had the ball back. UM kicker J. D. Carlson hit a 37-yard field goal, with no time left on the clock to ice the victory.

After three seasons, Cooper was winless against Michigan, and in 1991, things went from bad to worse as the Wolverines gave OSU fans more haunting memories. This time, their nightmares would be inhabited by a fleet-footed receiver with a wide smile who gave the Rivalry one of its most indelible images.

He was yet another Ohio kid who chose the winged helmets over the gray ones with a pastiche of Buckeye stickers. (Those stickers, by the way, are awarded to an OSU player who makes an outstanding play. It is a merit system that was put in place by Woody Hayes in 1968.) About 20 major colleges recruited the 5-foot-9-inch Clevelander named Desmond Howard, and conventional wisdom had him going to Ohio State, but that didn't interest the dynamic athlete.

"I didn't visit there," Howard said about OSU. "The year I graduated high school was the same year Ohio State fired Earle Bruce and brought in some guy from out west named John Cooper. No one knew who this Cooper character was, so I was very reluctant to be part of a program that was rebuilding with a new and relatively unknown coach."

At UM, Howard was an atypical football player, a serious kid who didn't socialize, didn't go to clubs, and wore a coat and a tie to class. On the field, though, he was all razzle-dazzle. In 1991, Howard made a game-clinching touchdown grab against Notre Dame by launching himself horizontally and catching the football on his fingertips with his arms completely outstretched and his body parallel to the end zone turf. At Michigan, this play is still simply called "The Catch."

The walking highlight film was marching through a Heisman Trophy–worthy year (one in which he would ultimately score 23 TDs), when the final game of the season against the Buckeyes arrived, and Howard told some buddies back home to pay extra attention to the Game.

"I told my friends in Ohio that if I got in the end zone against Ohio State, I'd do something special for them." Just before halftime, Howard got his chance. OSU's game plan going in was to keep punts out of Howard's hands, but unfortunately, Tim Williams's 41-yarder came down in the UM receiver's grasp—and he took off. Howard split two tacklers at the 10-yard line and then broke another tackle at the 18. He sprinted for the sidelines and picked up a key block from his Wolverine teammate Dwayne Ware at the 30. Howard was untouched the rest of the way, and the 93-yard punt return was the longest in school history.

After Howard crossed the goal line, a truly memorable thing happened. The receiver bent his left leg, high at the knee, and stretched out his left arm. He held the pose for only a second before his teammates mobbed him—but the world got the picture. Howard's friends back home got their special salute. And OSU fans got a serving of humble pie. The "Heisman Pose" was a precursor to the actual award that Howard collected one month later.

For Buckeye fans, that pose really hurt. They felt that the Wolverines were rubbing it in, and they may have been right. "That was the coolest thing we'd ever seen," recalled Chris Bruno, who was a sophomore at Michigan in '91. "A bunch of us started striking 'the pose' all the time as a kind of dis. We thought it was hilarious."

John Cooper wasn't laughing, and neither were Buckeye fans. Michigan crushed OSU 31–3 in that Game, and the Cooper critics were lining up outside his office door. In four seasons, the Ohio State coach was 0–4 against the Wolverines. Fans were beginning to seethe as the Rivalry, which was so even for two decades, started to look decidedly one-sided. A tie in 1992 did not help matters, even though university president E. Gordon Gee called it "one of our biggest victories." Fans felt otherwise, especially since Cooper had a chance to go for the win.

OSU began the fourth quarter down 13–3, but then Tim Williams hit a 30-yard field goal, and with 4:24 left to play, Buckeye quarterback Kirk Herbstreit threw a 5-yard touchdown pass on fourth down to tight end Greg Beatty. Down 13–12, Cooper sent Williams on the field to settle for 1 point.

So many fans in Ohio Stadium threw up their hands, there's a good chance the breeze was felt in Sandusky.

The game ended deadlocked, and afterward, Cooper was—not surprisingly—asked why he didn't go for two points.

"Never entered my mind," said the coach. And that wasn't all he had to answer for, because with 1:49 left, the Buckeyes were on the Michigan 49-yard line facing a fourth-and-four, and Cooper punted the ball away, rather than attempt perhaps his last shot at another score.

"You want to gamble with my chips," Cooper shot back, when reporters asked about the punt. "Gamble, coach, gamble, that's all I hear."

That's not all he'd hear.

Cooper really needed to get off the *schneid* against the team up north, or life in Columbus was going to get more and more uncomfortable.

"Do I like living in Columbus when we haven't beaten Michigan? Obviously, the answer is no," Cooper told reporters the following year before the 1993 Game. "I don't like living here when you have to hear that all the time. But I tell our team—our players and coaches and even myself—that if you don't like it, go change it. Go win the game."

Well, going into the '93 matchup, the Buckeyes had to like their chances. They were undefeated (although with one tie), and the Wolverines were a very un-Michiganlike 6–4. OSU even had a big-time playmaker in receiver Joey Galloway, who was being compared to Desmond Howard. A win or a tie would mean that the Buckeyes would go to the Rose Bowl. Finally, this was their shot to avenge the last few years and perhaps take a seat in the national championship picture.

They didn't score a single point.

OSU was intercepted on four consecutive first-half possessions and wilted in front of the Wolverines. When it was over, Michigan had gained 421 total yards, and Ohio State had only 212. The final score was 28–0.

"This is one of the most embarrassing games I've ever been involved with," Cooper said afterward. "They outplayed us on offense, on defense and in the kicking game. Running the ball, passing the ball . . . I'm shocked. If you had told me we'd come up here and get beat 28–0, I'd have probably stayed home."

Michigan's coach, Gary Moeller—a former assistant who was tapped to replace living legend Bo Schembechler, who retired after the 1989 season—was just as shocked over the victory, and his post-game comment surely didn't assuage the Buckeye fans. "It was probably our lack of success during the season that helped in our victory this time," he said. But Moeller and the Wolverines certainly wanted it going in. They didn't have a shot to go to Pasadena, but they could definitely play spoiler and they could hand it to their rivals. "We want to beat Ohio State," Moeller said before the game. "All of us at Michigan get great motivation just by beating Ohio State."

OSU fans were seething with frustration. Each loss to the Wolverines only made them resent their coach and hate the team up north even more. "You wouldn't have been able to find a single person on campus who liked John Cooper," remembers OSU grad Rob Paciorek of this period. "And what made it even worse was the fact that Michigan was now talking about Michigan State as their rival."

The worst kind of pattern for the Buckeyes was forming: a successful season and an upset at the hands of the Wolverines. Consecutive losses don't necessarily support a rivalry, and Cooper's 0–5–1 against Michigan meant that students were now graduating from UM thinking that OSU was a team you could count on beating the last game of each year—even though those early '90s Wolverine teams were inconsistent.

"In the Gary Moeller era, you never knew if Michigan would show up every Saturday," said '94 UM graduate Vinny Gauri. "The one thing you did know as a Michigan fan was that we could handle Ohio State. It was like a bad '50s sitcom, and John Cooper always ended up with egg on his face."

In Columbus, they were hopping mad, crying "Michigan sucks!" with increasing vigor and venom, while in Ann Arbor, fans were looking to Notre Dame and instate competitor Michigan State to satisfy their natural hunger for a rival.

When it came to the year's final matchup, even some of the Michigan players wanted a tougher fight. Before the '94 game, Wolverine wide receiver Walter Smith, who was sidelined with an injury, told the press, "We want to get Cooper fired. That's what I want to do."

During a news conference at an Ann Arbor hotel, he took the opportunity to get everybody riled up anew. "We want to keep on beatin' 'em and beatin' 'em until he's no longer there. If we need to stir this Rivalry up, I'm going to do what's necessary," Smith said. "I just care about Michigan. I don't care about no other coach outside of Michigan or no other team. I think if all our players had that type of attitude, we would be 11–0 this year."

Later he added, "I haven't lost to Ohio State since I've been here. We talk about that at our practices throughout the week and prior to the season starting. When we got here, we were taught that we always beat Ohio State. It's something we have to get into the minds of the young guys now, because they've never been in the big game."

Cooper refused to comment on Smith's statements but showed his obvious displeasure by abruptly ending a routine teleconference with out-of-town reporters after the questions drifted toward Smith's commentary and the coach's winless record against Michigan.

For Ohio State, it was time to draw a line in the sand. The coaches pulled out all the stops to motivate for this game and even asked ex-Buckeyes to visit the team during the week and give them a post-practice pep talk. Archie Griffin, then the OSU associate athletic director, felt that the talks were doing the trick.

"I know that they understand this is more than just another game," Griffin said of the Buckeyes during Michigan Week in 1994. "And that's the point. This week is like no other they'll ever experience. It's different. Special."

If the Michigan camp was looking for a bad omen, they

could point to an incident that happened the night before the game. Thieves broke into the Wolverine locker room and stole six helmets, including those of tailback Tyrone Wheatley and quarterback Todd Collins.

Bad luck continued after kickoff. Early on, Collins tripped over the foot of his own guard, Jon Runyan, and fell in the end zone for a safety. The Buckeyes went up 2–0 and rolled from there. OSU led 12–3 at the half, but Cooper took nothing for granted. His intensity was evident when he put his fist through the blackboard in the locker room.

"I've never seen him do anything like that," said QB Bobby Hoying after the game. "He's usually so businesslike at halftime."

"That got a real spark under us," said offensive tackle Korey Stringer (who died of heatstroke at the Vikings training camp in 2001). "Coach Cooper came in and he was excited as I've ever seen him. He put a good dent in the [blackboard], too."

The emotional speech worked, although it took a quarter to sink in. The Buckeyes let the Wolverines get back in the game in the third, and Michigan was attempting a field goal to cut the OSU lead to 3 points when Marion Kerner came from the corner and blocked the kick. Mike Vrabel recovered it, and 7 plays later, the Buckeyes scored a field goal to go up 15–6. On the next play from scrimmage, OSU nose guard Luke Fickell tipped a Collins pass in the air and then made a diving interception. The Buckeyes capitalized and scored another touchdown en route to a 22–6 victory.

After a seven-year hiatus, a post-game party was finally on in Columbus.

Cooper couldn't contain his excitement. "This one ranks right at the top," the happiest coach ever to be 9–3 said of the victory. "I don't look at it like I beat Michigan," he said.

"Our team beat Michigan today. This football program beat Michigan, and it was an outstanding Michigan team."

Cooper could breathe a sigh of relief; the monkey was finally off his back. "A lot of frustration is over," agreed OSU's great running back Eddie George, who scored the game's final TD. "Not beating Michigan has lingered in people's minds. The atmosphere is going to be more relaxed."

Relaxed? No, not when it comes to the Game.

A victory in '94 only placated frustrated fans for as long as it took their beer buzz to wear off and, in fact, the monkey would be back—only this time, the simian was madder than ever.

In 1995, things on paper looked lopsided again, and you know that's a bad sign. On OSU's side of the ball was George. The 6-foot-3-inch, 227-pound Philadelphia native worked his way from obscurity to the front of the Buckeyes' depth chart in his junior year and wound up rushing for 1,442 yards and 12 TDs. He was their man, but in 1995 he became *the* man. That year, Eddie George compiled a school-record 1,927 yards and 24 touchdowns. George and fellow senior quarterback Bobby Hoying were leading a Buckeye offense that averaged 39.8 yards per game. When it came time to play the Wolverines, the Buckeyes were 10–0 and ranked number 2 in the nation.

They were feeling confident, but they probably should have kept their mouths shut.

"They are nothing," wide receiver Terry Glenn said of the opponent before the game. "We expect to beat their butts like we've beaten everyone else this season."

The truth is, the Wolverines didn't have a whole lot to counter with. They had already lost three conference games and were ranked 18th in the country. Matching up against

George was a French-Canadian running back named Tshimanga Biakabutuka, or "Tim," as fans and teammates called him. He was having a solid season but not getting the kind of press George was—and not because his name required too much ink. Yet Biakabutuka took Glenn's words and the Buckeyes' confidence very personally. Michigan assistant coach Bobby Morrison even called him "Eddie" all week, in reference to OSU's back, to further needle Biakabutuka, and it worked.

"If you disrespect me and tell me I'm not something I believe I am," said Biakabutuka, "I'm going to prove you wrong."

Besides a running back with wounded pride, the Wolverines were also taking a rookie coach into the Game. Gary Moeller resigned before the season, following an altercation outside a restaurant in a Detroit suburb. He was arrested after being accused of causing a drunken disturbance and punching a police officer in the chest, although it is widely believed that two straight 8–4 seasons, not his supposed vulgar behavior, were his real undoing. After Moeller's resignation, UM named defensive coordinator Lloyd Carr head coach.

"Tim came into my office Sunday night," said the first-year field general, "and he said, 'Don't worry about it, coach. I'll be ready. I'm taking this game as a personal challenge.' I asked him why. He said, 'I want to prove I'm the best back in the Big Ten.'"

On that particular day, he was.

Eddie George rushed for 105 yards and won the Heisman Trophy, but Biakabutuka rushed for 313 yards—the most ever in the rivalry—and won the Game.

On the first two plays from scrimmage, Biakabutuka ran for 22 and 19 yards on his way to 109 in the first quarter alone. Nothing could stop him. Not cornerbacks Ty Howard and Shawn Springs. (Both of whom Biakabutuka carried on his back at one point for about 15 yards.) Not a strained calf muscle. Not a pulled groin muscle. Not a damn thing.

It was a throwback game, with Biakabutuka single-handedly reviving smashmouth football, and he carried his team to a 31–23 victory. And it was also the biggest upset for Michigan in the series since Woody shocked Bo in '69. The Wolverines—on their way to the not-so-sexy Alamo Bowl—celebrated as if they'd won a championship and carried Coach Carr off the field. UM's new coach said later, "I don't know how I could ever have a win bigger than this one."

And then came 1996. The game that Mike flew in from New Jersey to see. The "coronation," as he called it. Ohio State was ranked number 2. Michigan? A lowly 21. You really couldn't blame Mike for booking that ticket from the Garden State to the Buckeye State.

Once again OSU brought out the big guns. Fedora-wearing former coach Earle Bruce, now a fan favorite after being fired, made an impassioned speech in front of the team and thousands of fans Friday night at Senior Tackle.

Senior Tackle is a ritual that began in 1913 when some of the graduating football players asked coach Wilce for one last chance to hit the blocking sled. It had since grown—a lot. In 1996, Senior Tackle was an enormous Beat Michigan pep rally, and 20,000 people arrived at Ohio Stadium on a gray, cold Friday afternoon just to see some guys hitting a dummy. Not playing a football game, just hitting a sled! It was a huge event that resembled a religious revival meeting more than anything, and the pastor was named Earle. Screaming and red-faced, the former coach energized the throng of fans.

"Anybody who says this isn't *the Game* is nuts," he told the crowd. "It is the Game. One of your victories in a season has got to be against Michigan. You're 10–0. You've been great. But to be great at Ohio State, you've got to beat Michigan."

Nothing could be more accurate. But now that the truth was out there, the pressure grew enormously, and even the competition noticed. "It's really surprising how much emphasis they put on the Game here," said Wolverine center Rod Payne. "We got into Columbus on Friday afternoon and from the time we got here until we got up [Sunday] morning, it was nonstop press coverage: 'Let's check back with our roving reporter at the Horseshoe and see what's going on.' It was like a campaign or an election or something."

Payne and some of his teammates even saw Bruce's Senior Tackle speech on TV while resting in their hotel rooms and they claimed that it fired them up and put the real pressure squarely on the shoulders of the 17½ point–favored Buckeyes.

And those very same Buckeyes slipped. This time, literally.

Coming out of halftime, OSU was leading the game 9–0. On the second play of the second half, Michigan's backup quarterback Brian Griese (in for injured starter Scott Dreisbach) threw the football to receiver Tai Streets, who was being covered by OSU's Big Ten defensive player of the year, Shawn Springs.

Springs had almost wound up on the same side of the field as the Wolverines. In fact, when he was a kid, he loved UM, and that *really* irked his father. Ron Springs played at OSU for Woody Hayes, and, as he said, if his son went to Michigan, he "wouldn't have been able to drive through Ohio again."

At the last moment, Shawn committed to Ohio State. "I guess it was my Buckeye heart," he said.

That Buckeye heart was beating pretty fast when Springs boasted to the OSU coaches during halftime that he could cover Streets like a blanket. The only problem was, he couldn't do it from his back. When Streets made a move on a post pattern, Springs slipped, and the Michigan receiver took off. Streets caught the ball, and Springs finally caught up with him—in the end zone, after he completed the 68-yard play.

"The lesson I learned was that you have to wait to talk trash until after the game," Springs said later.

The momentum quickly shifted.

Michigan added two field goals, and the Ohio State offense shut down. Buckeye Nation was thinking, "Same shit, different year." This time, however, OSU had already clinched the Big Ten championship and would go to the Rose Bowl anyway, but to many fans, it didn't even matter. "If we lose to Michigan, a lot of fans don't even watch the bowl game," said a Bucks fan, who admitted to tuning it out. Once again, the Buckeyes didn't do what every OSU team is invariably measured by: they didn't beat Michigan.

But why? Was it a curse? Lack of concentration? Pressure? Overhype? "It's a big game," said senior OSU linebacker Greg Bellisari after the '96 debacle. "It's a one-game season. All that stuff is true. Both teams play differently than they play all year. Michigan obviously played one of the better games they've played all year."

Fans like Toledo native Bryan Hamilton who were in the 'Shoe remember their whole world crashing down around them when Springs hit the turf. "It went from the biggest party ever, to everyone just wanting to go home."

It really was like a bad B-movie where the monster kept coming back, each time stronger and angrier. The Rivalry didn't disappear; it got nastier, more heated, and definitely more bitter, as OSU fans displayed more anger and UM fans displayed more of a superiority complex.

The following year, the script was rewritten slightly, but the outcome for OSU was painfully similar. This time, it was Ohio State that had a shot at playing spoiler. Michigan entered the Game undefeated, dreaming of the school's first national championship since 1948. Ohio State was also ranked in the Top 10 and eager to avenge 1996's loss.

Amid all the hype, and apparently oblivious to the Game's recent history, up stepped OSU receiver David Boston. Even after what happened to Springs, Boston somehow felt that it would benefit him and his teammates if he were to call out Michigan's All-American cornerback Charles Woodson.

"I've played better corners than him," Boston said, after Ohio State beat Illinois 41–6 one week before the Game. "I think [OSU's] Antoine Winfield is as good as him. He's certainly faster than him. And he's no Shawn Springs."

Woodson, another Ohioan playing for the maize and blue, was in the midst of an all-world year, in which he could do no wrong on the football field while playing both defense and offense. He finished 1997 with 42 tackles, 7 interceptions, and 11 receptions for 231 yards and 3 touchdowns, along with his 36 punt returns for 301 yards.

Maybe not the right guy to call out. Woodson dominated the Game. He set up the Wolverines' only offensive score of the day with a 37-yard reception in the second quarter and then scored Michigan's second TD with a 78-yard punt return 3 minutes later. As a capper, the soon-to-be-Heisman-winner prevented an Ohio State touchdown with an interception of a Stanley Jackson pass in the Wolverine end zone.

After the game, Woodson held a bright red rose beneath his nose and took a deep breath. "Can y'all smell that?" he asked the gathering reporters and TV cameramen. "I know you can. Smells good, doesn't it?" Woodson and his teammates were off to their first Rose Bowl since 1993 as the Big Ten champions, and they eventually won the national championships.

Cooper and the Buckeyes went back to Columbus 1–8–1 against Michigan over the last decade. The questions were not going to go away. For all of his success, Cooper's career at OSU was clearly tainted.

"People come up to me all the time and say, 'So, Coach, are we going to beat Michigan this year?'" said Cooper. "Now what kind of a stupid question is that? No one wants to beat Michigan more than I do. But if you're going to coach football at Ohio State, it's something you have to accept. Michigan means everything to people in Columbus. That's the way it's always been."

A combined record of 111–43–4 was not nearly enough. The only record that mattered was, by the 2001 season, a painful 2–10–1. John Cooper beat Michigan only twice in 13 tries. Maybe he sounded too southern, he wasn't an Ohio boy, and his graduation rates were too low—all of which were criticisms lobbed his way—but if that record against Michigan were reversed, Cooper would undoubtedly still be pacing the sidelines for the Buckeyes.

OSU officials had seen enough. Fans like Mike had certainly seen enough. "You gotta win *that* game," he said, just before he ordered yet another beer at the Buckeye Hall of Fame.

■   ■   ■

One thing nobody could fault was John Cooper's ability to recruit Ohio's best talent. During the Tennessean's tenure, OSU became a veritable NFL factory—smoking and coughing out some of the most highly touted footballers in the professional game. In the 1990s, while Cooper suffered from the I-can't-beat-Michigan blues, Ohio State University was the nation's number 1 producer of NFL-bound talent. During Cooper's watch, 15 OSU players were taken in the first round of the NFL's annual draft.

Part of this was due to the superior talent he lured to the program, but part of it was also Cooper's openness to NFL scouts. (Which no doubt helped to land the talent in a chicken and egg–like paradigm.) In 1997 alone, 7 Ohio State players were taken in the draft (including the first pick overall, Orlando Pace), and 8 more were signed as free agents. That same year, 36 OSU players were on NFL active rosters.

"We recruit good players," said Cooper, to explain his success, but the truth is, the coach welcomed NFL personnel to campus and reportedly posted scouts' business cards in the lobby of the Hayes Center. They even set up a comfy room where scouts could watch videos of Buckeye players.

It was not that unusual. Not in the modern college game and certainly not in the halls of Top 20 football programs. Michigan was no different. The rival school came pretty darn close to equaling OSU's success of placing players in the NFL during the same period. And there was no doubt when it came to a final showcase for players who were looking for signing bonuses and multiyear contracts, The Game could be the perfect venue to convince a scout that a player on the bubble was NFL-worthy talent.

On the surface, what Charles Woodson did on November 22, 1997, was propel the Wolverines to a big win over the

Buckeyes, but, ultimately, it was an even bigger win for Woodson and his wallet. The brash superstar had already been talking himself up for a year, and the media were taking the bait. Articles were written about how he'd be competing for the Heisman Trophy, how he'd dominate the Big Ten, and how he'd probably leave school early for the NFL. The pundits even speculated early in the season what round this defensive star would go in the 1998 NFL Draft.

And round matters. There is a lot of pride in young superstar players, and there are also houses and cars that they've dreamed about since the day they strapped on helmets. Woodson had already been on *SportsCenter*, had already been seen chumming with Puff Daddy, but the place he most wanted to be seen was sitting in a suit and a tie at the Theater at Madison Square Garden on April 18, 1998, waiting for his name to be called—early.

In an event that is like the strange lovechild of the Grammys and a Bingo game, the NFL Draft has become yet another media spectacle, fueled by sports fans who are hungry for analysis and speculation about their favorite game during the dark days of the off-season.

In 1980, ESPN had to beg the NFL to air an event that normally took place behind closed doors, where men in ill-fitting suits decided the fate of young wannabe superstars. As soon as it took to the airwaves, the NFL Draft was an immediate hit, and it has since been expanded. ESPN2 now picks up the proceedings after the big names have already been called, and a fan can watch the entire process, which, to the uninitiated, makes paint drying look like a fireworks display.

The draft, remarkably, is one of the network's highest-rated shows. The first few hours (when the big names are chosen) have drawn nearly 3 million viewers. In 2002, the entire coverage drew 25.4 million people, who tuned in for an average of 74 minutes. And that doesn't include the number of people who monitored the proceedings on the Internet. Today, terms like "Pick Clock," the "DraftTracker," and a "Draft-Room-Cam" are just more sports lingo.

The average signing bonus for a first-round pick in 2001 was $3.8 million and "only" $1.3 million for second-rounders. And as the hype builds, up can go the stock of a player like Woodson. For the fleet-footed cornerback, the momentum toward a payday began with the Game and a surprise Heisman victory.

"Exposure is everything in the Heisman," Woodson said. "If you are not on TV, then you disappear." Nearly 10 million TV viewers saw Woodson's 78-yard punt return against the Buckeyes, while not nearly as many watched Heisman-front-runner Tennessee QB Payton Manning barely beat Vanderbilt on regional TV. A few weeks later, Woodson became the first defensive player to ever win the coveted award.

After the Heisman ceremony, Woodson's stock kept rising, and the hype machine kept cranking. In no time, the Wolverine announced his intention to leave school early, and he found himself in every predraft Top 10 ranking. When the fateful day finally arrived, the Oakland Raiders selected Woodson with their fourth overall pick. A few months later, he signed a contract with the Raiders: six years, $14.5 million, with an $8 million signing bonus.

Ann Arbor suddenly seemed very far away.

Of course, Woodson is far from atypical. Graduates of the Game have been making their mark in the NFL since the league began. The 2004 Super Bowl was an exciting affair, thanks to Janet Jackson and a last-second New England Patriot victory—and the game's MVP just so happened to be a University of Michigan grad, Tom Brady. Game grads also on that championship team included Pro Bowl cornerback Ty Law (Michigan) and outside linebacker Mike Vrabel (Ohio State).

After guys leave the college game, they never forget the Game—even when postcollege life includes the even brighter lights of the NFL. OSU great Archie Griffin played seven years for the Cincinnati Bengals, but he always considered himself a Buckeye first. And everyone in the league knew he was a Buckeye—especially the Michigan guys.

"One of my favorite guys that I played with in the pros from Michigan was Ronnie Simpkins," said Griffin. "He'd let me know if Michigan won the Game, and [OSU's] Pete Johnson and I, we'd let him know if we won. Plus, other guys from other teams would let you know if you got beat by your rival. Coaches would even say something about it. There were some side things that go on and when you get in the locker room on that level. You really want to be able to walk into the hotel on Saturday and say, 'Hey, we got you!'"

Once those fires are ignited, they never go out.

"You have to support your team," said former Wolverine defensive end Glen Steele, who moved on to the Cincinnati Bengals after graduation. "If you've got a big rivalry with two guys on the same team, forget it. All you have to say is your team is going to win, and it's on."

"It's still a rivalry," said Brady, soon after he won his second Super Bowl MVP. "[Vrabel and I] always talk trash. OSU guys hate Michigan guys, you know. On Game day, if we're on the road, I'll wear my letterman jacket."

Even guys who've left football altogether always come back to the Game. "This rivalry is like none other," said former Cooper-era OSU punter Scott Terna. "When you go back to Ohio State, and you talk to all the other players from other years, it's always, 'How many times did you beat Michigan? How many pairs of gold pants do you have?' I'm lucky enough to have one. That's what we're judged on."

The punter remembers beating Michigan in 1994 as if it happened yesterday. "Tito Paul, my gunner, downed it on the one," he recounted. "We wound up getting a safety on Collins. Then they punted to us, and a couple of plays later Bobby Hoying ran around the corner and scored a touchdown and it was 9–0. We wound up winning 22–6—they didn't score a single touchdown on our defense."

Terna had a huge smile on his face as he thought back to that day nine years ago. It was the week of the 100th game, and Terna was in Ann Arbor doing some work for ESPN, but he was also taking the time to enjoy himself at a Michigan bar. "To have participated in that rivalry, it's very special and I'll take that to the grave with me," he said, with a look of unsurpassed pride.

A Michigan fan who overheard was not impressed. "Ohio State sucks!" he yelled at Terna and some Buckeye fans nearby. The former punter shook his head—but he was still smiling.

7

GO BUCKS! GO BLUE!

It was difficult to breathe.

The shocking change in temperature caused the young man's diaphragm to contract, and the result was a sudden shortness of breath. On top of that, the water was so cold, it felt as if hundreds of tiny needles were jabbing all over his exposed skin.

But that didn't stop him. In fact, that didn't stop any of them.

Some fans were fueled by alcoholic courage, but for most of them, it was unconditional devotion to the Buckeyes that dulled the pain. Thousands of Ohio State students were partaking in Michigan Week's biggest (yet officially unsanctioned) ritual: jumping into Mirror Lake.

The "lake" is a small but bucolic body of water on the Ohio State campus. A long time ago it was spring fed and a water source for the college, but now Mirror Lake has a concrete bottom and is actually more pond than lake. It's a fixture on the OSU campus, nonetheless—as in, "Meet me at Mirror Lake, and bring those Comp Lit notes!" And for one night a year, its waters are believed to possess the mysterious powers of good fortune. At least, that's the hope of a bunch of OSU students looking for the Buckeyes to kick some Michigan ass.

The Thursday before the 100th Game against the Wolverines, thousands of students were drawn to the edge of the lake. Around 10 P.M. they began to arrive in earnest. Groups of friends from the dorms and different apartments walked across campus toward Mirror Lake, and once they showed up, the songs and cheers began.

"O-H," one loud-mouthed student yelled. "I-O" came the refrain, in unison. And then, "We don't give a damn for the whole state of Michigan, the whole state of Michigan, the whole state of Michigan!" That particular singalong didn't need much encouragement. It took off with ease until throngs of students standing near the freezing-cold lake were singing the anti-Michigan song. There were also intermittent cries of "Fuck Michigan!" "Beat Michigan!" "Go Bucks!" and, yes, the occasional "Show us your tits!" College students will be college students. . . .

As soon as the clock turned midnight, the first group let out a collective howl, shed various amounts of clothing, and jumped in. The watching crowd cheered, and then more people followed suit. Soon the waters of the pond looked like a deleted scene from *Titanic*, littered with chattering, pale, partially dressed bodies. It went on for hours—until well past two o'clock in the morning. As more arrived, more took the plunge.

No one is sure exactly how and when the ritual started. Most likely, some kid in the '70s, who was having a little too much fun during Michigan Week, responded to a dare from his buddies. Today it's as integral a part of the fabric of a Buckeye football season as the team's mascot, Brutus Buckeye.

"It's really become a thing, especially for freshmen," said OSU sophomore Pat Saad. "I jumped in my first year down here. It hurt so bad! We had flurries that day. It couldn't have been more than 20 degrees, but it was such a high."

"It was incredible," reported junior Jeff Gardiner, after his 2003 plunge. "You froze your balls off in the water, but the rush you get from it is phenomenal."

Jumping into Mirror Lake is a perfect pregame ritual: something so ridiculous, so crazy, and so painful that it makes logical sense to obsessed football fans. After all, it takes place just a couple of days before the Game, during a week when basically all anyone on campus can think about is the big game against Michigan, anyway.

"Absolutely no work gets done that week," said one student, to many professors' chagrin. With the Game approaching, the Mirror Lake plunge is a chance to let off some steam, celebrate communal spirit, and do a little partying on a Thursday night.

The Rivalry brings out students' school spirit like no other game on the schedule, and it's the same for college football fans across the region. The Game is like no other event on the yearly calendar—holidays included. "There is only one week of the year that I look forward to," said thirtysomething Bucknut Dave Ruupel, who is neither an OSU grad nor a Columbus resident, "and everyone from Ohio feels the same way."

The ongoing question of which of the two schools has more spirit is as big a part of the Rivalry as the question of which school has a better quarterback. In Columbus, Buck-eye fan and OSU student Rachel Gibson claimed, "Our school has more spirit," as she handed a souvenir seller 10 bucks for a "Fuck Michigan" T-shirt before a late-season home game. Another Buckeye supporter disagreed. "The people up [in Ann Arbor] are really cool—they have the same spirit."

The point is moot. When it comes to lengths that the wearers of the maize and blue or the scarlet and gray would go for their teams, Mirror Lake is really just the tip of the iceberg.

In the beginning, the Michigan contingent was small but spirited. Irving Pond, the man who scored the first touchdown in the history of the University of Michigan, recalled not only that first UM team but its first fans. "A large number of spectators came out to see the boys practice," he said. And on the trip to Chicago, he noted, "A few of the students, among them our managing editor, accompanied them as spectators."

And although it got a slightly later start, football in Columbus characteristically began with a boisterous crowd. At that very first OSU football game, 700 showed up, even though it was played 30 miles outside of town—a trek in 1890. In no time, when game day rolled around, Columbus found itself literally painted scarlet and gray, and the Buckeye fanatics began marching and singing like their counterparts up north.

It's more than 100 years later, and through the years, that indefatigable spirit has had time to fester and grow. Nowhere does Buckeye spirit soar higher than in the practice facility of the Ohio State University Marching Band.

If you walk into the $1.5 million annex inside Ohio Stadium, you have to be careful—the exuberance might hit you in the face. No, really. OSU Marching Band members are running up the stairs, carrying big, heavy pieces of musical equipment.

Why the rush? Most of them just want to get there . . . early.

It was only a regularly scheduled evening practice, like the ones that occur every weekday from 4 to 6 P.M. during the football season, but these pimply-faced band kids were still ecstatic to be there. Fifth-year senior Michelle Morman, a trumpet player from Lima, Ohio, declared, "I've always been a Buckeye fan since I was a little kid. I love the Buckeyes. And I love the band."

They pretty much go hand in hand. The OSU Marching Band has arguably as strong a following as the football team. The 225-piece all-brass-and-percussion outfit is confidently nicknamed "The Best Damn Band in the Land" (TBDBITL, for short) and is introduced everywhere it goes as "The Pride of the Buckeyes."

With pressed black uniforms and crisp military-style movements, the band cuts quite an imposing figure, and its traditions have become integral to Ohio State football, beginning with the school's many fight songs.

TBDBITL favorites include "Buckeye Battle Cry," "Across the Field," and "Carmen Ohio"—an alma mater that, remarkably, fans and players actually know the words to. They are all stirring fight songs, which are played at different times and for different reasons. "Across the Field"— which originally contained the lyric "So let's beat that Michigan now!"—is a staple during tough drives, but the "Buckeye Battle Cry" could be considered the primary fight song, played as the band enters the stadium and after every

OSU touchdown. The song was written in 1919 by a Buckeye fan named Frank Crumit in 1919, and the words are guaranteed to inspire the troops:

> In old Ohio there's a team
> That's known thru-out the land;
> Eleven warriors, brave and bold,
> Whose fame will ever stand.
> And when the ball goes over,
> Our cheers will reach the sky,
> Ohio Field will hear again
> The Buckeye Battle Cry!
> Drive! Drive on down the field,
> Men of the scarlet and gray;
> Don't let them thru that line,
> We have to win this game today,
> Come on, Ohio!
> Smash through to victory.
> We cheer you as you go:
> Our honor defend
> So we'll fight to the end for O-hi-o!

The OSU Marching Band also performs a pop-song-turned-fight-song, the bouncy and omnipresent "Hang on, Sloopy," written in 1965 by the Ohio rock band the McCoys. The song excites fans into such a rhythmic frenzy that at a 1988 game, the band was asked not to perform "Sloopy," after reports that the press box was shaking.

But the thing that the OSU Marching Band is probably best known for is not even a piece of music; it is what's referred to as "the incomparable Script Ohio." During their elaborate halftime and pregame shows, the entire band plays while marching onto the field, making labyrinthine twists and turns until the high-stepping musicians form the letters, in cursive, of their beloved state. The spelling out of "Ohio" is then followed by the pièce de résistance: the dotting of the "i." This is a privilege comparable to other esteemed honors, like, say, lighting the torch at the Olympic Games or being elected president of the United States.

"I decided in the third grade that was what I wanted to do and worked toward that goal from then on," said three-time dotter Anthony Core, demonstrating the typical intensity of a would-be dotter.

The senior sousaphone player who gets the call makes the spirited walk to take his or her place atop OSU's most famous vowel, then bends and salutes the crowd. What follows is a cheer more intense than the one that accompanies a game-winning touchdown. It is truly one of the great traditions in college sports.

But in the Rivalry, "Script Ohio" has even become a spoil of war. Michigan claims they performed the Script first in 1932, and although OSU band historians don't dispute the claim, they counter that TBDBITL adapted the formation and made it better. And the Script continues to be used as a weapon.

"When we do the double scripts up there [in Michigan], we march extra hard so you can see the Script Ohio on the field after we're off," said Morman, beaming with pride. "If you look on TV, you can even see it after a few quarters."

It's very possible that no one on the OSU campus or in Columbus hates Michigan more than the Ohio State University Marching Band does. While Woody Hayes's famous fuel fiasco near the border has become legend, the band still treats it like a mantra. "We never stay in Michigan [when we travel there for a game]," said Morman. "We always stay in a hotel near Toledo. We never spend any money in Michigan. We don't buy food in Michigan; we have a lunch that we bring so we don't spend a dime in Michigan."

Upon being accepted into the tight ranks of the marching band, these kids are indoctrinated immediately into the unofficial Michigan Hate Club. "I got in the band and all the older people in my row wouldn't even let you say the word 'Michigan,'" said tuba player Matt Benson, decked out in OSU Marching Band sweatpants and a T-shirt. "If you say Michigan, they'd get mad at you and yell, 'I hate Michigan!' You get here and the first thing they tell you is that 'Michigan is north until you smell it and west until you step in it.'"

The band's feelings can, to a degree, be justified. After all, these students are really on the front lines of the war. They step into enemy territory, wearing a uniform that might as well have a big scarlet-and-gray target on the back, when they visit Ann Arbor every other year. Especially for a band, entering the opposition's house can be intimidating and even dangerous.

"The first year [we went up to Ann Arbor], they stuck all the new people in the middle of the line and put the old people on the outside so no one could cut through the ranks," recalled Morman. "We put the big guys on the end who can handle the people. I remember getting pelted with marshmallows that had pennies in them. People try and get your hat or pull out your beret. The way you enter the field there is through a little tunnel and people can reach in and touch you. So you have to be careful."

"I can remember marching down the ramp and onto the field, and as we were marching, there were members of the Michigan football team, along with their coach, marching up the ramp and throwing some snide nasty remarks our way," said Wes Clark, another OSU band member. "It was 'We're gonna kill you!' stuff like that. I also remember hearing people say that their fans were gonna make ice balls with pennies in them and throw stuff at you. They did throw stuff, but, luckily, it was mostly popcorn and broken-up hot dogs."

"Still, it can be very traumatic," added Morman.

If these guys were to stop and think about it, they should be able to understand the kind of fan frenzy that leads to this behavior. After all, their spirited performances help ratchet up fan fervor better than anything. And for proof, you have to look no further than the macabre-named "Skull Session."

Two hours before every home Buckeye game, the Best Damn Band in the Land participates in a practice/pep rally in St. John Arena, the old basketball arena across from Ohio Stadium. The excitement of the band entering the small—always packed—arena and striking up one of the fight songs inside would bring goose bumps to the most jaded fan. The screaming Bucknuts, clothed head to toe in scarlet and gray, salute their band with cheers that would startle an airport runway worker. And after the band plays the requisite fight songs and gets the fans on their feet, everyone in St. John is treated to an appearance by the Buckeyes themselves. On their way to the locker room at Ohio Stadium and still wearing their dapper street clothes, the team saunters through the arena with their game faces already on. Their coach will step to the microphone, plead for the fans' support, and get a huge ovation from the St. John crowd. The scene is pretty damn exhilarating. A first-timer watching wondered out loud what kind of power a packed Skull Session and the reverent reception of the football team would have on a young recruit. The answer was obvious.

■   ■   ■

The last Skull Session of 2003 took place before the final home game against the Purdue University Boilermakers on Saturday, November 15, but many fans could rightfully be accused of looking ahead to that final game of the season. When a local radio disk jockey who was emceeing the event told the crowd, we are "looking forward to next week and making it three in a row against Michigan!" the fans packed into the quaint arena exploded in a roar.

After Skull Session, many marched straight to Ohio Stadium. It was still at least an hour before kickoff, but at Ohio State, fans were eager to see the band's entrance into the grand old stadium, and, because it was Senior Day, the ceremony planned before the game would salute Ohio State's graduating players.

Renovated in 2001, with the addition of more seats and luxury boxes that brought the official capacity to 101,568, Ohio Stadium, or the Horseshoe or just the 'Shoe, is a truly awesome football edifice. Its huge, domed, concrete front entranceway echoes Roman architecture, and it's definitely the kind of building you expect to enter and see wild animals ripping men apart—not unlike when the Buckeye defense is really on.

It was a gray and wet Saturday when Purdue arrived in Columbus, and the weather only added to the feeling of foreboding that Ohio Stadium induces on any given Saturday—a feeling that is accentuated by the sea of very loud scarlet-and-gray-clad fans.

The Buckeyes needed their unruly crowd on that day,

and, fortunately, their fans brought an added intensity, as they almost always did. With one loss to Wisconsin already, OSU was looking to remain in the championship hunt (they came into the game third in the BCS rankings, behind Oklahoma and USC), and, of course, one week before the showdown with Michigan, OSU remained in contention for the Big Ten championship.

You could just feel it in the air; this would be another cliffhanger.

The Buckeyes had won 16 straight in their own house, on the way to a national championship, and remarkably, even with a lack of sustained offense and all the off-the-field distractions, they were still in the hunt for a back-to-back championship. But then it all nearly slipped away.

The defense scored the Buckeyes' only touchdown of the day to put them ahead 13–6. After Will Allen stripped Purdue QB Kyle Orton of the ball, defensive end Mike Kudla scooped it up and put OSU in front, with 11:23 left to play in the fourth quarter. But Purdue came right back and tied the game on a 92-yard drive, ending in the always-picturesque Statue of Liberty play from Orton to Jerod Void that resulted in a TD.

The Buckeyes nearly avoided OT, but Purdue blocked Mike Nugent's field goal attempt from 41 yards. It was back to extra time for the Buckeyes, who, after winning the stunner in double OT against Miami to win the championship, had already beaten North Carolina State earlier in the season in a triple overtime.

In the OT, Nugent did his part by hitting a 36-yarder on OSU's first possession, which then set up a game-tying kick by Purdue's outstanding kicker Ben Jones from the same distance. Jones had already set the school record for the most field goals in Boilermaker history, but somehow, this ball sailed just wide left, and OSU won their third game of the season without scoring an offensive touchdown. The Buckeyes—or, as the media and Michigan fans were calling them, the Luckeyes—still had that old black magic.

The crowd of 105,286 was wild and gave the senior Bucks a moving sendoff. "I really did not want to leave," said tight end Ben Hartsock. "I just stood on the field and absorbed the atmosphere in the stadium. It was amazing how 105,000 people waited until the game was over and sang 'Carmen Ohio' with the team. I am proud to be a part of this university, this tradition, and this team."

But as fans exited the stadium, it wasn't "Carmen Ohio" that they were singing. *"We don't give a damn for the whole state of Michigan . . . "*

■   ■   ■

Michigan fans can sing, too. In fact, they have a little ditty that they are pretty proud of, and it's been around for almost exactly as long as the Rivalry itself. Back in 1898, Michigan adopted what, along with Notre Dame's "Notre Dame Victory March," is perhaps the most well-known fight song in all of college football. The Michigan fight song was written by a UM music student named Louis Elbel, who followed the Wolverines to Chicago and saw them pull off a monumental come-from-behind victory against the University of Chicago to clinch their first-ever championship. Trailing by 5 points late in the game, Wolverine Charlie Widman scored on a 65-yard touchdown run to deliver a 12–11 Wolverine victory.

"There was never a more enthusiastic Michigan student than I," said Elbel, "but that team and that Chicago game pushed me way up in the clouds, and all I had to do was fill in the notes, and there was 'The Victors.'" More than 100 years later, it is omnipresent at Michigan football games, and, with fists punching the air on each "Hail!" Michigan fans sing:

> Hail to the Victors valiant,
> Hail to the conquering heroes,
> Hail, hail to Michigan
> The leaders and best;
>
> Hail to the Victors valiant,
> Hail to the conquering heroes,
> Hail, hail to Michigan
> The Champions of the West.

The song—and those fists—can be intimidating to opposing teams and fans. To the independent observer, a packed Michigan Stadium, with more than 100,000 people raising their fists in unison, can look an awful lot like a fascist political rally. But it's hard to deny the addictiveness of "The Victors." Even while watching a Wolverine game on TV, you can fall under the power of the simple fight song. The master of march himself, John Philip Sousa, recognized the brilliance of Elbel's composition and labeled it college's best fight song.

But in a rivalry, there will always be a dissenting opinion. "Everybody says you gotta like their fight song?" said a Buckeye fan. "It drives you nuts! All they know is how to play one song. They play it over and over and over in that stadium. You walk into that stadium, and that's all you hear."

Actually, the Michigan Marching Band knows a few other songs besides "The Victors," including "M Fanfare" and "Let's Go Blue," and as an outfit, they are on par with the Best Damn Band in the Land. The 235-member Michigan Marching Band is also a high-stepping juggernaut that can fire up the Big House in a nanosecond.

The Michigan Marching Band doesn't do a script "Michigan," but it is known for a nifty formation they call simply "Block M" (it's a big capital "M") and other spirited halftime routines. Wearing bold maize-and-blue outfits with traditional plumed hats, the UM band warms up fans on game day in front of their practice facility with a "step show" performed by the drum corps. As game time approaches, the band marches en masse down Hoover Street toward Michigan Stadium, where they make a dramatic entrance through the tunnel and onto the field.

"When you're in the tunnel, you're just overwhelmed by tradition," said 2003's drum major Matt Cavanaugh. "You look down the tunnel, and it's sloped and you see this patch of grass and you get the word, it trickles back, it's time to go. And you hear the rap of the entry cadence and you're going. You see the sun when you go in the tunnel and you know the next time you see it, it's going to be in front of 111,000 people. The first time I experienced it, I looked around and I couldn't believe it. My mouth hung open and I think I forgot to play the first two notes of 'M Fanfare.'"

It's not surprising that the UM and OSU bands are locked in a rivalry of their own, but according to most members of both bands, they keep it respectful. "They're a great marching band," said one member of the Michigan band. "They are fun to watch, and they have a high standard for themselves—as do we," said Cavanaugh.

On the record they'll say nice things, but the truth is, the bands want nothing less than to outperform each other on game day. "When you see them on the sidelines, you know they are making fun of you. You want to strive to do your best," acknowledged Matt Benson, from the OSU band. "Their band wants to be at their best because they don't want to be embarrassed by the Ohio State band."

So, which is better? "We would never say anything to their face," said OSU's Morman, with a knowing smile.

Another thing the bands can't agree on is which school's fans are crazier. If you talk to the OSU band, going to Ann Arbor is like a trip to Hades; if you ask the UM band, they make Columbus sound like a state penitentiary. Before they made the trip to the Game in 2002, the Michigan band got a lecture about how to use their instruments to protect themselves, just in case they got attacked by a crazy fan, but for the most part, they laughed off the predictably rude behavior by OSU fans.

On the buses on the way down, members of the band performed a "finger count," remembered a UM band member. "We were counting how many times people were flicking us off. There were so many, it was ridiculous. We also counted how many times we saw mullets and how many times we saw shirts that said 'Fuck Michigan.' It was great."

— — —

The marching bands are part of the more traditional experiences to be found at a college football game, but on an individual level, you'll find no shortage of solitary acts of spirit dedicated to the Game—from different people from all different walks of life.

Take, for example, the "mysterious little gray-haired old lady" of 1935. During the melee on the field in Ann Arbor after OSU's 38–0 rout in the Game, an elderly woman wearing "a red-feathered Ohio State hat," according to a report in the *Detroit News*, swung a satchel at any Michigan supporter who tried to tear the hat from her head. Presumably, she was moved by both an innate sense of self-preservation and by her love for the Buckeyes.

Even more painful than a throng of fans trying to tear down a goal post and getting in granny's way is the story of a dedicated OSU fan named Harold Henry. A Buckeye supporter from Marion, Ohio, Henry owned a service station, and on the morning of the "Snow Bowl," he fell over a car jack in the shop and broke both of his arms. What's a Buckeye fan to do? Go to the doctor, right?

"He had tickets," said his son Dick, years later, "and no matter what, he was going [to the Game]." So, Harold chewed a few aspirins and went to the game, where he sat in a freezing-cold blizzard, with two broken arms, and watched the Buckeyes lose—all in all, a pretty bad day. He had casts put on his arms after the game, but, according to his son, the limbs never straightened.

Also under the category of Painful Expressions of Team Spirit is the journey made by UM undergraduate Hank Lerret and 14 of his friends in the '60s. The students—whom the hometown *Michigan Daily* even called "those idiots"—decided to run from Ann Arbor to Columbus before the Game. They took three cars to ferry the runners, who rested between 3-mile shifts, in order to cover the 200 miles. Why do it? "We hope to generate a lot of school spirit," they said.

Sometimes, spirited acts surrounding the Game are just for laughs. In 1978, an unknown cartographer with a sense of humor added two fictitious towns to a map of the region. The one north of the Michigan border was called Beat Bo and the one just south was Go Blue, Ohio.

With so many acquaintances on either side of the Rivalry, it is often a case of friends having a little fun with each other. Bob Schlegel has been going to Buckeye games for 67 years and has an old school chum named Bill Minick who happens to be a Michigan fan. The two have been needling each other over the years, but Bob pulled off a coup on one trip to Ann Arbor for the Game. Bill was on his home turf and, with some other friends, had planned a big banquet before the game to get everyone pumped up for a Wolverine victory. Unbeknownst to him, Bob and some OSU fans sneaked in and redecorated the place in scarlet and gray. "He was standing right next to me," said Bob, about his friend, "and when we got in the door, he looked around and—I'll never forget this—he said, 'What the shit did you do?'"

A few years later, Bill got his revenge when Bob went up to Marshall, Michigan, to visit his old friend. The Buckeye fan drove into town behind the wheel of his red van "all decorated with OSU stuff," and as soon as he got across the town line, no less than three cops pulled him over. "Of course, Bill had set the whole thing up," he said, still laughing about it years later.

For one fan, the joke became ways to sneak into the Game. The series' greatest gatecrasher is an Ohio pharmacist named Jerry Marlowe. Jerry was an OSU undergraduate in the '50s, when he began his tradition in flamboyant fashion. He wore a top hat and tails to the game and confidently approached the ticket taker, who was just trying to do his job.

"I pushed his hand aside with my cane," said Marlowe, "and I said, 'Tickets, rubbish. Who needs them?'"

The ironic thing is that Marlowe actually had a ticket that day, but beginning in 1968, he started pulling off his stunt sans ducat. That year, he dressed as a Boy Scout troop leader and claimed he was an usher to get a free pass. The next year he sneaked in with the marching band. What followed was a litany of theatrical disguises and ruses to get into the Game. Marlowe passed himself off as a referee, Superman (apparently, something to do with the halftime show), a hot dog vendor, a cheerleader, a cameraman, an OSU place kicker, a parachutist, and a nun. "I loved that one," Marlowe said. "It's the only time I went in drag."

With tickets to the Game at such a premium, people will go to great lengths to get them, spending a fortune or sometimes, as one UM alumni demonstrated, getting proactive and being lucky enough to find a sympathetic ear in the ticket office.

Russ Levine graduated from Michigan in '94 and has been a season ticket holder ever since. Unfortunately, he holds just a single ticket, and he wanted to offer a pair to his brother-in-law and niece. The brother-in-law was an OSU grad, and Russ wanted to introduce his 9-year-old niece Amanda to his side of the Rivalry. So he wrote a letter.

He enclosed a picture of Amanda and wrote on the back, "Don't doom this child to a future in Columbus." Four days later, he got a phone call at home from the UM ticket director, who said, "We take matters like this very seriously where Ohio State is involved. We hate to see kids go the other way." A few days later, Russ got a pair of tickets to the '97 UM–OSU game in the mail, and Amanda was in Michigan Stadium to see it.

For some fans, going to the Game year after year became a real point of pride. It's not uncommon to hear the old-timers make statements like, "I started going in '54 and I haven't missed a Michigan–Ohio State game since." That was the streak Buckeye Booster president Dick Smith bragged about in '03, but many streaks are even longer. In 1988, Wolverine fan Herb Wagner said that he'd missed just 6 home games since 1916. People hold their streaks sacred, and sometimes maintaining them requires drastic measures.

John Crawford hadn't missed an OSU home game in 48 seasons, when, in 1992, his nephew had the gall to schedule his wedding the same day as the Michigan game—in New Jersey! Crawford devised a plan to stash his car near the stadium in advance, drive straight to the airport, and hop a flight to Newark, in order to get to the ceremony 15 minutes before it was scheduled to begin. He did not figure any extra time into his plan in case the flight was delayed, and he certainly never considered skipping the Game.

You just don't miss the Game.

That fact became a metaphor for one close-knit group of Michigan fans. In 1979, John Cole was a freshman at the University of Michigan, living in Mary Markley Hall on the Hill, where he met a core group of friends who, like many Michigan students, went to every home game while they were at school. Then, right before graduation, Cole saw the movie *The Big Chill*, and it changed his football-watching life forever.

The Big Chill (written and directed by Michigan grad Lawrence Kasdan) is the story of a group of Michigan alumni in their 30s who reunite after the death of one of their friends and grapple with their loss of youth and idealism. For Cole, it really hit home. He watched the dramatization of the inevitable drifting apart that happens among college buddies—and he couldn't stomach it.

Shortly after graduation, Cole drafted a letter to his friends, the crux of which was: we shall never miss the Game. No matter what, home or away, he said that they should all reunite for that one weekend a year to see Michigan play Ohio State. Remarkably, his friends agreed, and in 1984, about 35 of them made the inaugural trip to Columbus. They stayed in the same cheap hotel, partied late into the night, and watched the Buckeyes beat their Wolverines 21–6.

But it didn't end there. For Cole and his friends, it turned out to be more than just a bunch of newly graduated young people looking to keep the party going. "The group took the vow," said Cole, "and it had staying power. All through our 20s we were insane, partied hard, sang the fight songs in groups, everything. But the Game was the core and the passion. We invest emotionally. If we win, we leverage it into celebratory partying; if we lose, we've always got each other."

Fans who can't be in Columbus or Ann Arbor for the can't-miss event will plan huge get-togethers to watch the game at home. It's a major family gathering in the Midwest, on par with how the Super Bowl is viewed nationwide. In 2002, the Game was watched in Columbus in nearly half the homes with TVs. OSU fan Paul Mains recalled one such gathering and how it made him love the Buckeyes. "I remember a huge party at my parents' house in 1979. We beat Michigan, and everyone just went crazy. I knew then that I needed to be a part of this."

Michigan fan Bob Reising was living in Orlando in '97 during the national championship season but got together with a "few" other fans to watch the Game on TV. "I think we had about 60 crammed into a room," Reising remembered. "When they won, it was just incredible—the rush that goes through you."

■   ■   ■

Maize and blue. Scarlet and gray.

What's in a color? When it comes to allegiance, the colors are everything. Spirit, honor, camaraderie, support—they are all reflected in the scarlet and the gray and in the maize and the blue.

Wearing the colors, especially on game day, is a point of pride for both schools. Clothing, body paint, tattoos, hair dye, makeup—if there is a way to mark the body with the most obvious signifier of the team, the colors, it's been done by these college football fans. (And it's not even limited to marking the body on the outside; there was a rumor in the '70s that a doctor put methylene blue dye in his patients' medicine so that they would "Go Blue.")

When it comes to the Ohio State University and the University of Michigan, you couldn't find two more distinct palettes. Put scarlet and gray next to maize and blue, and what you have is a good ol' fashioned color clash—just like what happens down on the field. Seeing maize, blue, gray, and scarlet together is more than a designer's nightmare; it's a sacrilege. And yet there is a place where you will routinely see these colors rubbing up against each other—and, occasionally, Michigan and Ohio State fans, too.

"Excuse me," one shopper said to another, as they passed through a narrow aisle in the divergently named Buckeye & Wolverine Shop in Sylvania, Ohio. There was a moment of tension, but they both went about their business, shopping on their respective sides of the store.

It's a remarkable place. You could draw a line directly down the center of this square store, located in a nondescript strip mall, next to a Subway sandwich shop. On one side, it exclusively sells Buckeye souvenirs, and it features Wolverine stuff on the other. Whichever side a fan opts for, there is a lot to choose from.

If you are looking for something to wear with your school insignia, there are garter belts, hair scrunchies, dog collars, Mardi Gras beads, earrings, socks, and ties, to name a few items. And if you are in the market for a household item, there is a wide selection of mugs, magnets, throw rugs, bobble-head dolls, stadium replicas, door mats, mousepads, leather office chairs, cookie jars, tricycles, door knockers, wrapping paper, paperweights, cutting boards, and car flags. Perhaps it's a Buckeye football snack helmet that floats your boat? You'd be in luck. They've got just about any Buckeye product you can dream of.

In case you are still wondering, a buckeye is a type of tree, and it has been used to describe people from Ohio for decades. It was adopted by the OSU sports teams sometime before the turn of the 20th century, although not officially adopted by the university's Athletic Council until 1950. It may not be a Tiger, a Bear, or a Seminole, or whatever else makes knees knock, but Ohioans are pretty darn proud of their tree. It's native to the state and produces a five-fingered leaf and a nut that is dark brown with a tan patch that resembles an eye. Attractive? Perhaps. Useful? Not at all. The buckeye nut is inedible and mildly toxic. But OSU fans carry the nuts for luck and even wear them around their necks. "What, those anal beads?" venomously inquired one Michigan fan, when he first saw them. Whatever you want to call them, the Buckeye & Wolverine shop sells those, too.

This improbable shopping experience exists on what could be considered ground zero of the war. Almost 170 years after the states of Michigan and Ohio nearly fought a real war over this present-day suburb, it remains disputed country in the ongoing battle between rival football programs. It's only 45 minutes from Michigan Stadium, so there are plenty of Wolverine fans, and because it's still in the state of Ohio proper—thanks to President Andrew Jackson—there are an almost equal number of OSU fans. It is what a woman who works at a nearby highway rest stop calls "schizoid country."

During the week before the Game, neighbors who normally chat about current events while taking out the trash or wave hello on the way to PTA meetings start to argue.

"I had to come back and tell her she had some trash hanging from her house," said Paul Patterson, as he pointed at his neighbor Sue Broz's Michigan flag the week before the Game in 2002. If you drive around Sylvania, you can see houses flying big red block O flags and others with big blue banners for the Wolverines.

Even in the elementary school, kids come to class during Game week decked out in the colors of their favorite teams. Nick Zachrich, an OSU sophomore from a nearby border town, remembers that week well. There was a lot of trash-talking and kids wearing either Michigan or Ohio State clothing. And even for kids this young, the outcome of the Game was everything. "Whoever won the game, their fans would get to go first in the lunch line the next week," Nick said. For a 12-year-old, that *is* pretty big.

Inside the Buckeye & Wolverine Shop, a boy even younger than Nick wandered away from his father's side. The father looked up, saw his son stray, and said, "Come back here, son . . . to the good side." He might have been joking, but he definitely wasn't smiling. The son dutifully returned to his father's side, and the man went back to looking at Wolverine pen sets.

Nearby, the impossible appeared to be a reality. A couple was standing arm-in-arm. But not just any couple. She was holding an OSU T-shirt, and he was looking at Michigan sweatshirts.

They were a living, breathing example of a commercial that ESPN had recently aired. The spot showed a man and a woman making out on a couch, before the camera pulls back to reveal that one of the lovebirds is wearing a blue Michigan shirt and the other has on a red Ohio State shirt. The punch line, written onscreen, reads: "Without sports, this wouldn't be disgusting."

The real couple laughed off their "difference." Dan was a Michigan fan and Amanda a Buckeye fan. He claimed to have supported the Wolverines "since he was a kid," and she had some distant family connection to Ohio State, revolving around a cousin's wife's brother or some such. But most important, they said that they never fought about their respective teams, and, of course, they would be watching the game on Saturday.

So, what was their prediction for the 100th Game?

"Oh, Michigan is a shoo-in," Dan said.

"No way. Michigan sucks!" Amanda said, shooting him a dirty look.

Hopefully they'd make it to kickoff.

8

COUNTDOWN

It was once an actual school bus. You know, the regular ol' yellow kind that picks up kids in front of their houses and drops them off at a red brick building, where they attempt to master their multiplication tables.

Now it's got a very different job.

It's the same bus, structurally speaking, but now its primary function is to take Terry Russell and his merry band of pranksters to and from Ohio State football games. And since it's been decommissioned from its original job, it's been lovingly retooled for its second life. Gone is that institutional can't-miss-it yellow color, and in its place is gray with a striking scarlet trim. Gone are the neat, black, stenciled-on letters that say Property of Some School System or Another, and in their place is the phrase "Whoop Ass Wagon!" Even the small sign that pops out on the driver's side and commands drivers to "Stop" when the bus empties its precious cargo has been altered. It now swings out and reveals a more pressing slogan: "Michigan sucks!" Terry will gladly demonstrate the still-working mechanism.

Inside, the walls of the bus—which in the past had been unadorned, except for occasional graffiti about some schoolyard crush or an improper reference to a teacher—now have an impressive collection of OSU-related memorabilia. There's the mouthpiece of an actual i-dotter, a "Buckeye Blvd." street sign, baseball hats, and photos—lots and lots of photos. There are snapshots of Terry with players, Terry with coaches, Terry with friends, and Terry with his pregame coterie. You acquire a lot of stuff when you tailgate at every home game (minus one) in 20 years.

The bus itself has been in Terry's service only for the last seven years. Terry plucked it out of a junkyard where school buses normally go to die and gave it a $5,000 face-lift and a second chance. He remembers exactly why he chose this particular bus. He knew that it was the vehicle for him because it had a great place for the stereo. The area that once housed a hydraulic wheelchair lift is now the home of a kick-ass sound system that announces Terry's arrival at each game and has helped his vehicle earn the unofficial nickname "the music bus."

The magic starts the night before the game. Terry picks up the bus from a friend's house, where it lives comfortably on five acres. ("It would look a little funny in our affluent neighborhood," he says.) Then he gives his baby a good scrubdown and begins to load the gear: chairs, tables, coolers, BBQs, and tents. Terry shamelessly admits that on occasion, a little partying also begins about this time.

The next morning, Terry is up about 3 A.M. and, together with his son and son-in-law, drives to Ohio Stadium and is outside the gate of the RV lot by 4:30 A.M. Forty-five minutes later, the guards open up, Terry pulls into his favorite spot in the lot, and the real party begins.

Of course, he's not alone. Literally hundreds of buses and RVs roll into Columbus on game day. The traffic has been known to back up miles from the city limits. Like the fans, most of the vehicles are gussied up in their Saturday Buckeye best, and many have clever names like Ol' Woody, the Woody Wagon, and the Best Damn Bus in the Land. These are not your average oversized vehicles, like the ones driven by weekend warriors and retirees looking for the world's largest ball of twine; they are redone and retrofitted to become parties-on-wheels.

OSU grad Greg Kirby and his friends invested $6,800 into transforming a delivery truck per their meticulous good-time specs. The resultant vehicle now has pretty much the same comforts of a well-stocked rec room, including a satellite dish, a TV, and a bathroom—with running water. When they roll out, they're sure to have plenty of food with them, and each week it's a different menu. When the Buckeyes faced Purdue, Kirby and Company deemed it appropriately a "big game" and decided that a fitting menu would be game meat. That spread included pheasant and "a wonderful dove breast wrapped in bacon."

For Peter Crusse and his cronies, the food was a more traditional bill of fare, including sausage and eggs before the game and chili, brats, and burgers afterward. "Our wives keep wondering how we can cook out here, but we can't cook at home," Crusse said, unfurling his custom-made 20- × 15-foot Ohio State flag.

Buckeye fans who don't have the wherewithal to plan and purchase their own traveling circus have plenty of other legitimate opportunities to tailgate around Ohio Stadium, where every available nook, cranny, alley, porch, garage, and parking lot is transformed into a de facto party.

On and around Lane Avenue, thousands of students, fans, and alumni gather around the cooler, the BBQ, or a vacant spot of grass—anywhere they can park themselves to drink, talk football, and drink some more. At the fraternities lining Fifteenth Avenue, the game-day ritual known as Kegs 'n' Eggs—self-explanatory, although sometimes the eggs are omitted—begins in earnest around 8 A.M.

"People here think the more they drink, the better the team will do," said a Varsity Club bartender. By 9 A.M., the inside of the famous Lane Avenue bar is packed, and shortly thereafter, the festivities spill out into a newly renovated area around back.

Just down the street is a more-than-20-year-old OSU game-day staple called Hineygate. It's so old that nobody can really remember where the name came from—something about a radio skit, is the best answer you can get. On any other day, the site is just another nondescript Holiday Inn parking lot, but on football Saturdays, it's transformed into a cross between Mardi Gras and a monster truck rally. Scarlet-and-gray-clad fans pack into the cordoned-off parking lot area, where beer vendors work nonstop to keep the masses sufficiently lubricated. The gathering is considered by some to be the biggest organized football party in the country, and the entertainment is provided by a local party band, the Danger Brothers, that's well-versed in the classic rock oeuvre, as well as by an 18-foot-wide television screen that alternates between game-day coverage and live shots of the Hineygate crowd. From time to time, the big screen will spot a young woman in attendance who is moved to fire up the Hineygate faithful by lifting up her shirt. It works every time.

It's hedonism, but with a purpose. The partying is equal to the intensity of the devotion to the cause—namely, the

Buckeyes. Although a large contingent chooses to stay outside and keep the revelry going, the focus is squarely on the game inside the Horseshoe and when it comes to that last game of the season, the focus narrows to laserlike intensity.

■ ■ ■

The scene outside Ohio Stadium on November 23, 2002, was no different. The Buckeyes were once again preparing to face Michigan, and they were attempting to preserve an unbeaten season and secure a spot in the BCS title game for a shot at a national championship.

The Buckeyes had been in this position before, recently and with painful results, no less. But the Cooper era was officially over, after Tressel gave his January 2001 promise to make Columbus proud 310 days later in Ann Arbor. He delivered.

The Buckeyes made the trip up north the previous year and did what they hadn't done in Ann Arbor since 1987; they won the Game. And better yet, they did it as underdogs, spoiling the Wolverines' chance at a Big Ten title. Perhaps the tide was turning at last? The 6–4 Buckeyes came out and blasted the Wolverines 23–0 in the first half and hung on for a 26–20 upset. A quarterback named Craig Krenzel got his very first start in that game, and it couldn't have been more fitting. He was a Michigan native who got to stick it to his home state.

If you ask him, he'll tell you it's not a big deal. Krenzel even claims he was a Notre Dame fan, despite growing up 56 miles from Michigan Stadium. "When I was in the third grade," he said, "I would run around the yard wearing Tim Brown and Tony Rice jerseys." But since he was a Michigan boy with skills, the big school still came knocking.

Michigan wanted Krenzel at first, and perhaps the Ford High School standout would have been on the other side of the field, but UM backed off their recruiting pressure after snagging another, bigger Michigan star named Drew Henson first—the same Drew Henson from Birmingham who was recruited by Michigan and drafted by the New York Yankees. Henson started exactly eight games for the Wolverines before leaving to collect $17 million to play baseball in the Yankees' minor league farm system. Michigan fans—the same ones who probably believe that a UFO carrying little green men crash-landed in Roswell, New Mexico—will note that Yankee owner George Steinbrenner is an Ohio native and rabid OSU supporter, who suspiciously plucked the clearly talented quarterback from the Wolverines after one victory in the Game and nearly no professional baseball experience.

Leery of backing up Henson for years, Krenzel committed to go to the rival across the border in his junior year, basically eliminating the intense recruiting process. "Good school, good medical school, good football program, and just the right distance from home, where Mom and Dad can make all the games but can't show up on my doorstep unannounced," Krenzel said, summing up his choice.

Krenzel is not your prototypical big school QB; he is, of all things, an egghead. While most players were struggling with communications degrees and the like, Krenzel was studying molecular biology, with an eye toward eventually applying to medical school. But while at OSU, he also began dissecting opponents' defenses on the football field, and it all started at the Game.

Tressel was forced to start Krenzel in 2001, after QB Steve Bellisari was suspended following an arrest for drunk driving, and the start yielded 118 yards passing and led the

Buckeyes to their first victory against Michigan in Ann Arbor (an hour's drive from where he grew up) in the last 14 years.

"They've been disrespecting us a lot, telling us this isn't a rivalry game anymore," said Buckeye running back Jonathan Wells, who ran for 129 yards and scored 3 touchdowns. "Well, it is now."

It was payback at last. And perhaps that win against the Wolverines was the initial spark that led to the victorious blaze that erupted in 2002. With Krenzel's sudden emergence as a dependable leader and the standout rookie season of running back Maurice Clarett, in the fall of '02, the Ohio State Buckeyes found themselves in the midst of, not a good season, but a storybook season, with a legitimate shot at their first national championship since Woody took them over the top in '68. Per usual, it was the Wolverines who were the final test. The Buckeyes had to face their rivals and prove that Tressel's and Krenzel's triumph the previous season was no fluke.

Terry knew as much, as he loaded up the Whoop Ass Wagon as usual the night of November 22, 2002, but with an extra sense of urgency and perhaps a little more anxiety than usual. Who could blame him? All those perfect seasons spoiled, and now they were right back in the same precarious position. But the Whoop Ass Wagon rolled into its usual spot like clockwork, and the stereo was cranked up. Then, an hour before kickoff, Terry and Company joined a record crowd of 105,539 in the 'Shoe.

They were all part of living history now. At least, that's how OSU's senior strong safety Mike Doss described the feeling going into the Rivalry's 99th edition. And as if the point wasn't made clear enough by the implications of the game and the mood in Ohio Stadium, the Buckeyes got the message when they glanced at the sign above the locker room door on their way to the field. It is inscribed with the words of OSU legend Chic Harley, the man who "built" Ohio Stadium: "We're heart and soul for this stadium, the fellows who know what it is to go in there and fight with all that's in us for Ohio State and her glory."

Heart and soul, that's all the Buckeyes needed. Well, that and some good defense. Oh, and their star running out on the field.

The latter was in question. Terry, for one, was concerned. Word went around the parking lot earlier in the day that Clarett was going to be unavailable against Michigan. The back had been sidelined for two of the three previous games with a shoulder injury, and he wouldn't reveal the status of his injury but implied to the press during the week that he'd be good to go. "This is Michigan Week," Clarett said. "That's all I've got to say." Still, when OSU's offensive unit took the field, number 13 wasn't out there.

From scrimmage, it was backup Maurice Hall who took the ball two plays in a row, with negligible results. OSU went three-and-out, and the wind was knocked out of a huge crowd, which was collectively flashing back to 1996. On its first possession, Michigan began moving the ball down the field, and Navarre hit receiver Braylon Edwards for a key first down on the way to a 39-yard field goal by Adam Finley. After having trouble all year with their kicking game, Michigan had to be pleased with the outcome of their first drive.

On the second play in the next series, the Horseshoe faithfuls got the jolt they were looking for. Clarett trotted into the backfield and, on cue, delivered the Buckeyes a first down. A few plays later, he found a hole and ran the ball to the Michigan 11—he also took a big pop on his sore shoulder. But Clarett stayed in the game and ran the ball into the end zone from 2 yards out, to give OSU a touchdown and a 7–3 lead.

In the second quarter, Finley hit another field goal for the Wolverines, and following the 35-yarder, they were within a point. With little pressure on their QB, Michigan continued to dominate the game, and Navarre completed passes to several different receivers. A TD grab by Edwards was called back, due to offensive pass interference, and after another long drive, Michigan was forced to settle for a 22-yarder from Finley, his third field goal. As the teams broke for the locker rooms, it was 9–7 and shaping up to be a cardiac special in Columbus.

In the third quarter, Michigan kept moving the ball, keeping the OSU defense on the field, but did not score, while OSU was still looking for the big play. The Buckeyes finally got it with 6:25 to play. OSU had a fourth-and-less-than-a-yard on the Michigan 36-yard line, as Krenzel himself carried the ball to give the Buckeyes a crucial first down. Then, once again, it was the freshman—beaten up, but still dominant—who made the big play, grabbing a 26-yard pass from Krenzel on a fade, and, suddenly, OSU had the ball on the Wolverine 6-yard line. Maurice Hall finished the job and ran the final 3 yards to give OSU a 14–9 lead.

But no team goes down without a fight in the Game, and Michigan marched back down the field and appeared to be flirting with handing the Buckeyes perhaps their worst upset yet. But all it takes is one huge play, by one key role player, and on that day, it was lineman Darrion Scott, who didn't even start the game, due to a pulled groin muscle.

On the Buckeye 30 with a first down, Navarre stepped up in the pocket, and it was Scott who worked his way toward the unsuspecting QB and was able to strip him of the ball. Will Smith was there to recover, and the anxious OSU fans began to breathe again.

But there was still time on the clock, and any time is too much time. On UM's very next possession, Navarre made a big play to set the Wolverines up for one last shot at the end zone to win the game and perhaps officially obliterate the hearts of Buckeye Nation.

Not this day. Navarre scrambled and fired the ball to his go-to guy, Edwards, who was running a slant pattern, but no fewer than three OSU deep safeties were in the vicinity. Edwards was at the goal line, but so was Will Allen, and the Buckeye snatched it.

Then the victory bell rang—the same bell in the southeast corner of Ohio Stadium that has rung after every OSU home victory since 1954. Down on the field, it was pandemonium.

The 2002 game against Ohio State was just another tough loss for Michigan's quarterback John Navarre, who was 23 for 46 and netted 247 yards, but that big play eluded him again at the end of the game. That Saturday, he walked off the field crestfallen, but Navarre knew he'd have one more shot. One more chance win the Game and one more chance at writing a legacy that wouldn't carry a footnote.

But getting there hadn't been easy, and 2003 didn't look much better than the year before, as the inconsistent Wolverines sputtered in that game against Oregon and then again two weeks later facing Iowa on October 4. Michigan built a big lead but then let the Hawkeyes claw back. Still, they were in the ball game, and Navarre took his team down field with 2 minutes to go before throwing three straight incompletions to settle a 30–27 defeat.

Any good football fan could see that the potential for a magical 100th edition of the Game, which existed at the beginning of the season, was looking dimmer and dimmer. The Wolverines were in danger of not even showing up at the party. "It was just classic Michigan," said the *Michigan Daily* sports editor. "All they needed down the stretch was a field goal. As a journalist you watch this team and all you can say is, 'Why do they keep doing this to themselves?' Perry broke off a 20-yard run, and it was brought back by holding. It was just pure frustration. What does this team have to do? What does John Navarre have to do? It was crushing."

The Wolverines, ranked 4th at the start of the season, plummeted to 20th and were staring a third loss squarely in the face only one week later.

The Wolverines were down 28–7 going into the fourth quarter against the University of Minnesota Golden Gophers on October 10, 2003. No Michigan team had ever come back from such a deficit. Not Fielding Yost's Wolverines or Bo Schembechler's. None. Ever.

It doesn't take a lot of imagination to picture a clandestine meeting of the football gods taking place sometime during the fourth quarter. Perhaps they sat around a conference table, eating chips and salsa, having a beer, and wondering aloud if after 99 years of epic football, they could really let the centennial game slide into mediocrity. You don't have to buy it, but *something* happened.

"We still don't know *what* happened," UM defensive end Larry Stevens admitted after the game. "How many points did we score in the fourth quarter? I don't even know."

The answer was 31.

None of them bigger than Navarre's 52-yard TD pass to Edwards to close the game to 35–28, with 10 minutes to play. Michigan then got the ball back, with 8 minutes to go, and Navarre completed an 18-yard pass to Chris Perry, who finished the game-tying drive with a 10-yard TD run, before almost blowing it.

Perry, who was still having a Heisman-caliber season, fumbled the ball on the Gophers' 14-yard line, but tight end Tim Massaquoi recovered to set up a game-winning kick by Garret Rivas, with 47 seconds left to play.

"It ranks high up there. It was an emotion win," Navarre said afterward. "At times in that game, you were thinking you're down and out, and this could go one of two ways: it could get real ugly or we could turn it around. The remarkable thing and the reason why it ranks up there as one of the best wins is the team stood by each other and had faith in the guy next to him that we'd be able to get it done. Now whenever any team from here on out is presented a situation like that, they can always look back and say, 'Hey, this is what can happen and what can be accomplished.' That's huge for the program and huge for this team, so we are going to take that momentum and carry on with it."

Momentum did carry the Wolverines for the next four games, which they won by an average of 20 points. Or maybe it was those old football gods—you can also call it fate, kismet, juju, whatever makes you more comfortable—because UM, improbably, after a rocky start, managed to preserve their season, just as the Buckeyes did with their own dramatic overtime win against Purdue.

The stage was now officially set. The hyperbole could begin in earnest. The 100th meeting between the Wolverines and the Buckeyes *would* be the game that every sports fan from Dayton to Dearborn prayed for three months ago. The Ohio State University and the University of Michigan would face off for the outright Big Ten championship. And, for good measure, OSU was clinging to hopes of going to the Sugar Bowl and defending their national championship after they rose to the number 2 slot in the BCS rankings, following the overtime win over Purdue. (USC dropped to third, even after they blew out Arizona, due to weaker strength-of-schedule numbers.)

It was time to set your phasers on hype because this was shaping up to be biggest tsunami to hit Ann Arbor in a long time. Forget '69. Forget '97. This was '03. It was the 100th anniversary of the Game, and the game was on.

▬   ▬   ▬

"Yeah, doll. Come down and pick up your tickets."

Jerry was talking on the phone. For a barber, he seemed to be working the phones an awful lot the week before the Game. But Jerry is not just any barber; he's the proprietor of the venerable Coach & Four in Ann Arbor. This State Street staple has been the place to get a trim and talk Michigan athletics for 31 years. The walls are plastered with yellowing posters of teams gone by and dotted with jerseys and gear of past stars, most of whom Jerry knows or whose hair Jerry has cut. Even Bo Schembechler himself still comes in for a cut, as he has since he arrived in Ann Arbor in 1969.

Besides doing 'dos, Jerry's got another vocation: he's the unofficial official ticket clearing house in town. And although selling tickets in the state of Michigan for more than face value is illegal, this grandfatherly looking barber has been grandfathered in by the cops. "My place is sacred ground, like an Indian burial ground," he said. "After 31 years, I've earned it."

This particular week he was also earning a pretty penny. Tickets were going for anywhere from $300 to $400, in what Jerry labeled the biggest markup ever. "They're coming in like crazy for these things," the barber said.

For this game, ticket demand definitely outweighed supply. And some entrepreneurs who didn't go through Jerry were trying to sell their extras through the online auction eBay. To circumvent the antiscalping laws, sellers were offering for sale items like a key chain, with bidding that started at $12,000; fortunately, four Ohio State–Michigan tickets were also thrown in for free.

"This thing is like the Super Bowl," remarked the man whose hair Jerry was trimming.

The barber agreed, and he would know. From his prime vantage point on State Street, Jerry had seen a lot of excitement outside the window, but so far, this week was overshadowing just about everything he'd seen in three decades.

The campus was buzzing. Everyone was talking about the Game . . . and about the parties. In a college football town that's best known for the pregame ritual of brunch at a restaurant named Angelo's, something was amiss. (For the record, the deep-fried french toast does live up to the hype.)

"Everyone has been talking about it since Saturday night," said one Michigan undergrad. "People have been planning all week what they're going to do Friday and Saturday."

"I usually get 4 or 5 party invites on e-mail each weekend, but this week it's already up to 8 or 9," said sophomore Michael Carroll, the Tuesday before the Game. He hadn't yet decided which one to attend.

A remarkable number of students were already sporting

the maize and blue. On the Diag, the nonprofit Habitat for Humanity was helping the cause—and their own—by selling maize-colored shirts that said "Beat Ohio State" in big blue letters. In front of the Michigan Union, a more traditional "Ohio State Sucks" T-shirt, featuring cartoon miscreants Beavis and Butt-head, was for sale, as well as a crass T-shirt that made a weak attempt at class with the not-so-thinly-veiled phrase "Buck the Fuckeyes" and another that read "100 Years of Busting Their Nuts."

Ryan Curtis, a sophomore from Trenton, Michigan, contemplated buying one. Although he'd already planned to wear a basic Michigan sweatshirt to the Game, he thought a "Buck the Fuckeyes" tee would make a good impression at his fraternity's preparty. "It should be crazy," he said about the upcoming fete. "I'll be up around 8 or 9, we'll have food and a keg out front."

Party plans were beginning to gel. Tickets were swapping hands. And Ann Arbor's streets had started to get crowded. By Friday afternoon, the Game was omnipresent. Even the guys behind the counter at the town's café culture hub, Espresso Royale, were talking about it, and they considered denying the first customers who were openly Buckeye fans access to their cappuccinos.

The Game was on everyone's lips, and the hype was further fueled by TV crews, the newspaper commemorative editions, and the wall-to-wall talk on sports radio. ESPN's *GameDay* crew setting up on the UM golf course was further proof that Ann Arbor was the center of the sports universe.

By late afternoon, the alumni began arriving from out of town—a couple of old-timers in maize-and-blue-checkered golf pants and berets looked particularly spiffy—and Moe Sport Shops on North University was packed with fans looking for a piece of last-minute gear.

Some brave Buckeye fans in their familiar colors were also skulking through the streets, looking like strangers in a strange town. A few Michigan fans took note of the rival fans and nodded in a friendly "May the best man win" kind of way, while a more hostile bunch in a black Range Rover saw the invaders and purposely turned up their car stereo to blast "The Victors."

And in the parking lot of Ann Arbor's Pioneer High School, which sits catty-corner to Michigan Stadium, the RVs were already parked like beached whales on the cold asphalt.

Tom Richards and his wife, Luette, were some of the first people in. Tom staked out his spot while waiting for school to let out. "We have to wait for the students to leave," said Tom, "but we park up on the hill and wait, and then 2:15 or 2:20 I'll come out here and stand in the spot and wait some more." Tom admitted that he was more worked up for this game than for almost any previous Michigan game—and he has two sons who are ex-Wolverines.

Near Tom and Luette, some fans from Ohio were already grilling sausages, but the real surprise was not their love of encased meats; it was the fact that not all of them were Buckeye fans. They were a mixed bag of high school buddies from one of those border towns that straddles allegiances.

They played a midwestern tailgating game called cornhole, in which beanbags are tossed at a wooden box with a target painted on it around a big hole. If you get the beanbag on the box, it's 1 point; in the hole, 3 points. It's more fun than it sounds, especially accompanied by beer. As they played, they began to talk trash in earnest.

There were jokes about those Buckeye "anal beads" and how OSU fans are so obsessed because "they have nothing else to live for," while the Michigan fans had to hear cracks about how one of their school colors is the same as a bodily function and how they're all just a bunch of snobs anyway. It was mostly good-natured ribbing, but then again, it was still early.

"It's not a real hate," said Pat Landolph. "It's friendly—unless you run into some brutal meathead fans. I've been up here and been treated like shit, and I've seen it down in Ohio State, people treated like shit."

For the most part, it can be classified as good clean fun by the participants on either side of the Rivalry. Bragging rights are on the line, and fans brag. But there is, and there always was, a seamy underbelly. Not every sports fan knows the definition of tact, and Michigan and Ohio State fans are no different. Sometimes the slurs get nasty, sometimes there's an abundance of profanity, and, most objectionably, sometimes there are even acts of aggression that mostly fall under the category of thrown objects and occasionally thrown fists.

"It's one thing to have beer poured on you," said one Michigan fan about the hostility he faced in Columbus, "but when we were up there, we had full cans of beer thrown at us." To be fair, the fan admitted to wearing Michigan gear and taunting the opposition with a few Heisman poses à la Desmond Howard. "Can you imagine a college student wasting a full beer can on an opposing fan?" said the Michiganite, only half-joking. The truth is, idiots will always be idiots, and rivalry and alcohol occasionally don't mix.

One old-timer was convinced that violent conflict between OSU and UM fans started in Columbus in '74. "OSU gave Michigan fans tickets," he said "and they were spread throughout the stadium, and there were fights and yelling contests. I think that's when the animosity started." That might have heated it up, but it also coincided with a period in time when sports fans in general began to show a dangerous pluck that was new to spectator sports—not to mention that 10-Year War between Woody and Bo.

As the sun set, it was surprisingly quiet in Ann Arbor on November 21, 2003. The streets were mostly empty, but that's because the bars were packed—including Scorekeepers on Maynard Street, home of Mr. Neck and Mr. Lips.

Even if they are well behaved, sports fans are never quiet. The night before the big game, the noise inside Ann Arbor bars was comparable to a jet engine's roar. Any lull was filled by alternating chants of "The Victors" and "O-HI-O." One thing was obvious, no matter what happened on the field the next day: Ohio State and Michigan fans proved that they can drink—and drink together. Sure, there were occasional insults hurled, but mostly, there were a lot of impatient, excited fans.

Guys like Ann Arbor resident Steven Sonntag. "I live and die for this game every year," he said, bellied up to a bar with a beer in his hand and the Rivalry on his mind. "One year, I was in Las Vegas," he remembered, "and I was standing next to this guy at the craps table. We started talking, and he said he was from Columbus, Ohio, and I said, 'Oh.' Then he asked where I was from, and I said, 'Ann Arbor, Michigan,' and this look of pain came across his face. I have to admit, I got a sick satisfaction out of that."

One of the loudest Ohio State fans in the joint was a student named John Stevens. Stevens went to OSU undergrad and was now in Ann Arbor for graduate school. Figuring that there was safety (and a better party) in numbers, he got a bunch of OSU fans to drive up, offering them a good time and housing. Well, if you could call it housing. There would be 11 guys in his apartment, split between 1 couch and 1 futon. It would be cozy, but John and his friends didn't care. "I'm losing my voice already," he said, "and it's not even Saturday."

Exchanging barbs with John was a Michigan student named Dave Jensen. "You gotta love it!" he screamed over the din. "It's all in good fun and everything, but we're gonna come and bring it," he said, referring to the Wolverines—and using the proverbial *we*. "We're gonna come and hit you hard. It doesn't matter how many Ohio State fans they have here. It just matters what the scoreboard says." And with that, he led the group at his table in a new chant: "Fuck! Ohio State!"

■   ■   ■

Six hours and four minutes later, the sun rose in Ann Arbor, as it has for eons. But this time, things looked a little different, almost clearer. The weather was beautiful. No, the weather was perfect. The chill and haze were both quickly burning off, and the sun shone even in the early morning.

By 8 A.M., there was already a lot of movement in town. Fans were beginning to stumble out of bed, a fraternity on State Street was moving the beer pong tables out onto the front lawn, and on Hill Street, some guys in a house were readying their "You Honk, We Drink" sign. Down at the Crisler Arena parking lot, next to Michigan Stadium, elaborate tailgates were being constructed, many with a decidedly different flavor than the ones in Columbus.

The basketball arena's parking lot contained some of the fanciest tailgates in college football—more wine and cheese than chips and beer. In a short while, the cool sounds of jazz, not AC/DC, would be wafting through the air, and Dave Schultz and his cohorts would be grilling 1,500 filets of fresh lake perch and laying them out on blue linen–covered tables—complete with maize skirts—then sitting back in wicker chairs with knit Wolverine seat cozies. An ice sculpture of Bo Schembechler would not be out of place.

By 9:17 A.M., four guys on Packard were tossing a football. Two women wearing bathrobes emerged onto a balcony overlooking the street and lit cigarettes. "Let's Go Blue!" they screamed with shrill voices that cut through the morning silence. It was the last time the morning would be quiet.

The fraternities on State Street turned their PA systems outward, facing the street, and soon the neighborhood was a battleground of a war to see who had the most powerful sound system. Fans of all ages and sizes were milling about. The traditional route to the Stadium at UM takes fans from the central campus area down State Street and right onto Hoover Street, where—closer to kickoff—the masses look a lot like people starting the New York City Marathon. The mass of humanity will then make its way up the hill toward the bowl. Tailgaters at the golf course and in the Pioneer High lot make their assault on Michigan Stadium from the other side.

By 10 A.M., every available porch and driveway is a familiar scene, set up with the requisite booze and snacks. One apartment building near Hoover featured a novel approach to pregame drinking, as a beer bong—a funnel with a long plastic tube dangling below it—extended to the ground from the third-floor balcony. Revelers up top heckled the fans below and dared them to put their mouths on the tube, as pitchers of beer were poured down the chute. Many fans took them up on their offer, including a group of

40-something soccer mom types who looked like they'd never had so much fun in their lives.

A couple of Buckeye fans in football jerseys got beer sprayed on them, but they just smiled and waved. Not satisfied with their reaction, an onlooker yelled, "Ohio State sucks!" It was a scene that was repeated throughout the morning, but fans on both sides expected it and, in a way, enjoyed it. You don't come all the way from Columbus looking like a starting linebacker for the Buckeyes without anticipating the abuse. "Oh, yeah," one such fan said, "bring it on!"

A pair of fans standing outside a frat party chose a less traditional getup. The taller of the two men was wearing only a red g-string. His entire body was painted red, and the ensemble was topped off with a clown wig. His buddy was shorter and thicker—but just as naked—only his color palette was blue. They were getting a lot of attention, and they loved it. "There really is a true hatred," said blue man. "But you don't hate the person, you hate the rivalry." Then he looked at red man and said, "Well, you can hate the person for a day."

Next door, some fans were taking their game-day frustrations out on the shell of an old Mercury sedan parked on the Beta fraternity's lawn. It was sloppily painted with the words "Fuck OSU," and $5 afforded fans a few swings at the car with a big sledgehammer. Proceeds went to charity; the venting of Rivalry-fueled rage was just a happy accident.

By 11 A.M., the party was in full swing. At the corner of Hoover and State, huge crowds of students had gathered in front of the porches of a few neighboring houses. It felt like the place was going to explode—and it nearly did.

A popular song of the moment, Outkast's bouncy single "Hey Ya!" suddenly came through the stereo, and a group of spirited students, some with roses in their mouths, began to jump up and down and scream. Soon they were joined by more dancing students until a mass of undergrads spilled into the street and began to bounce up and down in unison like giant human wave pool. Suddenly, somebody lit an Ohio State winter hat on fire, and the crowd roared its approval. At that moment, an SUV with a Buckeye flag approached the busy intersection, and a few eggs were hurled at the windshield, along with the flaming hat.

Then the car door opened.

As the music blasted, the fans screamed and circled, and the man stepped out to confront the mob. The delicate balance between pregame revelry and actual mass rioting seemed to hang in the balance. The somber driver looked around and assessed the situation, then his once-serious face broke into a grin from ear to ear. He quietly got back into his car and waited for the fans to disperse. The song ended, and the bouncing mob ebbed and headed back toward the curb.

Everyone was ready. It was time, once again, for football.

9

ONE HUNDRED

It takes only a fraction of a second for the available light to pass through the cornea, the pupil, and finally a small lens before striking the retina in the back of the eye and then be translated into electric impulses that are carried by the optic nerve to the brain, where the image is processed and a single, unambiguous thought is produced: that's a shitload of people.

As you walk up any of the ramps that are spaced around the enclosed oval and approach the daylight at the top of the walkway, the enormity of the bowl explodes in front of your face. It's like a gigantic basin that was dug into the ground, and when it's filled to capacity, it's a sea of humanity, circling an inordinately green gridiron.

And yet, surprisingly, the Big House doesn't look like much from the outside. The exterior of the blue steel structure resembles a giant tool shed. It looks as if you could dunk a basketball into it, if you got a good-enough running start. But that initial disillusionment about a building bold enough to be called the Big House—a nickname bestowed by ABC's venerable college football announcer Keith Jackson—only makes the act of actually walking into Michigan Stadium that much more intense.

Built in 1927 or, perhaps more accurately, dug out of the ground, Michigan Stadium has been expanded over the years and following the most recent renovation in 1997, it regained its title as the largest college-owned stadium in the country. The official capacity is 107,501, but it is routinely packed beyond capacity.

On November 22, 2003, it was literally bursting with people and enthusiasm. When the figures were finally tallied, the number of spectators in Michigan Stadium that Saturday was announced at 112,118, more than at the Notre Dame game earlier in the season, and, officially, the largest crowd ever to watch a college football game on a campus in the history of the known universe. For scale, that also happens to be about the same number of people who live in the entire city of Ann Arbor. In addition to all the football fans, there were an unprecedented 1,170 members of the media. Even New York Yankees shortstop—and Kalamazoo, Michigan, native—Derek Jeter was there.

The anticipation was palpable, and the energy bouncing around the stadium was intense to the point of restlessness. The mood didn't change when the "pride of the Buckeyes" was introduced, and the Best Damn Band in the Land took to the field. But when the Ohio State band began playing "The Victors," a traditional homage to their hosts, the enormous crowd finally got a chance to let off some steam, as fans pumped their fists in the air on cue with the fight song.

Even the most cynical Michigan diehards had to be impressed by the infamous "Script Ohio," and the TBDBITL exuded an all-business veneer and performed a dual script that day, with two i-dotters.

The band looked great, despite the fact that they'd really had a tough morning. While being bused from across the border, they got stuck in the massive amount of traffic trying to get to Ann Arbor all morning and had worried that they wouldn't make the kickoff. Although they arrived at the stadium in the nick of time, their lunch (purchased outside the state, of course) was somewhere else altogether, also caught in traffic. None of it mattered at this point; after they completed their legendary formation, you could still faintly see the impression of the two "Ohios" on the turf. Even the opposing band brought their A-game.

When the stadium announcer called on the "235-member Michigan Marching Band," the crowd was already mostly standing, but the appearance of drum major Matt Cavanaugh and his brass-and-reed posse brought the remainder of the fans to their feet. Matt personally energized the Big House with his traditional back bend. The drum major stood on his feet and slowly leaned back until his head made solid contact with the turf—he even removed his hat with the big maize plume so as not to cheat in his feat. In 2002, when Matt and the UM band performed at Ohio Stadium, they got booed so loudly that it drowned out his name being announced on the public address system. In the last home game of his senior year, Matt got a lifetime's worth of appreciation from the crowd.

Only one thing could complete a pregame ceremony for such a big game: the appearance by a former president, of course. The crowd had to settle for a videotaped message from one-time UM center Gerald Ford, as it was replayed on the large screens on either side of Michigan Stadium. "This is one of the greatest games in college football," the aging ex-leader told the fans—who for the most part were already pretty aware of that fact—before giving his best "Go Blue!" at the end of the short address, to the delight of the throng.

In a break from the usual pregame activities, a few hundred people strolled onto the turf, looking like the lost contingent from an insurance convention. It was actually five decades of former Wolverine football players, but the burly men in street clothes were largely ignored, as almost all eyes in the Big House were trained on the unmistakable maize-and-blue winged helmets that were poking out of the tunnel leading into the stadium.

Inside one of those helmets was the big head of senior defensive tackle Grant Bowman. Although he had stood in that very spot at least a dozen times before, it was never with the added emotion of his last home game at Michigan Stadium, not to mention the pomp and circumstance of the 100th meeting between Michigan and Ohio State—with a championship hanging in the balance. Earlier in the week, Bowman and some of his teammates had begun thinking about this very moment, and he planned to cherish it.

"It's unique," he said. "It's a long walk down there. You step out of the tunnel, and you start to walk down there. It's almost like you're looking through a peephole, and you can see a couple of the fans. As soon as the fans start to see the helmets, it starts to get louder and louder."

He was dead on. It didn't seem possible, but as the Wolverines, clad in their unmistakable home uniforms (bright yellow pants and blue jerseys with yellow numbers) bounded out of the tunnel and ran through the center of the throng of Michigan football alumni, sitting in the Big House felt more akin to being at the Indianapolis 500. "That was as loud as the stadium has been this year," said

Brian Schick, a Michigan student sitting with his classmates in the particularly noisy student section.

As they reached the center of the gridiron, the Wolverines jumped into the air and touched a big blue banner at midfield with the words "Go Blue" written on it—a tradition they repeat before every home game—and the team then gathered near the sidelines, jumping on each other's backs and pounding helmets like giddy Pop Warner kids.

The senior Wolverines and their parents were introduced, and then the predictable jeers began as the Ohio State Buckeyes in their road uniforms (gray pants, white jerseys with red lettering) calmly sauntered out of the tunnel behind their coach (dressed in his own usual road wear, a scarlet Ohio State sweater vest) and into enemy territory. Their eyes certainly looked past the hostile crowd and sought the significant scarlet-and-gray contingent in the north end zone. They had to be glad to see a large group of fans, including many members of Block O who had made the trip from Columbus.

"Well, it's an exciting atmosphere," Tressel said about Michigan Stadium during the week. "A lot of our guys have been there; a lot of them haven't. I think a lot of them don't even know how difficult the task is, but that's part of growing up. You go find out just how difficult things are. They have a great crowd, like we do. They're into it. They love their team. They love their school. They want to win very, very badly, and they're going to be noisy when we don't need them noisy."

Too bad for the Buckeyes, but Tressel was right. After all the criticism that the sportswriters and the diehards had directed at the crowds earlier in the year, fans were really up for it on this Saturday. How could they not be? And the players were feeling it, too.

"It feels like something takes over your body," linebacker Carl Diggs said before the Game, when trying to explain the emotion. "Especially after the Northwestern game. Running off the field, my face just lit up with a big smile because I knew the time had finally come. Throughout the season, you always have that Michigan and Ohio State game in the back of your head. It's something you think about every week and it's a good feeling that it's here."

"This is what you come to Michigan for," said Michigan tackle Tony Pape, "a chance to play Ohio State for the Big Ten championship in the last game of the season. You couldn't ask for anything else. You couldn't write a book better than this; it is just very exciting to be a part of."

Pape's counterpart across the field, OSU center Alex Stepanovich, agreed with the statement in principle, but from his own perspective: "This is why you come to Ohio State, to play against Michigan with everything on the line. It's going to be a war."

As if to underscore the point, four F-16 fighter jets—flown by UM alumni—suddenly roared overhead. The aural exclamation point was not necessary. At this point, all anybody in the building really wanted was for that 15-ounce pebble-grained leather oval to be kicked in the air. Michigan won the coin toss and elected to play defense first and receive the ball in the second half.

As the two schools' special team units came out on the field and faced each other—for the 100th time—everyone in the Big House was on his or her feet. Michigan place kicker Troy Nienberg trotted toward the tee, and the crowd uttered an expectant "ahhhhh" that hit a crescendo as he kicked the ball and it was lofted high in the crisp November air before coming down near the 1-yard line, just in front of the Michigan end zone and into the waiting arms of Ohio State running back Maurice Hall.

Hall started running up field, saw Michigan's oncoming defense, and cut left to the outside before being tackled by Prescott Burgess and Jerome Jackson near the sideline. There was a bit of shoving as the players got up off the turf. All the hype had melted away, as football players smashed into each other on the gridiron. "I expect this to be a phys- ical game," OSU fullback Brandon Joe had said before the game. Some of his teammates were finding out just how right he was.

Craig Krenzel quickly trotted onto the field with the rest of the Buckeye offense. The Michigan-born QB, who had already beaten the Wolverines twice and was a national championship game MVP just one year ago, was confident. "We never feel like we can lose," Krenzel said about his team, which was still technically the reigning national champion. Of course, how they fared in this, the biggest game since the Fiesta Bowl, rested to a large degree on the shoulders of the quarterback.

On the first play from scrimmage, Krenzel received the ball from center, spun, and made a quick throw to receiver Michael Jenkins, who was almost as quickly dropped by the covering corner, Markus Curry, but not before picking up a 6-yard gain. "The last two Michigan games I really haven't made really that big of a play," Jenkins said before the start of the game. "I'm trying to go out and have a good performance."

One receiver who was not available to Krenzel on the first series was Santonio Holmes. He was one of the OSU players involved in an incident outside a school dorm the week before the Game and later charged with a misde- meanor disorderly conduct, along with kick returner Troy

Smith. Tressel told the media that whether the players would be disciplined in some way by the team would be a game-time decision, and when Bam Childress lined up as wide out on that first play, it appeared that Tressel was at least offering a slap on the wrist. But how long would he keep a freshman with 19 catches, 339 yards, and 3 touchdowns in the Buckeyes' last four games out of the Game? After all, this sometimes anemic offense, averaging 24.2 points per game, which even the coach admitted needed to "score more points," was going up against a Wolverine squad that was averaging a much more robust 37.4 points per game.

On second down, Krenzel handed the ball to Lydell Ross, who surged forward a few yards but was short of the first down. The junior had become the team's primary back in Clarett's now-permanent absence and had contributed 722 yards for 9 TDs so far this season (still a far cry from 1,071 yards and 13 TDs, the numbers Clarett had going into last year's Michigan game). The Buckeyes needed to exploit a UM rush defense that was only the 35th best in the country if they wanted to win the Game for a third straight time.

It was now third-down-and-two as Krenzel took the snap and dropped back, finding one of his favorite receivers during the season, tight end Ben Hartsock, who was second on the team with his 31 receptions. His 32nd, however, did not yield a first down, as safety Ernest Shazor (leading the UM secondary in tackles) sprinted in to make a big hit and drop the 264-pound tight end short of the marker.

"The speed of this game is different from the others," Ben Hartsock had said before the game. "When I trotted on the field for my first Ohio State–Michigan game as a freshman, it was a nerve-wracking experience. As soon as that ball is snapped, people are flying around faster than they usually are. Whether that's just something in your head or not, I don't know. But it sure seems that way."

It looked that way, too. The Buckeyes were a quick three-and-out, and the Big Ten's best third-down defense made it look easy.

B. J. Sander came on the field to punt, and he sure wasn't the fanciest weapon in OSU's arsenal, but when you play a field position game the way Tressel does, it may be the most effective. The punting game for the Buckeyes had been superb all year (ranked fourth nationally in net punts), thanks to Sander. The week before, in the overtime victory against Purdue that helped set up the dramatic 100th game for the championship, Sander punted the ball 10 times, and 5 of those kicks pinned the Purdue offense inside their own 10 yard line. No, it's not flashy, but it wins football games.

This punt was a high one, and Michigan's Steve Breaston caught it near the 22-yard line. A number of Buckeyes were there to cover, and in the commotion, Breaston's knee hit the turf, and that was exactly where the Wolverines were going to begin their first series of the afternoon.

Big Wolverine quarterback John Navarre then calmly took the field in what, as advertised, was the biggest game of an already eventful college football career. If you opened the Michigan record book that day, you'd see the name John Navarre listed in second place in all-time completions, yardage, and TDs. Of all the illustrious quarterbacks to play at the University of Michigan, this 6-foot-6-inch, Cudahy, Wisconsin, native was nearing the very top of the list. Yet a few years ago, if someone had said that Navarre would be in the UM record books, you would have had to assume that that person was spending way too much time at Hash Bash.

Sure, in Wisconsin he was a star, but even though a 33–4 high school record as a starting QB might get you in the door at UM, it doesn't equal success in the Big House— especially when you're not even supposed to be on the field in the first place. When Drew Henson, considered one of the greatest pure athletes in school history, went down with a broken foot, Navarre, a red-shirt freshman, all of the sudden found himself quarterbacking the Wolverines for four games. He was impressive, even throwing four TD passes in his very first game against Bowling Green. But it was one thing to be the young guy who unexpectedly fills in for the star QB; it was another to flat out replace him.

In 2001, Drew Henson left Michigan to begin his wayward partnership with the Yankees (a relationship that has since been severed, as Henson became the property of the Houston Texans, who drafted him in 2003), and suddenly, Navarre wasn't the fill-in; he was *the* Michigan quarterback—and the expectations increased exponentially.

"I'm not saying it's just my team, but you've got to step up and be a leader," Navarre said before the start of the '01 season. "The offense is looking to you for all the answers, because you're running the offense, you're running the show. You have to have all the answers. Even if you don't, you've still got to pretend you do."

It wasn't easy to pretend anything under the spotlight. At the end of a jittery season, Navarre had thrown 11 interceptions in Michigan's final 6 games, including 4 against Ohio State in the year Jim Tressel first took over the program and nipped the Wolverines in the Game. The quarterback was booed in his own stadium, and thanks to the open disclosure of e-mail addresses on college campuses, Navarre's critics felt that it was within their right to e-mail their strong feelings to him as well. People who didn't have access to a computer called and wrote letters.

The Wisconsinite worked on his footwork, worked on his concentration, and improved his game, but even in '02, the criticism lingered, as the Wolverines came up short again against OSU. And it seemed to continue to linger until that miraculous fourth-quarter comeback against Minnesota in October. Suddenly, it looked as if Navarre had been reborn. Maybe he really was the bona fide star Michigan fans had been looking for since Henson left the program.

But none of it mattered right now. The records, that comeback, the passing yards that were piling up like chips in a no-limit poker tournament—all meaningless. For better or for worse, *this* was the game that would cement John Navarre's legacy. It would either erase the doubts about his ability to "win the big game," or it would write them in indelible ink.

Even his teammates could tell you that.

"Somebody asked about the legacy of John Navarre, whatever that means, would it hinge on this game," Bowman said before the Game. "It probably does, and it's probably unfair, but a lot of things are unfair, and that's the way it is and what you have to realize. With a game like this, the opportunities are bigger and the chance for loss is bigger."

If that was support, it was of the tough-love variety, but John Navarre had shown that he could handle it. The quiet kid, now a quiet man, deflected everything like a pro, which was probably the reason he was still wearing maize and blue. And was still sane.

"You have to block that out because that's just part of the hype," Navarre said of the legacy talk during the week. "You can't focus on that when you're preparing for this game.

But, obviously, how you do against Ohio State is a big part of any career here," he relented.

His coach didn't want to hear about one game defining anyone's career. "What defines you is character," Carr said.

Sure, tell that to the 112,118 who cheered as Navarre and his offense broke out of a huddle and took their positions on the field for their first offensive series of the Game.

He took the snap from center, dropped back a few steps, looked left, and then turned and made a quick pass to the right side toward Tim Massaquoi. The ball was rocketed to the junior tight end, and it hit his hands and bounced behind him, where a diving Dustin Fox moved in to try to pick the ball off. The football hit the turf just before the Buckeyes' cornerback could make his fourth interception of the year.

The Wolverine fans collectively winced. Navarre's pass was on target, but a pick early in the game would be devastating to the quarterback with the weight of the Big House on his shoulders.

On the next play, he went right back to the well and hit Chris Perry out of the backfield for an 8-yard completion. Perry, the not-so-secret weapon of the Wolverines, had done it all, all season long. He went into the Game as the Big Ten leader in rushing, all-purpose yards, and touchdowns and like his quarterback was making haste up the Wolverines' all-time leader board. Before the Game, the senior tailback was in Michigan's all-time top five in rushing attempts, yards, and touchdowns.

And not only was Perry going into the game knowing that he would have to carry the load on offense, but he had a heavy heart, too. The reason was written on a sweatband right around his bicep: MOM.

Things might have seemed tough for Chris Perry when he was a kid. His grades were slipping, he was a class clown, and, like many problem kids, he got shipped off to military school. Then, during his sophomore year at Michigan, he complained about a lack of playing time and got called selfish by his coach, who then called his bluff and told the back to go ahead and transfer if he wanted to. But all that was just a warm-up. The summer before his senior year, his Heisman-hopeful year, Chris Perry found out that his mother, Irene, had breast cancer.

"When I was diagnosed with breast cancer, I think it did something to him," said Perry's mom, "maybe changed him a little bit. It gives him a perspective about mortality. It gives him a perspective about football, that football is good, but there are a lot of things that are important in life."

"It's hard not to think about it," Perry said about his mom during the week of the Ohio State game, but in many ways the football field had become his place of solace, where he could retreat from the harsh realities of life and maybe do something to make his mom proud.

This was a good start. It was only the Wolverines' third play of the game, and Chris Perry, with the help of his big offensive line, ran the ball right up the middle and gave the Wolverines a first down.

This was one of the marquee match-ups: Perry versus OSU's running defense, led by linebacker A. J. Hawk and defensive end Will Smith. While Perry averaged 130.5 yards per game on the ground, OSU's defense had surrendered a stingy 50.55 yards per game—the best in the nation. It felt like the war would be won on the ground, again. But so far, Perry made finding holes in the defensive line look suspiciously easy.

On the first play after the first down, Navarre made another quick throw, this time to Jason Avant. The sophomore wide receiver was quickly tackled by Robert Reynolds, who twisted him to the turf, leaving his left leg caught under the big linebacker.

Avant had made a circus grab in the end zone the week before against Northwestern and was a rising star in what was already a solid Wolverine receiving corps. He came into the game fifth best in the Big Ten in receiving yards per game. But if there was one position for which UM could afford to lose a player, wide receiver was it. It's a good thing, too, because Avant was not getting up off the turf.

"This is going to be a tough, hard-hitting game just like the tradition of the previous 99 meetings," noted Wolverine fan Phil Calihan, as he watched the receiver writhe on the turf.

When he finally got up, Avant was escorted off the field, and the sophomore made no attempt to hide his tears from the fans or the TV cameras. Did the leg hurt that bad? Perhaps, but that's not why Avant was in tears.

"Jason was crying not because of the injury," Perry said about his teammate after the game, "but because he wanted to play."

On third-and-two, Navarre turned to his number 1 receiver, Braylon Edwards (68 catches for 901 yards and 12 TDs), but threw the ball behind the speedy wide out. It was Michigan's turn to punt from their own 45, as Adam Finley hit a high and deep kick to OSU's Jenkins, who made a fair catch at the 14.

It was a traditional UM–OSU war of attrition—so far.

Krenzel rolled out and hit Jenkins in traffic on the first play for a first down and a little breathing room for the Bucks. On the next play, Krenzel handed the ball off to Ross and Pierre Woods, the junior linebacker who led the Wolverines in sacks, got around the tight end Hartsock, and threw Ross to the turf, but not before their helmets collided with the net force that results when something that weighs 232 pounds intercepts something that weighs 225 pounds.

On second down, Krenzel took his spot behind the offensive line, and the crowd started to heat up. The quarterback didn't like what he saw—or what he heard from the energized crowd—and he took a timeout. The play they finally ran was a pass to Holmes, now in the game after his slap-on-the-wrist sit down, on the outside, who delivered to the Buckeyes a first down at the 40. On a reverse, Childress gained 6, and then Hall was stopped by Woods and Norman Heuer. On third-down-and-seven, Krenzel showed his mobility by rolling to the right but was forced to throw the ball away.

Sander came on for another kick and pinned Breaston inside his own 10-yard line—another beauty. On the Wolverines' first play, Perry did what Perry does best: started moving forward, shuffled his feet, broke a tackle, got a block, and then ran the ball up field. He wound up just a couple of yards short of the first down. But, eventually, he got it. And caught another screen pass (the record 40th reception for a UM back). And another. Michigan was moving the ball up the field. Then the Wolverines went deep.

Navarre to Edwards: it was a refrain heard often during the season by Wolverine fans, and the receiver was a speedy playmaker, reminiscent of the Cris Carters and the Desmond Howards who had passed through the Game before. But on him was OSU's own weapon in the secondary: Chris Gamble. The ball was thrown too far by Navarre, but Gamble was right there. Like Boston and Woodson in

1997, they would do the dance all day, working each other over like two bullies in a schoolyard.

Gamble was, in fact, very Woodson-like. Playing on both sides of the ball, the junior had opened a lot of eyes during the national championship season and was mentioned as a Heisman candidate following the Fiesta Bowl. But after playing mostly corner in '03, he didn't appear to be the same playmaker he once was. Teammates defended him and his blown coverage against Wisconsin's Lee Evans that led to the game-winning catch that cost the Buckeyes their second perfect season in two years.

"You can't blame him for the play," Buckeye Will Allen said, after the game against the Badgers.

Still, for a guy who had been trailed by whispers of Heisman and who was already being projected as a possible first rounder in the NFL draft, this was the time to step up. And it was clear that he knew it as well as anybody did.

A few plays later, while Perry was blasting up the middle for another first down, Gamble and Edwards looked like Ali and Frazier on their side of the field. Gamble made contact with Edwards, and the receiver pushed him aside, getting his hand caught on the Buckeye's helmet. Then Gamble retaliated with an almost full punch. This, on a play when the ball was nowhere near the two rivals. There was also some verbal jabbing, but the referee stepped in and broke up the heavyweights.

The sparring went on, but in the meantime, the Wolverines threw the Buckeyes for a loop. The receiver Breaston lined up under center (as Navarrre lined up on the outside, as if to receive), took the snap, and ran the option play, sneaking over the goal line for the 2003 Game's first touchdown. In 7 minutes and 4 seconds, Navarre brought his team 89 yards in 18 plays.

As Krenzel went back to work, he was getting the protection from his offensive line that he needed, but he missed a wide-open Jenkins anyway. Then on third-and-a-short-two, he handed the ball to Brandon Joe, who was stuffed short of the first down. Still, as the first quarter came to a close, Buckeye fans were not worried; their team had only given up one touchdown and was one big defensive play away from their usual script.

A few minutes later, things began to look a little more uncertain. Fox again got his hands on a potential interception that was tipped by linebacker Hawk and wound up kicking himself after the very next play, when Navarre connected with Edwards in the middle of the field, and the receiver broke tackles by Allen and Nate Salley before going 67 yards down the field for a touchdown.

The Big House roared. Then the Buckeyes went three-and-out, and the Big House roared again.

The Wolverines got back to work and Perry made a nice run toward the sidelines, picked up the first down, and came up limping but insisted he could stay in the game. A few plays later, it was again Gamble who was in a scuffle, but this time with Wolverine Tyrece Butler. Butler rolled under Gamble, knocking him off his feet. It was a cheap shot, but when the OSU corner made a little jab with his fist in retaliation, that was what the refs saw, and Gamble was rung up for a penalty and a Wolverine first down.

Navarre could have had a picnic in the pocket with all the protection he was getting, and on third-down-and-nine from OSU's 23-yard line, he made use of that time and found a streaking Edwards, who scored the Wolverines' third unanswered touchdown.

It was time for Ohio State, defending national champions

and winner of 10 of 11 games during the season, to show how much heart they had left. And Krenzel knew it.

He completed three passes before rolling out and taking the ball himself for a first down on his 43-yard line. He then hit Holmes for 12 yards, Jenkins for 5, and Jenkins a second time for 11. In almost no time, Ohio State was sitting on the Michigan 29-yard line.

The Jenkins reception put him just behind David Boston and Cris Carter on the all-time OSU list. The six-foot-five-inch senior was leading the team in catches and became a hero in Columbus in '02 when he caught a Krenzel pass on fourth-and-one against Purdue, with his team down 6–3 and with 1:36 left to play. That perfect season was more than a little in jeopardy when Jenkins shoved Purdue corner Antwaun Rogers and got open just enough to make the game-winning touchdown grab.

Now he appeared to be stepping up in a spot that fans were hoping they would look back on when they talked about the glories of the '03 season. And he knew it. "When it comes down to Michigan," the receiver said—as so many receivers had before him—"it feels like a one-game season."

After Krenzel rushed for another 6 yards, he found his money man for another first down inside the Michigan 17-yard line. Two plays later, the OSU quarterback threw a perfect ball to the back right corner of the end zone, over Holmes's shoulder, and it landed softly in the receiver's hands. It was the first time all season that the Wolverines had been scored on in the Big House in the first half of a football game. The Buckeyes were alive and kicking, as the second quarter of the Game was winding down. But Lloyd Carr still felt confident and with 44 seconds left on the clock, he told his QB to take a knee.

Michigan fans were loving it. "How's that defense now!"

someone in section 11 yelled. Buckeye fans, who were used to watching their team play catch up, prepared themselves to do it again.

"Now that they are on the board," said an OSU fan trying to keep his voice down because he was sitting in a sea of blue, "their offense will open up, and the defense will shut it down." His buddy was less optimistic. "Our band is better, right?" he said. "I hope to God it is. I hope *something* is."

At the start of the second half, Michigan just continued to make it look easy. This time, it was Perry who strutted his Heisman-like stuff. He spun and juked his way on a couple of big runs, breaking tackles and sidestepping linebackers. He then got the ball on a second-and-ten from OSU's 30, and the Michigan line created a hole that an SUV could have safely driven through. Perry took off straight up field. In the secondary, he had one man to beat, and he cut to the left, headed for the sidelines, and outran the safety Salley, diving into the end zone for a touchdown.

It was four touchdowns on the last four possessions for the Wolverines, and it was starting to look eerily like an Ohio State–Michigan game from the early 1900s—if you could call those games.

Would the national champions go out like that? Would Jim "I'll make you proud in Ann Arbor" Tressel start to look more like John Cooper on the sidelines? Not so fast.

Krenzel began to get a better read on the Michigan defense and—avert your eyes, Woody—threw the ball successfully, hitting Jenkins for a big first down at the 31, and then, a couple of plays later, he connected with him again on a crossing route that got him to the Michigan 28. But then the UM defensive line turned up the pressure, and Krenzel was sacked twice before having to punt, deflating Block O and the rest of Buckeye Nation.

While the OSU fans were busy wallowing in their pain, Perry experienced some discomfort of his own. On second-down-and-eight from the OSU 10, Perry got the ball and tried to jump over a tackle, as OSU's Smith came underneath, grabbed him, and pulled him to the turf. Somewhere in a pile of Buckeyes was Perry's leg, at an odd angle from his body. He remained on the ground, and the Big House encouragingly serenaded him with chants of his name.

Perry! Perry! Perry!

He still wasn't getting up. Fans continued to chant, even as they looked at each other nervously.

Perry! Perry! Perry!

Finally, the star back popped up off the ground. He slowly walked to the sideline, while screaming back at Smith for making what he thought was an intentional swipe at his leg.

"I was saying a few things to him about how I got hurt," Perry said after the game. "I can't repeat [what I said]."

Carr went over to try to calm down his running back, but Smith had a few choice words of his own for Perry. "I just told him he didn't have to play it out like that," Smith said later. "He could have just hopped up and jogged off the field. Did I hurt him? I made a tackle." A big, hard tackle.

And on the very next play, it appeared as if Michigan got out the hammer and nailed the coffin shut, until OSU pried it back open. Navarre threw a long bomb to Edwards that resulted in an 86-yard touchdown—but there was a yellow flag resting on the green turf back near the line of scrimmage. The play was called back due to holding by the Wolverines.

With a 21-point-lead, it didn't seem to matter, but OSU came out on their next series with a short field and scored a touchdown almost identical to their first. A ball thrown perfectly over Holmes's shoulder in the end zone cut the Buckeyes' deficit to two touchdowns, with 6:55 left in the third quarter.

On Michigan's next possession, the Wolverines went three-and-out, and now Ohio State had a chance to make the Wolverines really sweat, but Krenzel hit the turf—hard. He took a short drop to avoid stepping into the end zone and was drilled by the six-foot-five-inch 288-pounder Heuer. He lay on the ground holding his shoulder, before eventually being helped to the sidelines.

The game then went into the hands of backup Scott McMullen, which was not the worst thing in the world for Ohio State. McMullen had filled in for an injured Krenzel starting against Bowling Green and Northwestern. He came into the Penn State game, following a Krenzel concussion, trailing 17–7 before leading the team to a 21–10 win with a late-game touchdown. McMullen's solid play ignited a mini quarterback controversy. "I prefer to do what's best for our team and the guys involved," Tressel said about the situation after that game, but announced that Krenzel was still the starter. Some fans thought that was incongruous.

As opposed to Krenzel the scrambler, McMullen was a gunner who could perhaps more easily bring a team back from a two-touchdown deficit. "He's going to thread the needle and make the big pass that other quarterbacks might not think about making," said his teammate Ross.

But it didn't happen in the first series.

OSU was forced to punt, and Michigan got the ball back on the 45-yard line but quickly went three-and-out, giving McMullen another chance, as Krenzel retreated to the locker room to treat a separated shoulder of his nonthrowing arm.

McMullen and the Buckeyes went to work from their own 7-yard line and began moving up the field again. A screen pass to Ross, a couple of Ross runs, a pass to tight ends Hartsock and Ryan Hamby, and a Michigan pass interference penalty, and the Buckeyes were across midfield as the Game moved into the fourth quarter.

It was first down from Michigan's 42-yard line when McMullen faked a handoff, scrambled right out of the pocket, and looked up field and spied a wide-open Holmes—the very same Holmes who had started the game in the doghouse and was now having a solid game in the Big House—near the 12-yard line and hit him on the run. The receiver made it to the 3-yard line before being brought down by Michigan.

"I saw that Scott was under pressure," Holmes said, after the game, "so I didn't want to keep running my route. I broke off my route and found some space." It was then first-and-goal, and Ross finished the job with a run into the end zone.

McMullen engineered a taut drive that put the Buckeyes within one touchdown of the Wolverines, and an eerie hush swept over the crowd. "That was the quietest I've ever heard Michigan stadium," said one alumnus, who had been attending Wolverine games in the Big House regularly since 1990.

Carr gathered his defense around him on the sideline. "You want to win the Big Ten championship?" he asked them. "You've got the lead in the fourth quarter. You've got to protect it!"

The coach had reason to be worried. There were still 13:53 to play in the game, and a team that had been making improbable comebacks for two years was in striking distance.

And then they struck.

On Michigan's second play of the next possession, Navarre took his time and threw deep to Edwards, but Gamble, who'd been bumping and grinding all game and been burned a couple of times already, got in front of the intended receiver and made an easy interception on a ball that Navarre left short. It was the corner's chance at turning from goat to hero, and suddenly, OSU, down all game, was somehow looking like they were the team in the driver's seat, while Navarre's so-far brilliant game was close to caving in all around him.

"I smell overtime," yelled one excited Buckeye fan.

Even with Krenzel now back out of the locker room after receiving treatment and standing on the sideline ready to play, McMullen took over at the 37-yard line of what looked to be OSU's most important drive of the season.

But should the Fiesta Bowl MVP have been back in the game? "I thought I would get back in the game sooner than I did," Krenzel said afterward. "There was some miscommunication between Coach Tress and the trainers, and he was just being cautious for my health. Scotty had been playing fairly well, but he had not really done anything to blow the doors off the game." This was McMullen's shot to do just that, but on third-and-nine, the backup was sacked by a streaking Grant Bowman, and the momentum swung back the other way with a thud.

"Getting that stop there [was] huge," said the lineman. "That's probably one of the biggest plays of the game, to stop them on third down."

On the ensuing OSU punt, Breaston fumbled the ball at the 11 (another chance!), but Leon Hall, remarkably, was in the right place at the right time to recover it and prevent what would have been a mammoth play by the Buckeye special teams. "I was speechless," Breaston said after the game, about the potential disaster. "But Leon came through. I should take him out to dinner, shouldn't I?"

He should buy the freshman steak dinners for a year. Instead of facing a turnover and probably a tie game, the Wolverines went right back to work and delivered what was the game's biggest play. UM had the ball on third down with 4 yards to go and was sitting on their own 46-yard line with 9:16 left. It was not the showiest play in Carr's thick offensive playbook, but this was the one that cemented Navarre's status as a playmaker once and for all, and he got the assist from a really big man named Tyler Ecker.

Navarre shouted one last time to his teammates on the line of scrimmage to get them in position for the play, the ball was snapped, and he dropped straight back. Amid mounting pressure, he fired the football up the middle over the head of OSU's five-foot-eleven-inch Donte Whitner to his six-foot-six-inch tight end, who caught the ball in stride over his shoulder. Size mattered.

It was a 30-yard play, and it appeared to completely knock the wind out of Ohio State. Now, with the drive after the interception and the near fumble recovery on the punt, the what-ifs were starting to pile up as the seconds on the clock began to disappear.

Perry kept charging forward. The running back's helmet, once sparkling maize and blue, now looked dinged and chipped with splotches of red and gray paint smeared on the surface. A lot of it came from OSU's safety, Nate Salley. On the next play after Ecker's big catch, Perry took the ball and ran right up the middle. Salley came charging in full speed to meet the back, and their heads collided with a jarring impact that reverberated throughout the Big House. Both were shaken up. Perry was wincing, and Salley was dazed.

But they kinda grinned at each other.

"Nice hit," the back said to his rival.

"Nice playing," the corner shot back.

"All day, every time we had contact, I'd say, 'Keep on bringing it,' said Salley, after the game.

But in the end, Perry couldn't be stopped. After that big hit, Perry got the ball again, made a few sidesteps laterally, and was back in the end zone. The Wolverines were again two touchdowns ahead of the Buckeyes.

Krenzel got back into the Game, a decision that would irk some Buckeye fans for the next year and beyond. Why take the gunner out when all you needed right then were big guns?

"I love Craig Krenzel for who he is and everything he has done for Ohio State," said fan Nick Taylor, "but he was out of his element against Michigan. As soon as we had to play catch-up, it seemed obvious that Scott McMullen was the quarterback to do that. Krenzel is a gamer, but he is not the QB to sling it around the field in a game of catch-up. McMullen is."

From Krenzel's perspective, he felt that his coach should have gotten him in there even sooner and he was put in the impossible position of having to bridge a gap of now two TDs, with less than 8 minutes left in the ballgame. On top of that, the defense stepped up the pressure, and Krenzel, scrambling to make big plays, threw three incompletions on his first series. Michigan then ate some clock, and when Krenzel came back in with his offense, he was sacked for a loss on third down, and some of the Buckeye fans started to slip out of the Big House, hoping to go unnoticed.

Fat chance. "Bye, bye! Drive carefully," was a popular taunt from the Wolverine fans.

Michigan's next possession wasted even more time, and

then, tipping his own indecisiveness or desperation, Tressel went ahead and put McMullen back in the game.

The backup brought the Buckeyes to the Michigan 45-yard line. It was first-and-ten, and McMullen had four wide receivers lined up, looking for one more big play to prolong the game. With the crowd roaring, feeling the anticipation of an impending celebration, McMullen fired to Childress, and the ball was tipped in the air before landing in the arms of Wolverine Shazor. As in many editions of the Game, it was a late interception that sealed it.

"Where are those roses?" Edwards screamed from the sidelines—sounding a lot like Woodson in '97. "I said, 'Where are those roses?'"

A minute later, John Navarre cradled the ball in his arms and knelt on the turf. The University of Michigan Wolverines had beaten the Ohio State Buckeyes in their 100th meeting.

Chris Perry held a rose in the air, as his mother, Irene, looked on. "She is always in my heart," he said, "and inspires me all the time."

And beleaguered quarterback John Navarre breathed easy for the first time in years. "It feels great," he said. "It's a dream come true."

10

POST-GAME

The red brick wall separating the seats and the playing field in Michigan Stadium is only about seven feet high; in other words, it was no match for jubilant fans.

First, just a few jumped down from the ledge to join their beloved Wolverines, who began celebrating on the field after the final whistle. But then, like maize-and-blue-colored lemmings, the entire student section began to follow. From the other side of the stadium, it looked like a giant mass of humanity bleeding onto the turf.

Once on the field, the fans joined the football players and the marching band in an impromptu party. They carried roses, they pumped their fists, they sang "The Victors," and they chanted: "It's great to be a Michigan Wolverine"—over and over. It was the combined joy from a victory in the Game, winning a Big Ten championship, and just being able to express unbridled joy in the occasionally reserved confines of Michigan Stadium.

Earlier in the week, an e-mail had circulated on campus

imploring students to rush the field after a Wolverine victory. It said, among other things, "Let's make the biggest crowd in college football actually make its presence felt for once." And was signed simply: "See you on the field—Go Blue." By the end of the week, just about every student on campus had been forwarded the missive.

University officials also got wind of the e-mail and asked students not to mar the potential celebration and risk injury or worse by trying to get down on the playing field. They were particularly troubled by the part of the e-mail that read, "If you're not in the first few rows, just start heading down, because that'll force people in front of you to do so and then the momentum can't be stopped."

University Department of Safety spokeswoman Diane Brown was quoted in the *Michigan Daily* as responding, "That's not true. That has the potential for creating a crash situation at the bottom. The wall doesn't move."

The wall was rock solid and so was the spirit of these fans, who, remarkably, waited in a peaceful and respectful manner for their fellow revelers to move in orderly, almost single-file lines down the aisles in order to get to the top of the wall, where they assisted each other over the top, down the other side, and onto the field to join their classmates.

"I've wanted to do this since I started school here. This has been my goal for every game," one recent graduate said on the field. "This is why I came to school here."

After about 15 minutes, the public address announcer asked the celebrators to clear the field and made everyone left in the stadium chuckle by adding, "Those of you who think you are on TV . . . you are not." But that had nothing to do with it. This was a moment of true bliss, with no mugging or fan posturing.

The players knew it too. Many Wolverines remained on the field; some waved roses in the air, as the fans did, just taking it all in. Tight end Andy Mignery observed the fans and noted "how much emotion was going through their bodies, [they were] going crazy." He added, "It meant a lot [to me] as a player."

Perry, who had remained on the field in Ohio Stadium the year before, watching the Buckeyes celebrate with their fans, said that he used the image throughout the season as a motivational tool and was now on the other side. Fans mobbed the running back, hugging him and patting him on the back. Along with the rest of the players, he had to struggle to get back down the tunnel and into the locker room.

"I think our fans were rougher out there than OSU's defense," joked Perry. "I was more worried I was going to get injured with them celebrating. Everybody in there was yelling for us, and I just looked around at the other guys [on the team] and told them to enjoy, soak it all in. Because it isn't every day 110,000 people give you an ovation . . . This game was some kind of special."

On his way off the field, Larry Stevens looked around and just yelled, "We beat Ohio State!"

The fans didn't want to leave. Slowly, a large group made its way toward the south end zone, where many Buckeye fans still sat in the stands. The Michigan contingent began to taunt their rivals with cheers of "Overrated! Overrated!" and for a moment, tension filled the air, but the deflated Buckeye fans sat back and allowed their rivals to have their day. Because they knew, without a doubt, that they'd be back.

Things have not always been so peaceful after the Game.

Beginning with the melee on the field in Ann Arbor in 1935, the passion surrounding the Game has frequently boiled over, and on occasion, the results have been destructive and dangerous. During the 10-Year War, when the intensity surrounding the Rivalry was at an all-time high—and people were used to taking to the streets—things tended to get out of hand in Columbus. The action centered around North High Street, a strip with numerous bars that was routinely flooded with fans after the Game in the '70s.

In 1975, following OSU's 21–14 win, thousands of people took to the streets. At first, the gathering was peaceful, but later, the remaining masses "started rocking cars, harassing drivers, and throwing rocks and bottles at our men," reported Columbus Police Captain James Jackson. Police tried to clear the streets, but the crowds swelled and became more violent. "It looked like it was the booze finally being felt," Jackson said.

By 11:30 P.M., the throng had been sufficiently warned to disperse and Captain Jackson ordered his men to fire one-inch-diameter wooden projectiles known as "knee-knockers" at the remaining revelers. In the end, 48 people were arrested, and 4 were treated for minor injuries.

In ensuing years, it only seemed to get worse.

In 1979, Columbus saw the worst post-Game rioting of the decade when 338 arrests were made. The Game wasn't even in Columbus, but OSU had a dramatic win, thanks to a blocked punt by Jim Laughlin in the fourth quarter that preserved a perfect season (Bruce's first year as Buckeye coach) and sent OSU to the Rose Bowl, where they came 1 point away from a national championship.

As in earlier years, the celebrations were nothing but

festive at first. On the street, a happy fan approached one of the 500 cops on patrol, hugged him, and yelled "Great game!" As the day went on, the party continued and stores near campus reported brisk sales of "primarily beer and pops you can mix [drinks] with."

Just as in '75, the drinks eventually took their toll, and by nightfall a car with "Go Michigan" written on it was flipped over and lit on fire. According to the *Lantern*, "flame and smoke rose from the car and heat warmed faces 30 feet away." In a few hours, police in riot gear stood across from the celebrators. Glass was being thrown, as were the occasional cherry bomb and firecrackers. Police officers freely used clubs on the rioters, who would not disperse when asked to move out of the street. By 1 A.M., the streets were finally cleared of the overzealous fans.

Disturbances following the Game continued over the years, but the Cooper era didn't necessarily lend itself to many post-Game celebrations in Columbus. When the Buckeyes finally did beat the Wolverines in 1994, there were reports of Columbus police using chemical spray to break up crowds in at least two incidents, including one at an apartment off campus. "The trouble started when people lit a fire in the yard of the complex," said a student. "People were throwing furniture off balconies, and burning anything they could find."

In Ann Arbor, post-Game celebrations have been less destructive. In 1980, UM safety director Walter Stevens claimed that in his 10 years at the university, he had seen some damage done to the stadium itself and to dormitories following the Ohio State game, but nothing like what went on in Columbus during the same period. He said that before and after the game, UM safety personnel geared up for the "usual number of drunks." Stevens theorized that the relative size of Ann Arbor and the fewer nonticket holders who invade the city on game day help keep the post-Game incidents to a minimum, relative to those in Columbus.

However, after the win against OSU in 1997 that set the Wolverines up for their most recent national championship, over 8,000 fans rushed the field, and there were many small confrontations with the 50 University of Michigan police officers who were handling crowd control. Witnesses watched police spraying fans in their faces with pepper spray, as well as tackling and punching students who wouldn't leave the field. A UM graduate said that it looked like they were "trying to hurt people." The school mounted an investigation, but, fortunately, there were no serious injuries.

In 2002, violence reared its ugly head again after the Game. OSU's big win, on the way to the Fiesta Bowl and a national championship, was to a degree overshadowed by what happened in Columbus afterward. At first, fans flooded the field following Will Allen's memorable interception of John Navarre's last-gasp pass. But the problems weren't on the field, where fans mostly hollered, threw the occasional bottle, and did more damage to the stadium's turf than to anything else.

As day turned into night, a ghastly tradition from the '70s was reborn, of property damage and fires. First a mattress was thrown into the street by some fans and set on fire. Then, before long, partygoers added street signs, trees, chairs, and couches to the growing blaze. They chanted "O-HI-O," and firecrackers and beer cans were tossed haphazardly into the air. Shortly after midnight, police arrived, wearing full riot gear, and anyone who did not retreat inside was sprayed with tear gas.

And that was just one corner of town.

This sort of activity continued throughout the night, all over areas of Columbus that were near the campus. By morning, the stats being bandied about, along with yards and completions, included: 20 cars turned over, 9 cars burned, 107 fires reported, and 7 street lights ripped from their bases. The police had arrested 48 people by Sunday afternoon.

The riots made the national evening news and even the *Tonight Show with Jay Leno*, where the host joked: "Yesterday, President Bush signed a law to create the Department of Homeland Security . . . their first job: to protect Americans from Ohio State football fans."

University and city officials did not think it was very funny. "We had an opportunity to shine to the nation, and we did that on the field," Columbus mayor Michael B. Coleman said the next day. "Our shine was tarnished last night."

In '03, University president Karen Holbrook turned the screw, commissioning a task force to look into the riots and, most important, more strictly enforce open container laws around the stadium. The result was a riot-free football season in 2003.

▬   ▬   ▬

After the 100th Game in Ann Arbor, things remained basically under control. Students eventually cleared the field, and outside the Big House, fans made their way, in an orderly fashion, back to tailgates, cars, bars, dorms, or homes to celebrate. Of course, some needled any Buckeye fans they could find along the way.

"It's getting pretty disgusting around here right now," said one OSU fan, who continued to tailgate near the stadium after the game, even in the face of the abuse. "Just all the Michigan fans coming out, they're just taking their shots."

Some Wolverine fans were even polite. On Stadium Boulevard, a celebrating horde of fans walked past a group in Buckeye jerseys and gave them a sincere, "Great game." The scarlet-and-gray crew shot back, "You, too. But wait 'til next year!"

Players and coaches retreated to the locker rooms to meet with the media, and the dissection of the game began. Coach Carr was obviously pleased, and he choked back tears of joy. "It was a great win and a great football game," he said. "If you love passion and intense concentration and effort for two or three hours, it does not get any better than that."

In the other locker room, the coach was wishing his team had made a couple more big plays. "They came out and did the things that championship teams do," said Tressel about the Wolverines. "They stayed away from turnovers and were able to run and pass. We did not come out and do the things that you need to do to be the Big Ten champion, so obviously we have to tip our cap to Michigan." While the Wolverines were floating on air and kissing a championship trophy that was being presented in the locker room, the Buckeyes were licking some wounds.

Nate Salley's right eye was nearly swollen shut from that helmet-on-helmet hit with Perry. He could barely lift his left arm, and the knuckles on both of his hands were skinned and raw. "That was a heavyweight battle out there," he said.

They knew what the knockout had cost them: a chance to go to the BCS championship game and a successful season by the 100-game-old standard set in Columbus.

And yet back in the football-crazed metropolis, things were quiet. The parties that were thrown to watch the Game were breaking up, leaving in their wake a slew of empty plastic cups and brokenhearted fans slumped on sagging couches.

Some fans did venture outside to take out their frustration on any inanimate object they could find. Fifth-year senior Adam Bakewell, with some others, smashed a wooden stool on his front porch steps. "I'm already drunk," he said, "so I don't have to drink that much more to get to my happy place. I'm drinking away my pain. I cry for what could have been."

Police heavily patrolled the streets on foot, on bicycles, on horseback, and in cruisers, but things remained quiet—except for the grousing. "We've been struggling all year, and we've only been winning by a little bit," said an OSU student, wearing buckeye beads and a red Ohio State sweatshirt. "It was only a matter of time before the defense couldn't pull the load. It puts a bitter end to a pretty fun season."

The players, still in Ann Arbor, knew how bitterly a loss to Michigan was and always will be felt by OSU fans and Buckeyes alike. "We could have been 11–0 coming in, but when you lose *this* game, your season is for naught," said offensive tackle Shane Olivea.

"We had a chance to solidify our status today," said tight end Ben Hartsock. "We would have been the Buckeye team that won three straight from Michigan. We got outplayed."

"We deserve to be in one of the big bowl games," said Olivea. "I didn't want to play in the Outback [Bowl] again. We're a good football team."

The senior brought up an excellent point, and it wasn't

just the fact that the 10–2 Bucks *were* a good football team. It was hard think about it on that night in Ann Arbor, amidst all of the partying and bragging and wallowing, but both of these football teams would play one more game in the '03 season.

The big question was where and when.

■   ■   ■

BCS was akin to a curse word that fall. The ranking system, which was meant to bring to college football one unified, undisputed champion, was taking a lot of heat. Teams were constantly flip-flopping, even after wins, and the BCS rankings looked as similar to football's other established ranking systems as fraternal twins. OSU went into the game against Michigan ranked number 2 in the BCS, behind Oklahoma (and somehow ahead of USC, which was universally believed to be a better team and ranked ahead of them in the other polls), and with a win, the Buckeyes had a good shot at going to the Sugar Bowl in New Orleans to defend their title. As a result, the Game was almost as big on the West Coast, where USC fans were hoping that Michigan could knock off their rivals to put the Trojans back in the catbird seat.

"I was pumped," USC defensive tackle Shaun Cody said, after beating UCLA 47–22 and seeing Michigan take care of Ohio State. "I was a big Wolverine fan the whole day."

But thanks to the convoluted system, things were far from solidified, and there were regular season games yet to be played for both USC and the other one-loss team in the mix, LSU. Even though Michigan was officially offered a Rose Bowl bid following the Game, they actually held an outside shot of leap-frogging ahead of those two other teams in front of them and getting to the big dance themselves. Ohio State, at this point, was just hoping for an at-large bid to a BCS bowl; this was a far cry from their hopes before going into the Game.

A couple of weeks later, the convoluted picture became absolutely Jackson Pollock–like. Oklahoma was stunned by Kansas State; the same day, USC walloped Oregon State; and LSU handled Georgia. Suddenly there were three teams with one loss, and only two spots in the Sugar Bowl. Although USC was playing some of the best ball late in the season and was ranked number 1 in both of the other polls, the Trojans found themselves number 3 in the BCS rankings, thanks to strength of schedule and other formulas that go into the complicated ranking system. It was enough to make Einstein scratch his head.

The shambles caused by the BCS wasn't just a problem for college football at large; it was also worrisome to devotees of the Rivalry. It was clear that the NCAA would have to come up with a new system, and every possible solution was being considered, including a playoff-type structure and a possible reshuffling of the NCAA football conferences. All of this meant that there existed a very real possibility that one day the Ohio State–Michigan game would not be a permanent fixture as the last game of the schedule for both teams, as it has been since 1935—which is one of the primary factors that makes this Rivalry what it is. It is hard to imagine a future without the Game and hopefully the powers-that-be will see what a disservice this would be to college football.

In the end, it was the number 1–ranked Trojans—in the AP and ESPN/USA Today polls anyway—who would play Michigan in the Rose Bowl, with the very real prospect of a split national championship (between the winner of the Rose Bowl and the winner of the Sugar Bowl), the very thing that the BCS system was supposed to make extinct.

And it also meant that the Wolverines would continue to play a major role in the national championship picture. "[USC] are one in both polls and we are going to treat this as a championship game and as a chance for us to go out and show the country that Michigan is for real and we can play with top-ranked teams," said—of all people—John Navarre.

The Buckeyes were patient and did get their own BCS-bowl bid. OSU was invited to play in the Fiesta Bowl for the second consecutive year, only this time it was in a decidedly less significant game, this time against the Kansas State Wildcats.

"It will be nice to play at a place we have played before," said Buckeye Will Smith. "I like Arizona: we had a great time there last year and are excited to be back. Hopefully, I can finish my playing time here at Ohio State with a win."

In the meantime, Wolverine Chris Perry had to make an unscheduled trip to New York. As the crowd in the Big House chanted his last name in the Game, the incantation reverberated across the college football landscape, and Perry was among only four finalists invited to the Heisman Trophy presentation.

The Big Ten's leading rusher steamrolled his way into the ceremony, while his competitors, Oklahoma's QB Jason White, Pittsburgh receiver Larry Fitzgerald, and Mississippi QB Eli Manning, all looked fallible in their late season games. "If he wins the Heisman Trophy, he will certainly be very deserving," said Perry's somewhat biased coach.

White won the award, but Perry, the tailback who almost left Michigan and who gained only 22 yards in an early-season loss against Oregon, was at the table, thanks in large part to his inspiring performance in the Game.

"There's no disappointment," Perry said, about coming in fourth place in the voting. "I kind of expected it, really. It would've been nice to win, but I thought it was a foregone conclusion. It was just fun to be here." A few days later, Perry and the rest of the Wolverines flew west.

It wasn't California dreamin', however. After never seeing a hint of the turf against Ohio State, Navarre was sacked nine times and finished 27-of-46 for 271 yards, with one touchdown, while Perry ran for only 85 yards, and Michigan lost in the Rose Bowl to the eventual co-national champion Trojans 28–14.

"I am happy that we won the Big Ten championship," said Perry, "and that we got here and that the seniors were able to play in the Rose Bowl. I am not going to let this one game hamper my whole career and what it took for us to get here."

The next day, Craig Krenzel was taking snaps for the Buckeyes in Tempe, Arizona, on his way to his second Fiesta Bowl MVP in two years, with a four-touchdown pass performance—the most ever by an OSU quarterback in a bowl game. The Buckeyes bounced back from their loss against the Wolverines and held off a late-game rally by Kansas—what else would you expect from the Luckeyes?—to win 35–28.

"We went out and played for our pride tonight, to show the country that we belong in a BCS bowl," Krenzel said, after the Fiesta Bowl. "We belong playing the best guys in the country." Krenzel and the rest of the Bucks, who played against the backdrop of the Clarett controversy and were the team to beat in NCAA Division I-A football, with the biggest bull's eye on their backs, won 25 games and lost only 2 over two seasons. They wouldn't get much of an argument.

But how long could the '03 Bucks and the Wolverines bask in their accomplishments? About 30 seconds.

"We have to open up against Dantonio and Cincinnati in 2004," said Tressel, toward the end of his post-game press conference in Tempe. He was referring to OSU's defensive coordinator, Mark Dantonio, who was leaving the Buckeyes to become the head coach of the University of Cincinnati, the team that just so happens to be the first opponent on Ohio State's '04 schedule—almost exactly eight months away.

Before cleanup crews had even picked up the hot dog wrappers off the floor of the Fiesta Bowl, reporters were asking how the Buckeyes could possibly replace the six starters on offense and the seven on defense who were graduating. A. J. Hawk, who would be back, said, "I don't think people should worry. We've got a lot of young talent. And Ohio State always has a great recruiting year."

That process was, of course, well underway and about to go into overdrive. Official school visits by recruits, if they hadn't happened already, would keep the coaches busy over the next month until February 4, the official signing day for prospective college football players.

■   ■   ■

"All right, the marathon is over," Carr announced at the start of his meeting with the media on signing day. "I'm delighted to bring a number of young men back to Michigan next fall. They've all been in here for visits. They've accepted scholarship offers to the university, and we look forward to the opportunity to coach them, to try to develop them into the type of students that will be successful here and that will represent our football program in a way that we can all be proud of."

Down south, Tressel made his pitch, too, lauding a recruiting class that he labeled "diverse" and saying that they were "guys who have chosen Ohio State because they have a passion to be here."

Both the statement and its timing were ironic. Two days later, one guy who apparently didn't have such a passion for being there and may very well have cost the Buckeyes back-to-back championships won his fight to go pro. In a 70-page ruling, U.S. District Judge Shira Scheindlin said that the NFL eligibility rule requiring draftees to be out of high school for three years "must be sacked" because it violates antitrust laws. This cleared the way for Maurice Clarett to enter the draft. He had opened the door for himself and perhaps more players to forego three years of college (or perhaps any college).

It was a pretty big moment in the history of the NFL, but the final chapter was still unwritten. For years, college ball had acted as the minor leagues of professional football, a training ground for players to grow, learn, and showcase their abilities. But at the same time, in other sports, high-profile players like the NFL's LeBron James were being drafted right out of high school. And in baseball, although seasoning in the minors is almost always required, a team can draft a player out of high school, or if the player is foreign-born, he can be signed to a pro contract before he even turns 17.

Would football also go this way? Many questions were still left unanswered after the court's ruling in the Clarett situation. Were players as young as 19 and 20 ready for the physical punishment of the National Football League? Were they fast enough and strong enough to make an impact?

Clarett was, in essence, the guinea pig. (USC's 20-year-old receiver Mike Williams was the next player to take advantage of the Clarett ruling, and he opted for the NFL draft with two years of college eligibility still left.)

But many questions would remain unanswered—for now. Again the topsy-turvy Clarett saga took a sudden turn. On the eve of the NFL draft, a three-judge panel of the U.S. Court of Appeals of the Second Circuit stayed Judge Scheindlin's earlier ruling. One member of the panel said that the NFL rule was probably legal, and that the union was merely exercising its right to protect its members from those not yet in it.

It was another loss of legal yardage for the running back, now over a year removed from playing football on any level. The NCAA also quickly pointed out that players like Clarett and Williams, who had signed with agents, were now basically professionals, thereby signaling that a return to OSU was also unlikely.

Clarett and his lawyers had no choice but to file an emergency appeal with the U.S. Supreme Court to lift the Second Circuit's stay. Two separate appeals made to two different justices were denied, and the once-promising career of Maurice Clarett looked to be in limbo once again. The NFL draft would go on without him.

This was not the case for several other Buckeyes and Wolverines—including Chris Gamble. The versatile corner who went head to head (and occasionally fist to fist) with Braylon Edwards in the Game decided to forego his senior year at OSU and enter the draft (he was eligible by the old NFL rule—no lawsuits necessary.

"I knew I was always ready to play in the NFL," Gamble said, following the Buckeyes' victory over Kansas. "I had some bad games this year, but I just wanted to bounce back and play real good this game. I think I did." The corner had an interception that set up a touchdown, recorded three tackles, and broke up four passes. "I think I'm just ready right now." The pundits agreed. On the eve of the 2004 NFL Draft, Gamble was being projected as a potential first-round pick. He would be joining defensive end Will Smith and receiver Michael Jenkins as the Buckeyes most likely to succeed in the NFL.

On the Wolverines' side, it was Edwards who was thought to be contemplating leaving school early, but the receiver opted to return to Michigan for his senior year, an announcement that couldn't have warmed the hearts of OSU fans.

"I'm coming back because I see the potential for the team and myself to get better," said Edwards. "I know we can do more than we did last year, and I know I can do more than I did last year."

Cornerback Marlin Jackson, who started the year in trouble, got hurt, but finished strong, also announced his desire to return. That left Perry, Navarre, and Tony Pape as the Wolverines most likely to show up in the early rounds of the draft. All of them already had big-game experience, thanks in large part to the Game—something that NFL scouts definitely look for in a college player.

"I think it benefited me," said Perry, who was looking like a late first–round or early second–round pick. "Coaches love somebody who loves pressure. If you want to be a big-time player or an impact player in any sport at any position, you have to love the pressure and you have to step up during pressure time in big games." You can't beat the pressure of the Big House, with 112,118 people yelling your name when it's Michigan against Ohio State. Perry had been there—but for the moment, he wasn't sure where he was going.

There are few things in the world you really can be sure about, but here's one: on a Saturday, late in November, Ohio State and Michigan will play a game of football. And it will be a war.

Again.

APPENDIX

All-Time UM-OSU Results

Date	Site	Result			
October 16, 1897	Ann Arbor	UM	36	OSU	0
November 24, 1900	Ann Arbor	UM	0	OSU	0
November 9, 1901	Ann Arbor	UM	21	OSU	0
October 25, 1902	Ann Arbor	UM	86	OSU	0
November 7, 1903	Ann Arbor	UM	36	OSU	0
October 15, 1904	Columbus	UM	31	OSU	6
November 11, 1905	Ann Arbor	UM	40	OSU	0
October 20, 1906	Columbus	UM	6	OSU	0
October 26, 1907	Ann Arbor	UM	22	OSU	0
October 24, 1908	Columbus	UM	10	OSU	6
October 16, 1909	Ann Arbor	UM	33	OSU	6
October 22, 1910	Columbus	UM	3	OSU	3
October 21, 1911	Ann Arbor	UM	19	OSU	0
October 19, 1912	Columbus	UM	14	OSU	0
November 30, 1918	Columbus	UM	14	OSU	0
October 25, 1919	Ann Arbor	OSU	13	UM	3
November 6, 1920	Columbus	OSU	14	UM	7
November 22, 1921	Ann Arbor	OSU	14	UM	0

Date	Site	Result			
October 21, 1922	Columbus	UM	19	OSU	0
October 22, 1923	Ann Arbor	UM	23	OSU	0
November 15, 1924	Columbus	UM	16	OSU	6
November 14, 1925	Ann Arbor	UM	10	OSU	0
November 13, 1926	Columbus	UM	17	OSU	16
October 22, 1927	Ann Arbor	UM	21	OSU	0
October 20, 1928	Columbus	OSU	19	UM	7
October 19, 1929	Ann Arbor	OSU	7	UM	0
October 18, 1930	Columbus	UM	13	OSU	0
October 17, 1931	Ann Arbor	OSU	7	UM	0
October 15, 1932	Columbus	UM	14	OSU	10
October 21, 1933	Ann Arbor	UM	13	OSU	0
November 17, 1934	Columbus	OSU	34	UM	0
November 23, 1935	Ann Arbor	OSU	38	UM	0
November 21, 1936	Columbus	OSU	21	UM	0
November 20, 1937	Ann Arbor	OSU	21	UM	0
November 19, 1938	Columbus	UM	18	OSU	0
November 25, 1939	Ann Arbor	UM	21	OSU	14
November 23, 1940	Columbus	UM	40	OSU	0
November 22, 1941	Ann Arbor	UM	20	OSU	20
November 21, 1942	Columbus	OSU	21	UM	7
November 20, 1943	Ann Arbor	UM	45	OSU	7
November 25, 1944	Columbus	OSU	18	UM	14
November 24, 1945	Ann Arbor	UM	7	OSU	3
November 23, 1946	Columbus	UM	58	OSU	6
November 22, 1947	Ann Arbor	UM	21	OSU	0
November 20, 1948	Columbus	UM	13	OSU	3
November 19, 1949	Ann Arbor	UM	7	OSU	7
November 25, 1950	Columbus	UM	9	OSU	3
November 24, 1951	Ann Arbor	UM	7	OSU	0
November 22, 1952	Columbus	OSU	27	UM	7
November 21, 1953	Ann Arbor	UM	20	OSU	0
November 20, 1954	Columbus	OSU	21	UM	7
November 19, 1955	Ann Arbor	OSU	17	UM	0
November 24, 1956	Columbus	UM	19	OSU	0

APPENDIX

Date	Site	Result			
November 23, 1957	Ann Arbor	OSU	31	UM	14
November 22, 1958	Columbus	OSU	20	UM	14
November 21, 1959	Ann Arbor	UM	23	OSU	14
November 19, 1960	Columbus	OSU	7	UM	0
November 25, 1961	Ann Arbor	OSU	50	UM	20
November 24, 1962	Columbus	OSU	28	UM	0
November 23, 1963	Ann Arbor	OSU	14	UM	10
November 21, 1964	Columbus	UM	10	OSU	0
November 20, 1965	Ann Arbor	OSU	9	UM	7
November 19, 1966	Columbus	UM	17	OSU	3
November 25, 1967	Ann Arbor	OSU	24	UM	14
November 23, 1968	Columbus	OSU	50	UM	14
November 22, 1969	Ann Arbor	UM	24	OSU	12
November 21, 1970	Columbus	OSU	20	UM	9
November 20, 1971	Ann Arbor	UM	10	OSU	7
November 25, 1972	Columbus	OSU	14	UM	11
November 24, 1973	Ann Arbor	UM	10	OSU	10
November 23, 1974	Columbus	OSU	12	UM	10
November 22, 1975	Ann Arbor	OSU	21	UM	14
November 20, 1976	Columbus	UM	22	OSU	0
November 19, 1977	Ann Arbor	UM	14	OSU	6
November 25, 1978	Columbus	UM	14	OSU	3
November 17, 1979	Ann Arbor	OSU	18	UM	15
November 22, 1980	Columbus	UM	9	OSU	3
November 21, 1981	Ann Arbor	OSU	14	UM	9
November 21, 1982	Columbus	OSU	24	UM	14
November 19, 1983	Ann Arbor	UM	24	OSU	21
November 17, 1984	Columbus	OSU	21	UM	6
November 23, 1985	Ann Arbor	UM	27	OSU	17
November 22, 1986	Columbus	UM	26	OSU	24
November 21, 1987	Ann Arbor	OSU	23	UM	20
November 19, 1988	Columbus	UM	34	OSU	31
November 25, 1989	Ann Arbor	UM	28	OSU	18
November 24, 1990	Columbus	UM	16	OSU	13
November 23, 1991	Ann Arbor	UM	31	OSU	3

Date	Site		Result		
November 21, 1992	Columbus	UM 13		OSU	13
November 20, 1993	Ann Arbor	UM 28		OSU	0
November 19, 1994	Columbus	OSU 22		UM	6
November 25, 1995	Ann Arbor	UM 31		OSU	23
November 23, 1996	Columbus	UM 13		OSU	9
November 22, 1997	Ann Arbor	UM 20		OSU	14
November 21, 1998	Columbus	OSU 31		UM	16
November 21, 1999	Ann Arbor	UM 24		OSU	17
November 18, 2000	Columbus	UM 38		OSU	26
November 24, 2001	Ann Arbor	OSU 26		UM	20
November 23, 2002	Columbus	OSU 14		UM	9
November 22, 2003	Ann Arbor	UM 35		OSU	21

Overall: Michigan leads series 57–37–6

Ohio State Buckeyes' 2003 Football Schedule

Sat., Aug. 30	Washington	W 28–9
Sat., Sep. 6	San Diego State	W 16–13
Sat., Sep. 13	North Carolina State	W 44–38
Sat., Sep. 20	Bowling Green	W 24–17
Sat., Sep. 27	Northwestern	W 20–0
Sat., Oct. 11	at Wisconsin	L 10–17
Sat., Oct. 18	Iowa	W 19–10
Sat., Oct. 25	at Indiana	W 35–6
Sat., Nov. 1	at Penn State	W 21–20
Sat., Nov. 8	Michigan State	W 33–23
Sat., Nov. 15	Purdue	W 16–13
Sat., Nov. 22	at Michigan	L 21–35
Fri., Jan. 2	Kansas State	W 35–28

University of Michigan Wolverines' 2003 Football Schedule

Sat., Aug. 30	Central Michigan	W 45–7
Sat., Sep. 6	Houston	W 50–3
Sat., Sep. 13	Notre Dame	W 38–0
Sat., Sep. 20	at Oregon	L 27–31
Sat., Sep. 27	Indiana	W 31–17
Sat., Oct. 4	at Iowa	L 27–30
Fri., Oct. 10	at Minnesota	W 38–35
Sat., Oct. 18	Illinois	W 56–14
Sat., Oct. 25	Purdue	W 31–3
Sat., Nov. 1	at Michigan State	W 27–20
Sat., Nov. 15	at Northwestern	W 41–10
Sat., Nov. 22	Ohio State	W 35–21
Thu., Jan. 1	at USC	L 14–28

Ohio State versus Michigan, November 22, 2003

Ohio State (10–2, 6–2) vs. Michigan (10–2, 7–1)

Site: Ann Arbor, Michigan

Stadium: Michigan Stadium

Attendance: 112,118

Kickoff time: 12:10 End of Game: 3:30 Total elapsed time: 3:20

Officials: Referee: J. Lapetina; Umpire: R. Haberer; Linesman: B. Durbin; Line judge: T. Ransom; Back judge: J. Lyman; Field judge: N. Nelson; Side judge: J. Duncan

Temperature: Low 50s Wind: ENE10–20 Weather: Mostly cloudy

Score by Quarters	1	2	3	4	Score
Ohio State	0	7	7	7	21
Michigan	7	14	7	7	35

Scoring Summary:

1st

00:39 MICH—Breaston, Steve 3-yd. run (Rivas, Garrett kick)
18 plays, 89 yards, TOP 7:04, OSU 0–MICH 7

2nd

13:33 MICH—Edwards, Braylon 64-yd. pass from Navarre, John
(Rivas, Garrett kick)
3 plays, 74 yards, TOP 0:47, OSU 0–MICH 14
05:49 MICH–Edwards, Braylon 23-yd. pass from Navarre, John
(Rivas, Garrett kick)
9 plays, 80 yards, TOP 3:49, OSU 0–MICH 21
00:44 OSU–Holmes, Santonio 8-yd. pass from Krenzel, Craig
(Nugent, Mike kick)
12 plays, 81 yards, TOP 5:05, OSU 7–MICH 21

3rd

13:04 MICH–Perry, Chris 30-yd. run (Rivas, Garrett kick)
5 plays, 62 yards, TOP 1:56, OSU 7–MICH 28
06:55 OSU—Holmes, Santonio 13-yd. pass from Krenzel, Craig
(Nugent, Mike kick)
4 plays, 43 yards, TOP 1:03, OSU 14–MICH 28

4th

13:53 OSU—Ross, Lydell 2-yd. run (Nugent, Mike kick)
10 plays, 93 yards, TOP 2:59, OSU 21–MICH 28
07:55 MICH—Perry, Chris 15-yd. run (Rivas, Garrett kick)
8 plays, 88 yards, TOP 3:53, OSU 21–MICH 35

Team Statistics

	OSU	MICH
FIRST DOWNS	22	24
Rushing	4	9
Passing	17	13
Penalty	1	2
Rushing Attempts	25	40
Yards Gained Rushing	81	179
Yards Lost Rushing	27	9
NET YARDS RUSHING	54	170
NET YARDS PASSING	329	278
Passes Attempted	46	32
Passes Completed	28	21
Had Intercepted	1	1
TOTAL OFFENSIVE PLAYS	71	72
TOTAL NET YARDS	383	448
Average Gain Per Play	5.4	6.2
Fumbles: Number Lost	0–0	1–0
Penalties: Number Yards	5–65	4–34
Number of Punts—Yards	9–442	6–247
Average Per Punt	49.1	41.2
Punt Returns: Number Yards	1–3	6–55
Kickoff Returns: Number Yards	6–112	3–68
Interceptions: Number Yards	1–0	1–9
Fumble Returns: Number Yards	0–0	0–0
Miscellaneous Yards	0	0
Possession Time	27:40	32:20
Third-Down Conversions	5 of 14	6 of 13
Fourth-Down Conversions	0 of 0	0 of 0
Sacks by: Number Yards	0–0	4-22

NOTES

Any quotations not cited in the text or in the notes below were obtained in interviews conducted by the author.

I. Hate: The Early Years

9 *"Never in the course of my life"* Michigan Department of Military and Veterans Affairs, "The Toledo War," http://www.michigan.gov/dmva/0,1607,7-126-2360_3003_3009-16934--,00.html.

19 *"Everyone wants a piece"* Ohio State Buckeyes, "Football Notes and Quotes (August 5, 2003)," http://ohiostatebuckeyes.ocsn.com/sports/m-footbl/spec-rel/080503aaa.html.

19 *"There may be focus but no pressure"* Ohio State Buckeyes, "Football Notes and Quotes (August 6, 2003)," http://ohiostatebuckeyes.ocsn.com/sports/m-footbl/spec-rel/080603aaa.html.

19 *"We're ready to take on the task"* Ibid.

22 *"Did you punch him in the eye?"* Maryanne George, "Jackson Cops Plea," *Detroit Free Press*, August 14, 2003.

23 *"I really think that the only person"* Michigan Football, "Media Day—Offensive Players," http://www.mgoblue.com/document_display.cfm?document_id=12261&season_id=227.

24 *"That motivated me throughout"* Ibid.

2. Born and Bred

29 *"We do not care what happens"* Wilbur Snypp, *The Buckeyes: A Story of Ohio State Football* (Huntsville, Ala,: Strode Publishers, 1974), 140.

38 *"historic rivals"* Vic Donahey, letter in the October 20, 1928 Michigan–Ohio State game program. Courtesy of the Ohio State University Archives.

3. Cold War

48 *"'You can leave,'"* Larry Lage, "Perry Leads Michigan After Deciding to Stay," Associated Press, September 14, 2003.

49 *"Our goal is to go undefeated"* Michigan Football, "Weekly Press Conference—September 15, 2003," http://www.mgoblue.com/ document_display.cfm?document_id=12433&season_id=227.

49 *"We want to win the rest"* Michigan Football, "Weekly Press Conference—September 22, 2003," http://www.mgoblue.com/ document_display.cfm?document_id=12489&season_id=227.

50 *"I think sometimes I forced"* Ibid.

51 *"When you've been around football"* Ibid.

54 *"I lost my poise"* Tim May and Bob Baptist, "Reynolds Issues an Apology," *Columbus Dispatch*, October 13, 2003.

56 *"Ben, at this rate"* Will Perry, *The Wolverines: A Story of Michigan Football* (Huntsville, Ala.: Strode Publishers, 1974), 123.

58 *"Freddie, I still have supreme"* Ibid., 170.

65 *"Having the ball today"* Ibid., 251.

66 *"When he kicked the ball"* Jason Maddux and Jay Hansen, "More Than 50 Years Ago, 'Snow Bowl' Heated Up OSU–UM Rivalry," Gannett News Service.

67 *"It was a big play"* Tim May, "Momsen Brothers Sparkle in the Snow," *Columbus Dispatch*, November 20, 1998.

67 *"enough time to close out"* Bill Levy, *Three Yards and a Cloud of Dust* (Cleveland: World Publishing Company, 1966), 239.

68 *"It's like a nightmare"* Ibid, 241.

4. Two Men and a Rivalry

71 *"No, goddammit!"* Jerry Brondfield, *Woody Hayes and the 100-Yard War* (New York: Random House, 1974), 4.

NOTES

74 *"There are three things"* Rick Telander, "Defining a Grid Legend," *Sports Illustrated*, March 23, 1987.

74 *"I'm not trying to win"* Jim Barstow, "Woody's hometown still reveling in 'The Game,'" *Coshocton Tribune*, November 19, 2002.

77 *"My name's Schmidt"* Bill Levy, *Three Yards and a Cloud of Dust* (Cleveland: World Publishing Company, 1966), 71.

80 *"I didn't come here"* Jerry Brondfield, *Woody Hayes and the 100-Yard War*, 72.

82 *"I despised him"* Bo Schembechler and Mitch Albom, *Bo* (New York: Warner Books, 1989), 15.

85 *"I reckon it's a good thing"* Will Perry, *The Wolverines: A Story of Michigan Football* (Huntsville, Ala.: Strode Publishers, 1974), 47.

87 *"When are you going to"* John J. Green, "That's Bo and the New Sound of 'M' Football," *Detroit News Magazine*, September 21, 1969.

88 *"He's rough, and he knows"* Ibid.

89 *"Because I couldn't"* Larry Lage, Associated Press, November 16, 2003.

90 *"If he was trying to rub it in"* Jim Mandich and Robin Wright, "Jim Mandich Speaks on Ohio State," *Michigan Daily*, November 21, 1969.

90 *"Nobody has a better defense"* Jim Forrester, "Wolverines Bust Woody," *Michigan Daily*, November 23, 1969.

91 *"I know it wasn't Woody's"* CTC Sports Productions, "The Ten Year War: Woody vs. Bo" (Family Express Video, 1998).

91 *"We were trying to psych"* Ibid.

95 *"No more, damn it"* Will Perry, *The Wolverines*, 17.

95 *"one of the greatest performances"* Schembechler and Albom, *Bo*, 67.

96 *"One of [Woody's] downfalls was"* Jeff Snook, ed., *What It Means to Be a Buckeye* (Chicago: Triumph Books, 2003), 116.

96 *"Bo came in knowing what"* Helene St. James, "In Memory, Pierson Runs 60 Yards Forever," *Detroit Free Press*, August 29, 1997.

96 *"All good things must come"* Kaye Kessler and William F. Reed, "Bye-Bye, No. 1," *Sports Illustrated*, December 1, 1969.

97 *"We will start preparing"* Jeff Snook, ed., *What It Means to Be a Buckeye*, 91

97 *"I've been thinking about"* Bill Cromartie, *The Big One* (West Point, New York: Gridiron-Leisure Press, 1981), 278.

98 *"I want to feel"* Snook, *What It Means to Be a Buckeye*, 164.

98 *"It was our biggest victory"* Cromartie, *The Big One*, 278.

100 *"learn discipline and teamwork"* Mary Bridgman, "With a Goal in Mind: Tough Times Don't Sideline Archie Griffin," *Columbus Dispatch*, February 16, 1997.

101 *"it gave me a whole lot"* Ibid.

101 *"If you're good enough"* Ibid.

102 *"He spoke of how terrible"* The Duncan Group, "Interview with Archie Griffin," http://www.duncanentertainment.com/interview_griffin.php.

104 *"Goddamn it! Goddamn it!"* Schembechler and Albom, *Bo*, 174.

105 *"Twenty-two Michigan Wolverines"* Joe Falls, "Let's Not Spoil Feud With the Buckeyes," *Detroit News*, November 19, 1999.

105 *"I hope we don't"* Todd Jones, "More Than a Punchline," *Columbus Dispatch*, November 21, 2003.

106 *"I have a temper"* Bob Dolgan, "Punch Still Lingers," *Cleveland Plain Dealer*, December 29, 2003.

106 *"Just like my father"* Jones, "More Than a Punchline."

106 *"If that was war"* Schembechler and Albom, *Bo*, 79.

107 *"I promise you'll be proud of"* Bruce Hooley, "He's Ready to Bridge OSU's Gaps," *Cleveland Plain Dealer*, January 19, 2001.

107 *"Like everyone else"* Joe Lapointe, "Coaching in Schembechler's Shadow," *New York Times*, November 20, 2003.

108 *"Lloyd Carr is as secure"* Ibid.

108 *"He was doing his thing"* Michigan Football, "Press Conference Comments—Bo Schembechler," http://www.mgoblue.com/document_display.cfm?document_id=13064&season_id=227.

5. Boys to Men

113 *"I was working out three times"* Tim May, "Haw Sprints into Spotlight," *Columbus Dispatch*, July 6, 2003.

113 *"Things are just happening"* Ibid.

115 *"I think it's the Michigan"* Angelique S. Chengelis, "Tradition

NOTES

Lures Top Quarterback to U-M," *Detroit News*, August 8, 2003.

116 *"I'm not going to say Orlando"* Tom Melody, "A Fish Tale on How OSU Landed the Big One," *Akron Beacon Journal*, July 12, 1998.

117 *"It's where I wanted to go"* May, "Haw Sprints into Spotlight."

118 *"Okay. How you doin'"* Austin Murphy, "Good Neighbor," *Sports Illustrated*, May 20, 1996.

118 *"I want to be on the field"* Steve Kornacki, "Rosy Promise Pays Off," *Ann Arbor News*, November 23, 1996.

119 *"I guarantee we will beat"* Doug Harris, "Great Memories from 'The Game,'" *Dayton Daily News*, November 17, 2000.

119 *"One thing about football"* Rusty Miller, "Sports News," Associated Press, November 21, 1986.

119 *"He's 22 years old"* Ibid.

120 *"I knew if I made"* Bernie Lincicome, "Harbaugh Talks, Michigan Listens," *Chicago Tribune*, November 23, 1986.

121 *"I can't recall"* Ibid.

122 *"Why Earle has a problem"* Hank Hersch, "Short on Style, but Plenty Long on Substance," *Sports Illustrated*, December 1, 1986.

122 *"The play depends on"* Ibid.

122 *"I thought it was good"* Sam McManis, "Michigan Wins, 26–24—On a Left Hook," *Los Angeles Times*, November 23, 1986.

123 *"This is the worst feeling"* Miller, "Sports News."

123 *"It's such a tough game"* Ibid.

123 *"I'd have said it myself"* Ibid.

124 *"Strap on your helmets"* Jeff Snook, ed., *What It Means to Be a Buckeye* (Chicago: Triumph Books, 2003), 272.

125 *"We didn't make"* Steve White, *One Game Season* (Collegeville, Minn.: One Game Season, 1995), 321.

126 *"The coach told us not"* Bob Logan, "Ohio State Bids Bruce Farewell Against Michigan," *Chicago Tribune*, November 20, 1987.

130 *"You learn how fast things"* Vicki Michaelis, "Brother Kindles Determination of Michigan's LeSueur," *USA Today*, December 30, 2003.

6. Broken Hearts and Ballooning Wallets

144 *"I didn't visit there"* Michigan Football, "The 100th Game—Voices: Michigan's Desmond Howard," http://www.mgoblue.com/document_display.cfm?document_id=13078.

145 *"I told my friends in Ohio"* Harry Atkins, "Sports News," Associated Press, November 24, 1991.

146 *"one of our biggest victories"* Ed Sherman, "Michigan the Odd Choice," *Chicago Tribune*, November 19, 1993.

146 *"Never entered my mind"* Bernie Lincicome, "Tie Displays a Disturbing Pattern," *Chicago Tribune*, November 22, 1992.

146 *"You want to gamble"* Ibid.

147 *"Do I like living in Columbus"* Tim May, "Cooper Wants Win over Michigan—Bad," *Columbus Dispatch*, November 16, 1993.

147 *"This is one of the most embarrassing"* Christine Brennan, "Wolverines Intercept Buckeyes' Bowl Plans," *Washington Post*, November 21, 1993.

147 *"It was probably our lack"* Ibid.

148 *"We want to beat Ohio State"* Sherman, "Michigan the Odd Choice."

149 *"We want to get Cooper"* Bruce Hooley, "Wolverine Targets Cooper," *Cleveland Plain Dealer*, November 15, 1994.

149 *"We want to keep on beatin'"* Bob Baptist, "Wolverine: We'll Get Cooper Fired," *Columbus Dispatch*, November 15, 1994.

149 *"I haven't lost to Ohio State"* Bob Baptist, "Beating Buckeyes Is Habit-Forming at Michigan," *Columbus Dispatch*, November 19, 1994.

149 *"I know that they understand"* Tim May and Bob Baptist, "Griffin Thinks Buckeyes Are Getting Fired Up," *Columbus Dispatch*, November 18, 1994.

150 *"I've never seen him do"* Steve White, *One Game Season* (Collegeville, Minn.: One Game Season, 1995), 349.

150 *"That got a real spark under"* Bruce Hooley, "OSU Rocks Michigan," *Cleveland Plain Dealer*, November 20, 1994.

150 *"This one ranks right at the top"* Ibid.

151 *"A lot of frustration is over"* Steve White, *One Game Season*.

151 *"They are nothing"* Ibid.

152 *"If you disrespect me"* Helene Elliott, "Wolverine's Biakabutuka Takes Comment Personally," *Los Angeles Times*, November 26, 1995.

152 *"Tim came into my office"* Lenn Robbins, "Michigan Spoils Ohio State Season," *Bergen Record*, November 26, 1995.

153 *"I don't know how I"* Thomas George, "Michigan Breaks Buckeye Hearts," *New York Times*, November 26, 1995.

154 *"Anybody who says this"* Bob Hunter, "Preacher Bruce Delivers One from the Heart," *Columbus Dispatch*, November 23, 1996.

154 *"We got into Columbus"* Ray Stein, "Wolverines: Game's Too Hyped Here," *Columbus Dispatch*, November 24, 1996.

154 *"wouldn't have been able"* Lisa Dillman, "Shawn Springs and His Father Ron Are Bound by Blood and Ohio State Football Glory," *Los Angeles Times*, December 25, 1996.

155 *"I guess it was my Buckeye"* Ibid.

155 *"The lesson I learned"* Chris Dufresne, "Michigan Is Thorn in Rose Bowl," *Los Angeles Times*, November 24, 1996.

155 *"It's a big game"* Bob Hunter, "Another Michigan Loss? Why Ask Why?" *Columbus Dispatch*, November 24, 1996.

156 *"I've played better corners"* Marc Katz, "Boston Blasts Woodson," *Dayton Daily News*, November 16, 1997.

157 *"Can y'all smell that?"* Keith Gave, "U-M Comes Up Roses in 20–14 Over Buckeyes," *Detroit Free Press*, November 23, 1997.

157 *"People come up to me"* Gerry Callahan, "Cooper's Town," *Sports Illustrated*, September 8, 1997.

158 *"We recruit good players"* Ibid.

160 *"Exposure is everything"* Jerry Greene, "UCF Has Heisman Hopes in '98," *Orlando Sentinel*, March 22, 1998.

161 *"You have to support"* Todd Archer, "Bengals Talking Serious Trash," *Cincinnati Post*, November 19, 1999.

7. Go Bucks! Go Blue!

166 *"A large number of"* Will Perry, *The Wolverines: A Story of Michigan Football* (Huntsville, Ala.: Strode Publishers, 1974), 26.

169 *"I decided in the third"* Brenda Donegan, "Harding Grad Gets the Honor Twice," *Marion Star*, September 18, 2003.

174 *"There was never a more"* Perry, *The Wolverines*, 26.

178 *"He had tickets"* Jason Maddux and Jay Hansen, "More Than 50 Years Ago, 'Snow Bowl' Heated up OSU–UM Rivalry," Gannett News Service.

178 *"We hope to generate"* Fred LaBour, "Would You Run to Columbus, Ohio?" *Michigan Daily*, November 19, 1969.

179 *"I pushed his hand aside"* Jill Riepenhoff, "Fan Never Needs Ticket to Big Game," *Columbus Dispatch*, November 21, 1992.

180 *"I loved that one"* Associate Press, "Gate Crasher Mulls Sneaking into OSU–Michigan Game," *Cincinnati Enquirer*, November 22, 2002.

185 *"I had to come back"* John Seewer, "Game Divides Neighborhoods, Families Near Ohio–Michigan Line," Associated Press, November 21, 2002.

8. Countdown

193 *"They've been disrespecting"* Larry Lage, "Ohio St. 26, Number 11 Michigan 20," Associated Press, November 24, 2001.

194 *"This is Michigan week"* Joe Lapointe, "Big Game Is Understatement," *New York Times*, November 23, 2002.

197 *"We still don't know"* Michael Rosenberg, "Navarre, Michigan Steal Win with 34 Fourth Quarter Points," *Detroit Free Press*, October 13, 2003.

198 *"It ranks high up there"* Michigan Football, "Player Comments—October 13, 2003," http://www.mgoblue.com/document_display.cfm?document_id=12658&season_id=227.

9. One Hundred

212 *"It's unique"* Michigan Football, "Player Comments—November 17, 2003," http://www.mgoblue.com/document_display.cfm?document_id=13062&season_id=227.

213 *"Well, it's an exciting"* Ohio State Buckeyes, "Transcript from the November 18th Ohio State Football Press Luncheon," http://ohiostatebuckeyes.ocsn.com/sports/m-footbl/spec-rel/111803aab.html.

214 *"It feels like something"* Michigan Football, "Player Comments—November 17, 2003," http://www.mgoblue.com/document_display.cfm?document_id=13062&season_id=227.

214 *"This is what you come to Michigan for"* Ibid.

214 *"This is why you come"* Ohio State Buckeyes, "Ohio State Football Player Quotes—November 18, 2003," http://ohiostate-buckeyes.ocsn.com/sports/m-footbl/spec-rel/111803aac.html.

215 *"I expect this to"* Ibid.

215 *"The last two Michigan games"* Marla Ridenour, "Ohio State's Big Three Return for Michigan Moment," *Akron Beacon Journal*, November 21, 2003.

216 *"The speed of this game"* Doug Harris, "Rivalry's Intensity Hits Players Hard," *Dayton Daily News*, November 22, 2003.

218 *"I'm not saying it's"* Michael Rosenberg, "U-M's Navarre Finds Confidence in Job Well Won," *Detroit Free Press*, August 31, 2001.

219 *"Somebody asked about"* Michigan Football, "Player Comments—November 17, 2003," http://www.mgoblue.com/document_display.cfm?document_id=13062&season_id=227.

219 *"You have to block"* Larry Lage, "Navarre's Legacy at Michigan Hinders on Ohio State Game," Associated Press, November 17, 2003.

220 *"What defines you"* Ibid.

221 *"When I was diagnosed"* Rick Morrissey, "Like Mom, Perry Hard to Bring Down," *Chicago Tribune*, November 23, 2003.

221 *"It's hard not to"* Jay Mariotti, "Perry Fights through Two Kinds of Pain," *Chicago Sun-Times*, November 23, 2003.

222 *"Jason was crying"* Vaughn McClure, "Did Buckeyes Try to Hurt Perry?" *South Bend Tribune*, November 23, 2003.

224 *"You can't blame him"* James Walker, "OSU's Gamble Comes Up Short," *Columbus Dispatch*, October 12, 2003.

226 *"When it comes down"* Melissa Isaacson, "Plenty at Stake—Just Like Usual," *Chicago Tribune*, November 22, 2003.

228 *"I was saying a few"* Vaughn McClure, "Did Buckeyes Try to Hurt Perry?" *South Bend Tribune*, November 23, 2003.

228 *"I just told him"* Ibid.

229 *"I prefer to do"* Marla Ridenour, "Controversy? There's No Controversy—Really," *Akron Beacon Journal*, November 7, 2003.

229 *"He's going to thread"* Ibid.

230 *"I saw that Scott was"* Aaron Portzline, "Held Out of Starting Lineup, Contrite Holmes Has a Big Day," *Columbus Dispatch*, November 23, 2003.

230 *"You want to win"* Liz Clarke, "Wolverines Deliver a Knock-out," *Washington Post*, November 23, 2003.

231 *"Getting that stop there"* Michigan Football, "#5 Michigan 35, #4 Ohio State 21—Quotes," http://www.mgoblue.com/document_display.cfm?document_id=13125.

232 *"I was speechless"* McClure, "Did Buckeyes Try to Hurt Perry?"

233 *"Nice hit"* Tom Archdeacon, "Buckeyes Bruised, Battered," *Dayton Daily News*, November 23, 2003.

233 *"All day, every time"* Ibid.

233 *"I love Craig Krenzel"* Ray Stein, "Buckeye Fans Put Forth Their Views on Loss to You-Know-Who," *Columbus Dispatch*, November 30, 2003.

234 *"Where are those"* Vaughn McClure, "Michigan Smelling Roses," *South Bend Tribune*, November 23, 2003.

234 *"She is always"* Rick Morrissey, "Like Mom, Perry Hard to Bring Down," *Chicago Tribune*, November 23, 2003.

234 *"It feels great"* Michigan Football, "#5 Michigan 35, #4 Ohio State 21—Quotes."

10. Post-Game

236 *"I've wanted to do this"* Emily Kraack, "Michigan Fans Jump Wall, Flood Field to Join Celebrating Team," *Michigan Daily*, November 24, 2003.

237 *"how much emotion was"* Ibid.

237 *"I think our fans were rougher"* Barker Davis, "Michigan Exposes Ohio State," *Washington Times*, November 23, 2003.

237 *"We beat Ohio State"* "Victors!" *Michigan Daily*, November 22, 2003.

238 *"started rocking cars"* "Police Arrest 48 after OSU Victory," *Columbus Dispatch*, November 24, 1975.

239 *"primarily beer and pops"* Elliot Blair Smith, "Celebration Ends with 338 Arrests," *Columbus Dispatch*, November 19, 1979.

239 *"The trouble started when"* Tiffany C. Miller, "Police Gassed Crowds During Celebrations On and Off Field," *Lantern*, November 22, 1994.

239 *"usual number of drunks"* John Gibeaut, "Ann Arbor Only Expects 'Usual Number of Drunks,'" *Lantern*, November 20, 1980.

240 *"trying to hurt people"* Stephanie Hepburn and Heather

Kamins, "Michigan Fans File Complaints of Police Brutality," *Michigan Daily*, November 25, 1997.

241 *"We had an opportunity"* Lorraine Sommers, "Ohio State U. Riots Lead to 48 Arrests, 20 Overturned Cars," *Lantern*, November 25, 2002.

241 *"It's getting pretty"* Ray Stein, "Michigan 35–Ohio State 21," *Columbus Dispatch*, November 23, 2003.

242 *"It was a great win"* Michigan Football, "#5 Michigan 35, #4 Ohio State 21—Quotes," http://www.mgoblue.com/document_display.cfm?document_id=13125.

242 *"They came out"* Ibid.

242 *"That was a heavyweight"* Tom Archdeacon, "Buckeyes Bruised, Battered," *Dayton Daily News*, November 23, 2003.

243 *"I'm already drunk"* Jonathan Drew, "Buckeye Fans Deflated after the Game," Associated Press, November 23, 2003.

243 *"It was only a matter"* Ibid.

243 *"We had a chance to"* Tom Archdeacon, "Buckeyes Bruised, Battered," *Dayton Daily News*, November 23, 2003.

243 *"We deserve to be"* Ibid.

244 *"I was pumped"* John Niyo, "USC Benefits from Michigan Win," *Detroit News*, November 24, 2003.

246 *"[USC] are one in both"* Michigan Football, "Weekly Press Conference—Players, December 8, 2003," http://www.mgoblue.com/document_display.cfm?document_id=13292&season_id=227.

246 *"It will be nice"* Ohio State Buckeyes, "Ohio State Fiesta Bowl Selection Quotes," http://ohiostatebuckeyes.ocsn.com/sports/m-footbl/spec-rel/120703aab.html.

246 *"If he wins the"* Josh Dubow, "Heisman Trophy Hopefuls Struggled in Big Games," Associated Press, December 12, 2003.

247 *"There's no disappointment"* John Niyo, "Oklahoma's White Wins Heisman," *Detroit News*, December 14, 2003.

247 *"I am happy that we"* Mark Anderson, "Rose Bowl Notes," *Las Vegas Review-Journal*, January 2, 2004.

247 *"We went out"* Rob Oller, "Ohio State 35 Kansas State 28," *Columbus Dispatch*, January 3, 2004.

248 *"We have to open up"* Doug Harris, "Buckeyes Have Many Holes to Fill," *Dayton Daily News*, January 5, 2004.

248 *"I don't think people"* Ibid.

248 *"All right, the marathon"* Michigan Football, "2004 Signing Day Comments," http://www.mgoblue.com/document_display.cfm?document_id=13742.

249 *"guys who have chosen"* Ohio State Buckeyes, "Ohio State Football National Signing Day Quotes," http://ohiostatebuckeyes.ocsn.com/sports/m-footbl/spec-rel/020404aab.html.

251 *"I think I'm just"* Ohio State Buckeyes, "Versatile Buckeye to Leave Early for NFL," http://ohiostatebuckeyes.ocsn.com/sports/m-footbl/spec-rel/010304aaa.html.

251 *"I'm coming back"* Keith Parson, "Pollack, Edwards to Stay in Schools," Associated Press, January 12, 2004.

251 *"I think it benefited"* Mike O'Hara, "Local Players Work to Improve NFL Stock," *Detroit News*, February 22, 2004.

ACKNOWLEDGMENTS

One hundred is a lot of football games, and I would first like to thank all the writers and the reporters who provided the eyes and the ears at each of them.

Many people lent invaluable support on this project, and I would like to single out a few. First, thanks go to my agent, Bob Mecoy, for tossing the idea into my lap, and to Stephen Power at John Wiley & Sons, for suggesting the whole ball of wax in the first place and then shepherding it through. My sincere gratitude also goes to Brett Martin, for hooking me up with these characters and then calling me all the time and almost preventing me from getting the damn thing written.

Big thanks also to Russ Levine and Vinny Gauri, for their indoctrination into the passionate world of college football and for quickie research and fact-finding. And I am forever indebted to Mike Gutter and Shawn Collier for their assistance in Columbus.

273

Thanks also to Bertha Ihnat, Tamar Chute, Michelle Drobik, Julie Petersen, Karen Jania, Malgorzata Myc, and Greg Kinney in the libraries, and Dave Ablauf in the UM Media Relations department, who came through at the last possible moment. (Not mentioning anyone in the OSU media relations department is not an oversight—hopefully, *both* universities will try harder not to ignore the little guys in the future.)

Thanks to *Michigan Daily* writers Ellen McGarrity and Brian Schick, for their reporting help, and to Melissa Mariola, Jon Neff, Lauren Proux, and the *Michiganensian* staff for their assistance and their office.

The following people also deserve recognition for going above and beyond: Steve Geddes, Andy Hebron, Chris Bruno, Matt Cavanaugh, Greg Masica, Pat Saad, Brady McCollough, Phil Calihan, Drew Montag, Molly Stevens, Tony Ding, Annemarie Cullen, Michael Thompson, Hope Breeman, Michelle Morman, Lee Starr, Robert Ducas, Gary Belsky, Paul Keels, Terry Russell, Scott Terna, Craig Krenzel, and Archie Griffin.

And finally, thanks to the usual emotional crutches: Mom, Dad, Deb, Rob, Isabel and Natalie Lutz, Grandma Min, Marcia and Peter Chesler, Paul Litton, Nikki Weinstein, John "That's What She Said" Sellers, Henry, K.C., and, of course, Jessica, who doesn't necessarily like it but somehow manages to absorb some of this stuff anyway—and I love her for it.

INDEX

Page numbers in *italics* refer to figures.

Adams, John Quincy, 9

All-American players, 56, 72, 75, 96, 156

Allen, Will, 19, 173, 224, 225, 240

Ann Arbor, Michigan, 1–3, 6–7, 31–38, 240–241

Autzen Stadium, 50–51

Avant, Jason, *140*, 222

bands, *139*, 166–172, 174–177, 210–211

Baraka, Kelly, 129

Bay, Rick, 122

BCS (Bowl Championship Series), 4–5, 191, 199, 242, 244–246

Beat Michigan Week, 26–27, 44–45, 153, 163–166

Bell, Calvin, 23

Bellisari, Greg, 155

Bellisari, Steve, 192–193

Benson, Matt, 170

"The Best Damn Band in the Land" (TBDBITL), 166–172, 176–177, 210–211

Biakabutuka, Tshimanga (Tim), *138*, 152

The Big Chill (Kasdan), 181–182

Big House, 33, 209–210. *See also* Michigan Stadium

Big Ten championship, 4, 40, 60, 118, 128, 155

no-repeat rule, 104

100th game and, *140*, 235, 247

Big Ten championship
(*continued*)
  10-Year War and, 97
  2002, 23–24
Bixler, Paul, 80
"Block M," 176
Block O, 26–27, 30–31, 37
Blood Battle, 41–43
Boston, David, 156, 226
Bowman, Grant, 212, 219,
  231
Brady, Tom, 24, 115, 161
Breaston, Steve, 217, 223,
  224, 231–232
Brown, Paul, 79–80
Bruce, Earle, 119, 121–126,
  129, *137*, 153
Brutus Buckeye, 165
Buckeye, meaning of, 184
"Buckeye Battle Cry"
  (Crumit), 39, 167–168

Canham, Don, 83, 87
Carr, Lloyd, 22, 48, 50–51,
  106–108, 129, 152, 220
  100th game, 226, 230, 242
  on 2004 season, 248–249
Carter, Anthony, 127
Carter, Cris, 120–122, 121,
  226
"The Catch," 145
Cavanaugh, Matt, 176, 211
Celeste, Richard, 127
Chattams, Angelo, 130
Childress, Bam, 216, 223,
  234

Cincinnati Bengals, 79, 80,
  161
Clarett, Maurice
  legal troubles of, 20–21, 53,
    130–131, 247, 249–250
  playing record of, 193, 194,
    216
Clark, Meyers, 54–58
Clark, Wes, 171
Cline, Oliver, 61
Cody, Shaun, 244
Coleman, Michael B., 241
Collier, Shawn, 25–27, 44–45
Collins, John, 22–23
Collins, Todd, 115
Columbus, Ohio, 27–31,
  33–38
  Blue Jackets, 29–30
  post-game rioting in,
    238–241
  reaction to 100th game,
    243–244
Cooper, John, 116, 142–143,
  143–149, 149–151, 157,
  158
Core, Anthony, 169
Craw, Garvie, 93, 94
Crisler, Herbert O. (Fritz),
  58–60, 62, 64, 85–87
Crumit, Frank, 168

Dantonio, Mark, 248
Darden, Tom, 98–99, *134*
"Dark 26" play, 93–94
Deleone, Tom, 97–98
Detroit, Michigan, 34

Diggs, Carl, 214
Division I-A, 4
Donahey, Vic, 38

Edwards, Braylon, 250–251
   plays by, 23, 194, 196, 198,
      223, 225, 228, 231
   reaction to 100th game, 234
Elbel, Louis, 174–177
Elliott, Bump, 87, 89
ESPN, 21, 159, 186, 201
Evans, Lee, 52, 53, 224

fans, 177–182, 187–191,
      205–208
   in Ann Arbor, 1–3, 6–7,
      31–38, 240–241
   Block O, 26–27, 30–31, 37
   Buckeye & Wolverine Shop,
      183–186
   in Columbus, 27–31, 29–30,
      33–38, 54–55, 238–241,
      243–244
   hype about 100th game,
      196–205
   post-game reactions by,
      235–237, 238–244
Farokhrny, Shahin, 22–23
Ferkany, Ed, 71–72
Fesler, Wes, 66–67, 69, 80
Fiesta Bowl, 18, 20, 52, 240,
      246, 247
Finley, Adam, 194, 195, 222
Fitzgerald, Larry, 246
football, origin of, 10–11
Ford, Gerald, 40, 211–212

Franklin, Dennis, 102, 103
Frantz, Matt, 122, 126
Fraser, Simon, 19
Frey, Greg, 143–144
Friedman, Benny, 56–58, 58

Galloway, Joey, 147
Gamble, Chris, 52, 223–225,
      231, 250–251
Gandee, Sonny, 68
Gator Bowl, 105–106
Gee, E. Gordon, 146
Geiger, Andy, 21, 53
George, Eddie, 151–153
Glenn, Terry, 151
"golden pants," 78
Grbac, Elvis, 24, 115
Greene, Cornelius, 103
Griese, Brian, 24, 115, 154
Griffin, Archie, 100–103, 106,
      110, 137, 141, 149, 161
"Guarantee Game," 119, 123

Haji-Sheikh, Ali, 128
Hall, Leon, 231–232
Hall, Maurice, 194, 215
Harbaugh, Jack, 118
Harbaugh, Jim, 24, 115,
      118–123
Harley, Chic, 75–76, 194
Harmon, Tom, 59–60
Hart, Randy, 122
Hartsock, Ben, 216–217, 223,
      230, 243
Haw, Erik, 109–112, 117, 131
Hawk, A.J., 221, 225, 248

Hayes, Wayne Woodrow
(Woody), 17, 71–75,
80–82, 99–100, 108, 124,
127, *134*
fuel legend and, 71–72,
169–170
Griffin and, 100–103
merit system of, 144
1968 game and, 89–90
1969 game and, 90–97
1978 game and, 105
resignation of, 106
"Heisman Pose," 145
Heisman Trophy winners
George, 152
Griffin, 100–103, 106, 110,
137, 141, 149, 161
Hayes and, 72
Horvath, 61–62
Howard, 144–145
Janowicz, 65–66, 68
Perry as finalist, 246–247
Woodson, 160
helmets, 85–87, 144, 150
Henne, Chad, 115
Henson, Drew, 192, 218, 219
Hill, Henry, 93, 95
Hineygate, 190
Holbrook, Karen, 241
Holland, Jamie, 120
Holmes, Santonio, 130,
215–216, 230
Horn, Jason, *138*
Horseshoe, 172
Horvath, Leslie, 61–62, 80
Howard, Desmond, 144–145

Hoying, Bobby, *138*, 150,
151, 162

Jackson, Andrew, 9–10
Jackson, James, 238
Jackson, Marlin, 22–23, 49,
129, 251
James, LeBron, 249
Janowicz, Vic, 65–66, 68
Jenkins, Michael, 215, 222,
225, 226, 251
Joe, Brandon, 215, 225
Jones, Ben, 173–174

Karow, Marty, 56–58
Karsatos, Jim, 120–122
Kasdan, Lawrence, 181–182
Keels, Paul, 30, 53
Kern, Rex, 92–96, 97
Klaban, Tom, 110
Krenzel, Craig, 19, 222–223,
225, 226, 227, 231,
233–234
in Fiesta Bowl, 247
100th game, 215, 216, 223
in 2001, 2002 games,
191–196

Lantern, 15, 239
Lantry, Mike, 110
Larkins, Dick, 64, 69
Laughlin, Jim, 238
Law, Ty, 161
Leach, Rick, 105
legal troubles, 117, 124,
129–131

Baraka, 129
Chattams, 130
Clarett, 20–21, 53, 130–131,
    247, 249–250
Cooper, 130
Holmes, 130, 215–216
LeSueur, 130
Marlin Jackson, 129
Moeller, 152
Pagac, 130
Schlichter, 128–129
Steve Bellisari, 192–193
Troy Smith, 130
Leno, Jay, 241
LeSueur, Jeremy, 47, 49, 130,
    131
Lucas, Robert, 8–9

Mandich, Jim, 90
Manning, Eli, 246
Mason, Stevens T., 8–9
Massaquoi, Tim, 198, 220
McCollough, J. Brady, 51
McMullen, Scott, 229–230,
    231, 233–234
Meyer, Jimmy, 116
Michigan, state of, 7–10
Michigan Daily, 13, 32–33, 51,
    85, 91, 178, 197, 236
Michigan Stadium, 33, 51, 85,
    88, 132, 202, 206
  Big House nickname, 33,
    209–210
  tunnel of, 139
  wall, 235, 236
Mirror Lake, 163–166

Moeller, Gary, 147–148, 152
Momsen, Bob, 65
Momsen, Tony, 66–67
Montag, Drew, 104–105
Moorehead, Don, 93, 94
Morman, Michelle, 167,
    169–170, 177
Morris, Jamie, 120–121
Morrison, Bobby, 152
"music bus," 187–189

Naked Mile, 31
national championships, 79,
    156, 240, 246
Navarre, John, 23–24, 50–51,
    139, 231, 234, 247, 251
  in 2002 game, 194,
    195–196, 196–198, 240
  in 100th game, 217–220,
    222–225, 228, 246
NCAA, 116
  BCS, 4–5, 191, 199, 242,
    244–246
  Clarett and, 20–21
  "golden pants" and, 78
  on NFL draft rule, 250
NFL, 21, 53, 115, 158–161,
    249–251
Nienberg, Troy, 214–215
Northwest Ordinance,
    7–10
Notre Dame University, 36,
    47–48

Ohio, state of, 7–10, 29–30
Ohio Pants Club, 78

Ohio Stadium, 76, *133*, 172, 196

Ohio State University Monthly, 39, 75

Ohio State University (OSU), 3–4, 11–15, 17, 30, 34–35, 165. *See also* fans; "the Game"; *individual names of coaches and players*

all-time UM-OSU results, 253–256

Block O, 26–27, 30–31, 37

in-state recruiting by, 115

Marching Band, 166–172, 176–177, 210–211

tailgating rituals, 187–191

team statistics, 259

2003 schedule, 256

"Old Button Shoe," 92

Olivea, Shane, 243

100th game, 17–24, 23–24, 51–54, *139, 140*, 205–208

fans' reaction to, 235–237, 241–244

hype about, 196–205

statistics, 257–258

Oosterbaan, Bennie, 56, 65, 87

Osman, T.J., 144

Otis, Jim, 89, 92–93, 96

Owens, Lee, 116

Oxley, William (statue), *136*

Pace, Orlando, 116, 158

Pagac, Fred, Jr., 130

Pape, Tony, 214, 251

Payne, Rod, 154

Perry, Chris, 23, 33, 48, 197, 220–221, 223–225, 227–228, 234

as Heisman finalist, 246–247

NFL and, 251

post-game reaction, 237

Salley and, 232, 242

Perry, Irene, 221, 234

Pierson, Barry, 94, 95

Pittman, Tony, 112–113

Plate, Todd, 143

"Point-A-Minute" team, 85

Pond, Irving, 166

Purdue University, 90, 172–174, 217

"razzle dazzle," 77

recruitment, 101, 109–114, 114–117, 116. *See also* NFL

Reynolds, Robert, 54, *140*, 222

Rose Bowl, 72, 98, 105

OSU in, 155, 238

OSU-UM tied, 104

UM in, 68, 87, 118, 244–247

Ross, Everett, 120, 125

Ross, Lydell, 216, 230

Salley, Nate, 225, 232, 242

Sander, B.J., 217, 223

Schabert, Matt, 51–54

Scheffer, Lance, 98

Scheindlin, Shira, 249, 250
Schembechler, Glen Edward
    (Bo), 81–83, 87–88,
    90–97, 102–103, 107, *134*
    Harbaugh and, 118–123
    retirement of, 147
    on 10-Year War, 106, 108
Schlichter, Art, 106, 124,
    126–129
Schmidt, Francis A., 77–79
Scott, Darrion, 195–196
"Script Ohio," 168–169,
    210–211
Senior Tackle, 153
Shazor, Ernest, 216–217, 234
'Shoe, 172
"Skull Session," 171–172
Smith, Dick, 180–181
Smith, Steve, 127–128
Smith, Troy, 130
Smith, Walter, 149
Smith, Will, 196, 221, 228,
    246, 251
Snow, Carlos, 125, 126
"Snow Bowl," 63–69, *133*, 178
songs, 38–39, 85, 105,
    167–169, 174–177,
    210–211
Sousa, John Philip, 174
Spath, Michael, 114, 116
Spielman, Chris, 123, 125
Springs, Ron, 154
Springs, Shawn, 154–155
Stagg, Amos Alonzo, 86
statistics, 253–259. *See also*
    "the Game"

Staysniak, Joe, 124
Steele, Glen, 161
Steinbrenner, George, 192
Stepanovich, Alex, 19, 214
Stevens, Larry, 197, 237
Stevens, Walter, 239–240
Stillwagon, Jim, 96
Stobart, Chuck, 101
Streets, Tai, 154
Stringer, Korey, 150
Sugar Bowl, 244–246
Super Bowl (2004), 160
Sylvania, Ohio, 183–186

10-Year War, 81, 106, 108
Terna, Scott, 161–162
"the Game," 13–15. *See also*
    100th game
    1900–1919, 16–17, 75, *132*
    1920–1929, 54–58, 76, *132*
    1930–1939, 39–40, 40–41,
        58–60, 77–78, 238
    1940–1949, 60–62
    1950–1959, 63–69, *133*, 178
    1960–1969, 89–90
    1969, 90–97, *134*
    1970–1979, 97, 98–99,
        102–103, 103–104,
        105–106, *137*, 238
    1980–1989, 119–123,
        123–126, 127–128, *137*,
        143
    1990–1999, 142, 143–144,
        143–146, 146, 147,
        148–151, 151–153,
        153–155, 158–159, 159

"the Game," (*continued*)
 2000–2002, 191–196
tickets, 64, 179–180, 200
"Toledo Strip," 8–10
"Toledo War," 10
Tressel, Jim, 18–19, 21, 52–53,
 106–108, 191, 218
 100th game, 213, 216, 227,
 234, 242
 on 2004 season, 248, 249
Trosko, Fred, 58–60
Tupa, Tom, 125–126

University of Colorado, 117
University of Michigan (UM),
 3–4, 11–12, 33–35, 75,
 205. *See also* fans; Michigan Stadium; "the Game";
 *individual names of coaches
 and players*
 all-time UM-OSU results,
 253–256
 first game with OSU, 13–15
 helmets, 85–87
 Marching Band, *139*,
 174–177, 210–211
 out-of-state recruitment by,
 115
 team statistics, 259
 2003 schedule, 257
University of Oregon, 49–51
University of Southern California (USC), 244–247
University of Wisconsin,
 51–54

"The Victors" (Elbel), 85,
 174–177
Vrabel, Mike, 150, 161

Wakefield, Dick, 99, *134*
Walsh, Bill, 80
Wells, Jonathan, 193
"West Coast offense," 80
White, Jason, 246
"Whoop Ass Wagon,"
 187–189
Widdoes, Carroll, 61, 80
Widman, Charlie, 174
Wilce, John W., 75–76
Willaman, Sam (Sad Sam),
 76
Williams, Mike, 250
Williams, Tim, 145, 146
Williams, Willie, 116–117
Wolverine, 114
Wolverine Death (drink),
 141–142
Wolverines, origin of nick-
 name, 10
Woodson, Charles, 156,
 158–159
Woody Hayes Athletic
 Center, 17
Workman, Vince, 120

Yost, Fielding (Hurry Up),
 83–85
Young, Jim, 94–95